This book is part of the Allyn and Bacon Series in Creative Teaching. The books in this series are:

I

Setting Conditions for Creative Teaching in the Elementary School
James A. Smith

II

Creative Teaching of the Language Arts
in the Elementary School
James A. Smith

III

Creative Teaching of Reading and Literature
in the Elementary School
James A. Smith

IV

Creative Teaching of the Creative Arts
in the Elementary School
James A. Smith

V

Creative Teaching of the Social Studies
in the Elementary School
James A. Smith

VI

Creative Teaching of Mathematics
in the Elementary School
Alvin M. Westcott and James A. Smith

VII

Creative Teaching of Science
in the Elementary School
Albert Piltz and Robert Sund

In a circus unit, children dramatize "The Merry-Go-Round," by Dorothy Baruch.

Creative Teaching of
Reading and Literature
in the Elementary School

James A. Smith
State University of New York at Oswego

foreword by E. Paul Torrance
University of Georgia

ALLYN AND BACON, INC., BOSTON

Library of Congress Catalog Card Number 67–13080

PRINTED IN THE UNITED STATES OF AMERICA

first printing: March, 1967
third printing: May, 1968

to Dot

Foreword

Many exciting, potentially powerful, and valid educational ideas have gone unused or have been forgotten altogether because no one has translated them into practical methods, instructional materials, textbooks, and the like. The idea of creative teaching has been among them. Creativity has been a persistent and recurrent issue throughout the history of education. Actually, the idea of creative ways of teaching has never had a very good chance to prove its worth. Teachers and educational leaders have continually struggled to understand the nature of creative functioning, the conditions that facilitate and inhibit creative growth, and the means of rewarding creative achievement. Bit by bit, advances have been made, and in recent years efforts to add to this kind of knowledge through research and experimentation have been accelerated. We need to know a great deal more than we do, but in my opinion we have made enough advances to make possible a more creative kind of education than has been known up to now. This is why imaginative, informed, and hard-working translators and creative synthesizers like Professor James A. Smith and his associates, who have created this series of books on setting the conditions for creative teaching and learning, are such a welcome asset to the educational enterprise.

The task of retooling—inventing and testing methods, creating tests and instructional materials, devising evaluation procedures and creating textbooks and methods of teacher education—for any new educational idea is enormous. It takes tremendous energy, creativity, courage, commitment, and willingness to risk on the part of many people. The inauguration of this series of books on creative teaching is a major venture for Professor Smith, his associates, and Allyn and Bacon. In the past, the adoption of new and improved educational ideas has been retarded by two powerful forces—teacher education institutions and textbook publishers. The case of Braille writing for the blind is an excellent example. Even after Louis Braille had perfected the method of writing that bears his name and had tested it successfully for five years, it was not adopted by schools for the blind. Opposition came from the training institutions because teachers would have to master this new way of writing and from textbook publishers because they would lose their investments in the enormous embossed books then used by the blind. It was not until many years after Braille's death that his method of writing for the blind was adopted.

Innovations in education are usually hailed as "fads" that will soon be forgotten. This is a common expression of resistance to change. Rarely, however, are valid and worthwhile innovations really forgotten, if they are translated into tested methods and materials. Braille had created an alphabet, a way of writing, that had been taught successfully to blind children. The idea of Braille writing could be rejected but it could not be forgotten. Similar statements might be made about the educational innovations of people like Socrates, Froebel, Montessori, and others. They created and tested methods and materials that have been rejected for a time, but the world has not been able to forget them. Many people have said that the idea of a more creative education is a fad that will pass and soon be forgotten. It *is* possible that creative ways of teaching may be rejected, but they will not be forgotten. Professor Smith and his co-authors in this seven-volume series have in a variety of ways expressed the definition, the spirit, and the truths of creative teaching in a way that will be difficult to forget.

The format of each book of this seven-volume series illustrates concretely many of the most important principles of creative teaching. Through the format and structure of these books, the author and publisher recognize the reader as self-acting and stimulus-seeking. The reader is provided both the guidance and the freedom necessary for creative growth. These books are a rich source of ideas, but this is not their greatest value. The reader who uses them for rapid reading or for occasional reference will miss an important opportunity for personal growth and professional development in creative directions. The "great ideas" quoted at the beginning of chapters are provocative. The suggested activities preceding most chapters provide worthwhile explorations in creativity. The content of the chapters provides a wealth of information that translates research findings into classroom methods and instructional materials. The exercises and questions at the end of each chapter will help the reader to make a creative synthesis of these experiences.

The authors offer themselves as models of creative teaching.

They bring to their task the fresh aroma of first-hand experiences in creative teaching in the college and university classroom and in elementary schools. They also offer the reader a variety of other models of creative teaching, making him feel almost as though "he were there." Participation in the experiences of the authors and the teachers they have observed, however, is not enough. The authors have added to this the kind of guidance that helps the reader identify, understand, and generalize the important principles at work in these experiences. This should increase the chances that the reader will develop useful skills and be able to transform his own classroom behavior.

Each of the seven books has its own unique contribution, along with a consistent philosophy. Book I is a creative synthesis of Professor Smith's rich experience in teaching children and teachers of children, a vast amount of research concerning creativity and classroom learning, and his theories of education. It is far more than this, however. The author has gone beyond all of these and, building onto the contributions of others, added his own innovations. He has distilled a great deal of the essence of the creativity of children. Book II, *Creative Teaching of the Language Arts in the Elementary School,* is a comprehensive, well-organized, and rich source of ideas. Book III, *Creative Teaching of Reading and Literature in the Elementary School,* is perhaps my own favorite. It is interesting and exciting and assumes a positive and consistent position on important issues in teaching reading. It will be difficult for the reader to resist becoming a creative reader. The way in which the author heightens expectations and challenges the reader to do things with what he reads is quite compelling. The books on social studies, science, the arts, and mathematics have their own unique features and should be valuable in courses on teaching methods in these areas and to teachers in service who want to become more skilled in setting the conditions for creative learning.

It is my own hope that your creative use of this series of books will help you realize more fully your own dream of helping your pupils live more creatively. This is the challenge of our day. In the past, we have been able to survive with static goals and concepts. This is no longer true. Things are changing so rapidly that our civilization can no longer survive if we insist on thinking and living in static terms and returning to the "old ways."

E. PAUL TORRANCE
University of Georgia

Preface

This is the third of a series of books on creative teaching. Its main objective is to translate into methodology those principles of creative thinking and creative development which the author has culled from research done in this area in the past ten years. This book will be most effective if it is read in combination with Book I of the series, *Setting Conditions for Creative Teaching in the Elementary School.*

Since reading has a definite place in the logical sequence of development of the language skills, the reader will also benefit by reading Book II, *Creative Teaching of the Language Arts in the Elementary School;* all the material discussed in that book is either pertinent to the creative teaching of reading or essential for its development. The basic material from the first two books is summarized in Chapter I of this volume.

Both reading and creativity are precious commodities. In the past decade more research has been done in these two areas than in any others of the elementary school curriculum. But, in spite of the new knowledges obtained in the area of reading as a result of this research, reading problems in our schools seem to mount, and concern over the lack of specific reading skills in our elementary school children grows. This dilemma may be due in part to the fact that the pseudo-scientific focus on reading has made teaching it a dull—often dead—communication process. Language is not dull or dead. It is dynamic, powerful, and constantly changing. Language is the tool of communication, and printed language requires reading in order to fulfill its communicative function. Reading can be vibrant and exciting to children *if* it is taught in a vibrant, exciting way.

The author believes that the answer lies in combining the knowledge gleaned from research in the area of reading with that in the area of *creativity. Changing* teaching is *creative* teaching. Creative teaching employs certain principles unique to creative development. Creativity in children can be developed in the teaching of reading, and, conversely, reading can be taught just as well and with more positive gains when taught creatively than when taught through the more conventional systems.

The material in this book is geared to two groups of people: the teacher-in-training and the teacher-in-practice. Parents also will enjoy its many illustrations of creative teaching and the philosophy it emphasizes. That philosophy promotes the concept that the great creative potential inherent in all humans at birth can be developed through all areas of the elementary school curriculum. The remaining books in this series illustrate how creativity can be developed through teaching in the social studies, the fine arts, mathematics, and science.

I am indebted to many people for the material in these books. First of all, I must thank the children with whom I worked and the cooperative teachers who allowed me to use their classes to try out many new and creative ideas, or who tried their own ideas and permitted me to observe the creative process that developed. I am grateful to my students at Syracuse University and especially to my student teachers, who were often uninhibited and daring in their work with children. They were a source of inspiration.

JAMES A. SMITH
Oswego, New York

Contents

Part One

The Nature of Creative Teaching

I

Basic Principles
of Creative
Teaching

It's a sad thing to say of the vocabulary of any set of reading books for an infant room that it must necessarily be a dead vocabulary. Yet I say it. For although the first quality of life is change, these vocabularies never change. Winter and summer, for brown race or white, through loud mood or quiet, the next group of words, related or not to the current temper of the room, inexorably moves into place for the day's study.

I tried to make this division between the climate of a room and an imposed reading book by making another set of books from the immediate material, but all I did was to compose another dead vocabulary. For although they are closer to the Maori children than the books of the English upper-middle class, their vocabulary is static too, and it is not the answer to the question I have asked myself for years: What is the organic reading vocabulary?

At last I know: Primer children write their own books.[1]

SYLVIA ASHTON-WARNER

TO THE READER

This chapter presents a review of Book I of this series. If he has not already done so, the reader is advised to examine that volume before reading the material presented here. Even if the reader has read Book I, he will want to read the first part of this chapter, which describes how the basic principles of creative teaching were applied in a culturally deprived area of a large urban community.

Introduction

"They are *such* slow learners," the teacher told me as I surveyed the group of six-, seven- and eight-year-olds. "I don't believe any of them has an IQ above ninety. And with their poor backgrounds and all added to that, I don't think they are *ever* going to read," she added, almost in despair.

"Well," I asked, watching the children who stared at me dull-

[1] Sylvia Ashton-Warner, *Teacher* (New York: Bantam Books, 1964), p. 54.

eyed but with a certain spark of curiosity, "just what *can* they read?"

"Oh, they *all* know the twenty words on this chart," she said, pointing to a chart labeled "Words We Know." "When *everyone* knows a word we put it up here. A few of them can read in the pre-primers, but that's all."

I turned to the chart and read *I, them, they, book, see, run, mother, father, it, me, my, to, the, see, baby, dog, walk, in, oh, book.* "May I watch for a while?" I asked.

And I did. Three children came to a corner of the room and played some commercial readiness games with the teacher while the rest worked on some dittoed readiness sheets at their desks. For two hours there was a shifting of groups as children came to work with the teacher. Little by little, the children at their desks became bored and restless; more and more, the teacher interrupted her group work with such phrases as "Daniel, you are not cooperating," "Maria, I know you have work to do," and "Kevin, why are you out of your seat?"

What work Maria was supposed to be doing was difficult to discern. Christmas was only a week away, yet the room was barren of things for the children to do. In the back of the room three small bulletin boards were fastened to the cloak closets. On one there was a commercial cutout of a Christmas tree, on another, a commercial cutout of a reindeer, and on the third, a commercial cutout of a Santa Claus. Along the window sill sat a row of scrawny plants. On a table in the front of the room stood piles of books—old, worn, faded, unattractive books. Over the chart, "Words We Know," was a shelf on which there was a box with SURPRISE printed on it, but it was out of reach, and in all the days of my visit I never saw it used. And that was all, except for thirty-five screwed-down desks and twenty dull, apathetic faces that stole timid glances at me from time to time.

And this was reading! Slow-learning indeed! "Culturally deprived," .hey said. "Educationally deprived," I said—and by people who should know better. How I longed to get at them, to erase that dull apathetic look from their faces, to make them come alive!

I got my chance the next day, after I had learned a little about the children. And little by little they became human beings, lovely human beings, *creative* human beings. Kevin, supposed to be the slowest in the room, fell in love with me—and I with him. He couldn't read anything, the teacher had told me, not even all twenty words on the chart, but she had to make exceptions—it wasn't totally fair to the other children not to! But Kevin had no father and I became the substitute.

I brought in a tape recorder before school started that day. "What is it?" they asked, crowding around.

"Haven't you ever seen one before?" I asked.

"No—no—what is it?"

How do you explain a tape recorder? "Well," I said, "it is really called a tape recorder but I call it my magic box. Do you know what *magic* is?"

"No—what is it?"

"Haven't you ever seen a magician on television or at the movies?" I asked.

"Maybe," said Thomas. "I think I saw one once. He had two big rings and he went like this and they were together and no one could pull them apart. I think they said he was a magician."

"He *was* a magician," I said. "A magician does tricks."

"Oh," said Peggy with the apathy leaving her eyes, "I think I saw one on TV too. He pulled a rabbit out of a hat!"

"Now you've got it!" I encouraged, "anyone else—"

Words, words, words—they spilled out, filled the very corners of the dull room with color and action, and I listened. With such a wealth of spoken words, why no reading words? We would see.

"O.K. Now listen and I'll tell you about the magic box."

Dead silence.

"It's magic because, when we talk into this little box, these wheels go round and our voice goes on this tape here. After we talk I can push this button and you can hear your own voice saying exactly what you said into the box."

"Can we try it? Oh, let us try it, please!"

"Of course, we've got to try it—but first we have to make sure everyone gets a chance. Why don't you make a line here and then listen to me once more."

Shoving and pushing and laughing eagerness, but only for a minute. Then Margaret said, "Sh! Be quiet! Mr. Smith wants to talk."

More silence.

"Thank you, Margaret. What I wanted to say was this: sometimes we can't think of anything to say when it's our turn. So you say anything you want to, but if you can't think of anything, tell me about you—where you live, how many there are in your family, about your pet or favorite toy, what you do after school—or tell me about

Christmas. Think about it for a minute. What are you going to say?"

Dead silence—eyes rolling, fingers tapping foreheads, the wheels grinding.

"Well, Charlie, you seem to be first in line. Are you ready?"

Push the button—hand the mike to Charlie, who is all grins. "My name is Charlie Martin and I go to Maple Street School. I live at twelve Pine Avenue, I have a mother, a father, three sisters, and four brothers in my family—"

I nod encouragement. Charlie finishes and passes the mike to Owen. One by one they speak. Soon it is all over. I stop the tape and rewind it. The suspense in the air is thick. "Now for the magic!" Each child leans forward in his seat. The tape talks. "My name is Charlie Martin—" Giggling, hiding of faces in folded arms on the desk, an occasional guffaw of laughter, squeals of delight. And, after it is over, chatter, chatter, chatter. The magic box is a hit!

"Let's do it again!"

"Later," I say. "That's why I wanted you to try it out now so you will know how to use it later."

It is now school time. Everyone in his seat, hands folded, but no apathy now. A sea of faces (Caucasian, Negro, Oriental) so far below me, all chins turned up, all faces smiling.

"I think we'll have some fun together this afternoon with many kinds of magic," I say, "and we'll start by making sure you can tell that wonderful word when you *see* it as well as when you *hear* it. This is how it looks." Dare I put it on the coveted list of "Words We Know"? No, better not! So I print it on the chalkboard. "Read it to me," I say, and they all shout, "Magic!"

"Good!" I say. "We have learned to read a new word. Now we're going to make some magic—would you like that?"

A chorus of "Yes—how?"

"Watch me carefully," I say, "for I'm going to draw something on the board and you're going to help me. And after a while you'll make some magic with what I am putting on the board."

They lean forward as I draw. "Two Christmas trees," they say when I have finished.

"Right," I say, "two Christmas trees, but I must tell you something about them. They're very, very sad Christmas trees. Could you guess why they're so sad?"

No response.

"Well," I go on, "just imagine you were a Christmas tree and it

was only one week before Christmas—why would *you* be sad?"
Hands pop up.
"Lucy?"
"They haven't got any decorations," says Lucy.
"Well, I guess that would make any Christmas tree sad," I
comment. "No decorations. Now that's a big word. I wonder if we
could read it?" And I print it under the word "magic" on the chalk-
board.
"That's a big word, all right," volunteers Jonah. "I bet that's a
fifth-grade word."
"It is, indeed," I say, "and now you can read a fifth-grade word.
Well, now, I don't like to think of Christmas trees feeling sad
around Christmas. What can we do about it?"
Kevin shouts, "Decorate them!"
"A good idea," I agree, "let's do that. Kevin, you pass this
box of chalk around and let everyone take a piece. Now the people
in these two rows can work on this Christmas tree and the people in
these two rows can work on this one. Each one of you draw one
thing on the tree—you can draw it more than once if you like, but
each draw *one* thing and then everyone will get a chance. O.K., let's
see how many *different* things we can draw!"
Four children go to the board and begin to draw, two to a tree,
then four more. While they are drawing, I put some chart paper on
the chalkboard.
"I'd like to do something else while those people are working
at the board," I remark. "I'd like to write a story on these papers
about our Christmas tree. Do you think those of you who are finished
drawing could help me?"
Eyes are now torn between the drawers and the teacher. "Watch
if you like," I say, "or help me if you like. Does anyone have a name
for our story?"
Arthur, sensitive, shy Arthur, says, "The Sad Christmas Tree."
I tell him I like it and print it with red flo-pen across the top of the
chart paper.
"And how shall we begin our story?" I ask.
"Once there was a Christmas tree," says Lucy. Of course, how
else? The joy of storytelling. Once there was . . . I print it on the
chart.
"And what about the Christmas tree?"
"It was sad." (Arthur again.) I print it.

"So what did we do?" I ask.

"We decorated it," says Nancy.

I print that too.

"Let's see how we decorated it," I say. "Charlie, what did you draw on the Christmas tree?"

"Stars."

"And Melba?"

"Candy canes."

"Kevin?"

"Candles."

"Let's put it in our story." And I print, "Charlie drew stars. Melba drew candy canes. Kevin drew candles."

Before long the trees are decorated; beautiful, childish, and creative, they cover the chalkboard. And the story is finished, too. Well, almost. . . .

The Sad Christmas Tree

Once there was a Christmas tree.
It was sad.
We decorated it.
Charlie drew stars.
Melba drew candy canes.
Kevin drew candles.
Daniel drew tinsel.
Maria and Jimmy put presents at the bottom.
Thomas drew snowflakes.
Peggy and Walter drew Christmas balls.
Owen and Willard drew bells.
Lucy drew strings of beads.
Jonah drew wreaths.
Arthur drew holly.
Nancy and Sarah drew lights.
Peter drew a Santa Claus.
June put a star on top.
Ellen wrote "Merry Christmas" over it.
Harry drew a manger.

I read it to them, using a liner. "My, that's a good story," I say. "And now how shall we end it?"

June's hand is up. I nod to her. "We could put 'So, it was glad!' " she says.

"Perfect," I say. "Now listen once again while I read it and this time will you each try to remember the line that tells what *you* did?" So I read it again—and the next time each reads his own line. Harry draws my attention to the fact that we have used the big word from the chalkboard in our story, so we spend some time talking about the difference between the word "decorations" and the word "decorated." They discover that it sounds different at the end—and looks different, too.

"I've got a good idea!" I exclaim. "Let's read our story like we just did and we will put it on the magic box. Let's all read the first three lines together, then each person will read his line alone. Then we can all read the last line together. Shall we try it once before we put it on the tape?"

We try it and it is good. But there is a problem where two people's names appear on one line. Daniel resolves this by suggesting that both people read the line together. Good! It adds variety and music to the tape. They clap after the playback.

"Play it again," they beg.

"All right, but only once because we have something else to do. Did you forget about the magic? We're going to make magic, remember?"

They have forgotten, so we listen to the tape once more and Jonah says, "Now, what about the magic?"

"Well," I say, "the Christmas trees you drew are beautiful, but they're not like the Christmas trees I see when I walk along Genesee Street where all the store decorations are. How are they different?"

We have a discussion about that, and Walter suggests they are only black and white chalk.

"I feel like Walter does," I agree. "Christmas trees generally have a lot of color. Let's do some magic. Kevin and Charlie, you pull down the shades; Jonah, you stand by the light switch and wait until I tell you what to do."

The children do not know that I have given them fluorescent chalk with which to draw, and so I slide a table under the chalkboard, on which I have snapped a black light. When the shades are down I tell all the children to say "Let There Be Magic" with me. I print the phrase on the chalkboard and ask if anyone can read it. They figure it out, and we say it together. Jonah snaps out the lights on the word "Magic," and the Christmas trees burst into color. Gasps of delight! "We made magic!"

We write a story then about the Magic Christmas Tree. We have to find good words to describe it, and we have to find words to tell how we felt when the magic came. It goes like this:

> *The Magic Christmas Trees*
> Once there were two Christmas trees.
> They were on the chalkboard.
> They were sad.
> They had no decorations
> So we decorated them.
>
> And we said,
> "Let there be magic!"
> There was magic.
> Suddenly they were all in colors.
> Beautiful, wonderful, happy trees
> All tinsel, stars, and colored toys.
> We were surprised and happy.
> Happy girls and boys!

Such a sense of achievement! So many "fifth-grade" words, and even some poetry in it (that was Lucy's idea). We have to put it on tape, too, and so we work out a pattern for saying it.

"Play it again—play both our stories." So we play it again while they read the words from the charts at the front of the room.

The afternoon is over—where did the two hours go? "Will you come back tomorrow?" They help me pack my things and take them to my car.

"Keep reading the stories," I comment, "I'll be back tomorrow and I'd like to hear each one of you read them to me. I'll leave the magic box so you can listen and get help with the words you forget. So many good words—and such big ones! I don't know how many you will remember. Try and see."

Kevin is waiting at the door. "Do you want me to read you the big words now?" he asks.

"Indeed I do."

We turn back to the charts. I hand him a pointer—he is so small! Meticulously, he points first to the word on the board. "It says 'magic,' " he says.

"Yes," I answer quietly, "it certainly does."

He points to the first chart. "That says 'Christmas,' " he says, pointing to it twice, "and that says 'decorated'—and this says 'Kevin made candles.' "

"You are so right!" I exclaim. "Such big words you learned today—can you read any of these?" We look at the other chart.

"That says 'magic' too," he says, pointing, "and that says 'Christmas tree' and that says 'Christmas tree,' and that says 'magic' and here is 'decorations' again."

They all want to read the words to me but it is time for the bus. We all hate to go. It is such fun making magic!

*   *   *

"And with their poor backgrounds added to that I don't think they are ever *going to read," the teacher had said. "Twenty words we know . . . Kevin is the slowest; he doesn't even know all the words on the chart. . . ."*

But Kevin had read the fifth-grade words. All told, the whole afternoon had been one of magic.

*   *   *

That's what creative teaching does: it catches the magic within children which makes them learn, and it brings it out into the open where you can get at it and work with it. It is different from other kinds of teaching. I have shown how it is different in Book I of this series[2] by extracting from current research those facts we know to be true of creativity, and compiling a set of principles about creative teaching—which, incidentally, I used in planning the above lesson in reading. The reader will want to refer to Book I of this series for a detailed explanation of these principles. But, because the material that follows in this volume is based on these principles, I feel justified in summarizing them here.

Principles Basic to Creative Teaching

1. Something new, different, or unique results.
2. Divergent thinking processes are stressed.
3. Motivational tensions are a prerequisite to the creative process; the process serves as a tension-relieving agent.
4. Open-ended situations are utilized.
5. There comes a time when the teacher withdraws and children face the unknown themselves.
6. The outcomes are unpredictable.

[2] James A. Smith, *Setting Conditions for Creative Teaching in the Elementary School* (Boston: Allyn and Bacon, Inc., 1966).

7. Conditions are set which make possible preconscious thinking.
8. Students are encouraged to generate and develop their own ideas.
9. Differences, uniqueness, individuality, and originality are stressed and rewarded.
10. The process is as important as the product.
11. Certain conditions must be set to permit creativity to appear.
12. It is success- rather than failure-oriented.
13. Provision is made for learning knowledges and skills; but provision is also made to apply these to new, problem-solving situations.
14. Self-initiated learning is encouraged.
15. Skills of constructive criticism and evaluation are developed.
16. Ideas and objects are manipulated and explored.
17. It employs democratic processes.
18. Methods are used which are unique to the development of creativity.[3]

My lesson was also guided by my knowledge of the material on creativity which I used in Book I. Some of this knowledge is summarized below as a review for the reader. It is essential to understanding the material in the remaining chapters.

Basic Principles of Creativity

Throughout this series the following definition of creativity is used: Creativity means tapping our experiences and rearranging them into something new.

1. All children are born creative.
2. There is a relationship between creativity and intelligence; highly creative people are always highly intelligent, though highly intelligent people are not always creative. But all children can create to some degree.
3. Creativity is a form of giftedness which is not measured by current intelligence tests.
4. All areas of the curriculum may be used to develop creativity.
5. Creativity is a process and a product.
6. Creativity is developed by focusing on those processes of the intellect which fall under the general area of divergent thinking. This area of the intellect has been greatly neglected in our teaching up to this point.
7. All creative processes cannot always be developed at one time or in one lesson. Lessons must be planned to focus on each process.

[3] Alex Osborn, *Applied Imagination* (3rd ed.) (New York: Charles Scribner's Sons, 1963), pp. 69–327.

8. Creativity cannot be taught; we can only set conditions for it to happen in and insure its reappearance through reinforcement.
9. More knowledge, more skills, and more facts than ever before are required for creativity to be developed.
10. The theories of creative development lead us to believe that children must be able to tap all of life's experiences in order to become truly creative; unnecessary rules and actions may force much of their experience into the preconscious or subconscious where it cannot be readily used.
11. Excessive conformity and rigidity are true enemies of creativity.
12. Children go through definite steps in the creative process.[4]
13. Creative teaching and creative learning can be more effective than other types of teaching and learning.
14. Children who have lost much of their creativity may be helped to regain it by special methods of teaching.[5]

Summary

Creative teaching is a special method of teaching. Although it utilizes many of the principles of all good teaching, it is attainable only when teachers understand those factors which make it different from other types of teaching. Every area of the curriculum can be a tool for developing creativity if the basic principles stated in this chapter are understood and applied. We have seen how, through creative teaching, a teacher can develop creativity *while* he is developing basic reading skills. The teaching of reading can indeed be a highly creative process.

TO THE COLLEGE STUDENT

1. Read *Spinster,* by Sylvia Ashton-Warner, and discuss it in class. Then read *Teacher,* by the same author. (See bibliography.)

2. Explain the quotation from Sylvia Ashton-Warner's *Teacher* at the beginning of this chapter. What does it mean to you?

3. Consider the material you read in Chapter II of Book II, *Creative Teaching of the Language Arts in the Elementary School,* and then discuss this statement: The chart, "Words We Know," which the teacher used at the front of the room, was a good technique for building reading vocabulary.

[4] *Ibid.*
[5] *Ibid.,* pp. 69–327.

4. In the account of the reading lesson given in this chapter, the children spent the entire afternoon developing language skills. Tell how the teacher taught good listening skills. How did he foster skills in effective oral expression? In reading? Is this total blend of teaching without specific class periods a good idea? Justify your reasoning.

5. Discuss the following statements:
   a. Mr. Smith used the logical sequential development of language skills while teaching his lesson.
   b. Mr. Smith considered the biology of the children while teaching his lesson.
   c. Mr. Smith used "contrived" teaching techniques or "normal" teaching techniques to develop his lesson.

6. What should have been done on the day following Mr. Smith's lesson to insure the fixation of vocabulary and its further development?

TO THE CLASSROOM TEACHER

1. Watch your pupils carefully while you are teaching reading and ask yourself these questions:
   a. Are they really interested?
   b. Are they bored?
   c. Do they see the purpose behind what I am doing?
   d. Is reading a discovery time, a highly exciting and strongly motivating time?
   e. Do the children love books and clamor for them outside of reading periods?
   f. How many of my lessons this week helped children to be creative?

2. How many of the principles of creative teaching listed in this chapter are applicable to your reading lessons?

3. How might you apply the principles of creative teaching to each of the following areas of reading:
   a. The teaching of phonics.
   b. The teaching of reading comprehension.
   c. The teaching of structural analysis.
   d. The teaching of map reading.

4. Take from your teacher's manual a lesson that you will teach in the next few days and make it as creative as possible by applying as many as possible of the principles mentioned in this chapter.

TO THE COLLEGE STUDENT AND THE CLASSROOM TEACHER

1. Examine each of the principles of creative teaching summarized in this chapter and apply them to the reading lesson at the beginning of the chapter. How many of the principles were apparent in the lesson? Were there some that were not?

2. Repeat the above with the principles of creativity. Which ones did Mr. Smith apply in his lesson?

3. Using the steps of language development as they are outlined in Book II of this series, examine Mr. Smith's lesson and note how he followed the logical language sequence.

4. Examine a teacher's manual for a reading series. How many lessons can you find which might be classified as creative? In making your judgment, apply as criteria the principles stated in this chapter.

5. Take any lesson from a teacher's manual and rewrite it so it employs the principles of creative teaching *and* develops creativity in the children.

SELECTED BIBLIOGRAPHY

ANDERSON, H. E. (ed.). *Creativity and Its Cultivation*. New York: Harper & Row, 1959.

ASHTON-WARNER, SYLVIA. *Teacher*. New York: Bantam Books, 1963.

———. *Spinster*. New York: Simon and Schuster, 1959.

GETZELS, JACOB W. and PHILIP W. JACKSON. *Creativity and Intelligence*. New York: John Wiley & Sons, Inc., 1962.

GRUBER, HOWARD, GLEN TERRELL and MICHAEL WERTHEIMER (eds.). *Contemporary Approaches to Creative Thinking*. New York: Atherton Press, 1964.

GUILFORD, J. P. "The Structure of Intellect," *Psychological Bulletin,* LIII (1956), 277–95.

———. "Three Faces of Intellect," *American Psychologist,* XIV (1959), 469–79.

LOWENFELD, VIKTOR. *Creative and Mental Growth.* New York: Macmillan Company, 1947.

MARKSBERRY, MARY LEE. *Foundation of Creativity.* New York: Harper & Row, 1963.

MEARNS, HUGHES. *Creative Power: The Education of Youth in the Creative Arts* (rev. ed.). New York: Dover Publications, 1958.

MIEL, ALICE (ed.). *Creativity in Teaching: Invitations and Instances.* Belmont, Calif.: Wadsworth Publishing Co., Inc., 1961.

OSBORN, ALEX. *Applied Imagination* (rev. ed.). New York: Charles Scribner's Sons, 1963.

RUGG, HAROLD. *Imagination: An Inquiry into the Sources and Conditions That Stimulate Creativity.* New York: Harper & Row, 1963.

RUSSELL, DAVID. *Children's Thinking.* New York: Ginn and Co., 1956.

TAYLOR, CALVIN W. (ed.). *Creativity: Progress and Potential.* New York: McGraw-Hill, 1964.

———— and FRANK BARRON. *Scientific Creativity: Its Recognition and Development.* New York: John Wiley & Sons, Inc., 1963.

TORRANCE, E. PAUL (ed.). *Creativity.* Minneapolis: University of Minnesota, Center for Continuation Study of the General Extension Division, 1959.

————. *Guiding Creative Talent.* Englewood Cliffs, N.J.: Prentice-Hall, Inc., 1962.

————. *Rewarding Creative Behavior.* Englewood Cliffs, N.J.: Prentice-Hall, Inc., 1965.

VON FANGE, E. K. *Professional Creativity.* Englewood Cliffs, N.J.: Prentice-Hall, Inc., 1959.

WERTHEIMER, M. *Productive Thinking.* New York: Harper & Row, 1959.

WILT, MIRIAM E. *Creativity in the Elementary School.* New York: Appleton-Century-Crofts, Inc., 1959.

ZIRBES, LAURA. *Spurs to Creative Teaching.* New York: G. P. Putnam's Sons, 1959.

II

The Nature of Reading

I see the mind of a five-year-old as a volcano with two vents: destructiveness and creativeness. And I see that to the extent that we widen the creative channel, we atrophy the destructive one. And it seems to me that since these words of the key vocabulary are no less than the captions of the dynamic life itself, they course out through the creative channel, making their contribution to the drying up of the destructive vent. From all of which I am constrained to see it as creative reading and to count it among the arts.

First words must mean something to a child.

First words must have intense meaning for a child. They must be part of his being.[1]

SYLVIA ASHTON-WARNER

TO THE READER

This chapter describes the reading process and the primary reading program. The seasoned teacher may want to omit this chapter and look at the ideas for creative teaching in Chapter III. The teacher-in-training will need to read the whole chapter and think through the experiences suggested.

Introduction

Reading falls into the natural sequence of language development after good listening and oral expression skills have been developed (see Book II of this series).[2] When a child is speaking many words and using them as an integral part of his personality, he is ready to read them. In teaching reading to young children, this is often the first place where we go wrong: we pull words from thin air and try to put them into the child. Often we make matters worse by putting these strange words into printed context outside the realm of the child's experience and expecting him to read—and he cannot.

[1] Sylvia Ashton-Warner, *Teacher* (New York: Bantam Books, 1964), pp. 29–30.

[2] James A. Smith, *Creative Teaching of the Language Arts in the Elementary School* (Boston: Allyn and Bacon, Inc., 1967).

Children can read any word they speak. One of the greatest hoaxes in all of educational pedagogy is that which says that reading vocabulary must be developed in a predetermined logical sequence. It just isn't so. Linguists tell us that when a child comes to school he has all the language equipment he needs in order to learn reading and all the other skills of language. The trouble is that we don't use his equipment. We contrive artificial systems of language development and methods of teaching reading, and we impose them on children. It is almost as though the child has to learn two languages in order to be able to read—one for communication and one to "get through" his reading books.

More research has been done in the area of reading than in any other area of the elementary school curriculum. This is justifiable because reading is an important skill needed for learning. But it is not the most important method of communication.[3] It is important only to the degree that it *communicates!*

Much confusion exists about this research. This is the second place where we go wrong; we have built up a vast storehouse of knowledge about reading, but *all* the needed knowledge is not yet known. And, because there are great gaps in that knowledge, we have turned to the next best source—the opinion of the experts in the reading field. What is more, where the knowledge is lacking, we have filled in with the opinions so that we often confuse the two. The result is that many experts have advocated their "systems" of teaching reading, basing them on known truths but filling in the gaps with their own ideas. Schools have often adopted these systems so wholeheartedly that teachers are not permitted to skip one page of a basal reading book or omit one single exercise in the reading manual that accompanies the text. Many teachers have simply become middlemen, transmitting the ideas of the authors of a basal series to the children and not daring to use their own ideas to teach reading as a communication skill. This takes all the sense out of language skill development and reduces the role of the teacher to that of a puppet. Certainly no creativity can break through such rigid conformity.

Teachers are *teaching* experts. Their training has made them this. Reading experts can help with a multitude of ideas but they cannot possibly know the problems of any *one* teacher with any *one* group of children. Basal readers and teachers' manuals work *only* if they are

[3] *Ibid.,* Chapters II and III.

adapted to the group of children using them, and they can be invaluable when used this way but are almost worthless when they are not.

Take the lesson described in Chapter I as a case in point. The children in this chapter were from culturally deprived areas. In the basal preprimers and primers of the series that the teacher was using *not one single* story (if we can call them that!) had any relationship to the experiences of these children. The children in the primer have pets; these city children are not allowed to have pets. The children in the series are all Caucasian; only five children in the class were Caucasian. The grandmother in the series is a little old white-haired lady who wears a shawl, lives on a farm, and doles out goodies. Most of these children never see their grandmothers, and those that do never see one like the one described in the text. The "basal" children live in the suburbs; these children live in the slums of the city. No wonder they do not identify with these books! They are, indeed, learning another language to be used in another world!

Most of the reading books on the market today are written by the experts, and these experts are all concerned with making a living. Consequently they plug their reading systems. One reading expert recently told me he was almost frightened by the dogmatic way in which his reading series was being used by school people. He has a good basic series, and in the introduction of the teacher's manual he clearly states that the series must be adapted to the children and makes many logical suggestions for this adaptation. Apparently some teachers do not read introductions to teachers' manuals; they plunge into Lesson I without first learning the primary objectives of the series and its basic philosophy.

We teach *children,* not reading. Any system of reading that does not consider the *particular* group of children and *each child in that group* first is pseudoscientific in its approach. And only a teacher can know the children she teaches—and know them she *must* before any significant gains can be accomplished.

The author feels strongly that reading becomes vital only when the teacher becomes the source of the plan of the teaching and when she is able to utilize the experts' books, materials, gimmicks, devices, and ideas to help her develop her *own* plan for her *own* particular group of children. Teaching is a creative role, not a mimetic one, and the teaching of reading must be a creative process.

Linguistic research of the past ten years has provided us with more implications as to how reading should be taught than has any other source. Two books have been published in the past decade which have contributed significantly to the creative approach to the teaching of reading: Sylvia Ashton-Warner's *Spinster*[4] and *Teacher*.[5] Miss Ashton-Warner calls her pedagogy "organic reading." I call it the creative teaching of reading. Miss Ashton-Warner knows how to teach reading creatively; more important, she knows how the reading process takes place.

What Is Reading?

Reading is the ability to recognize and understand the printed symbols of the child's spoken vocabulary. Printed words, as well as spoken ones, are meaningful to the young child only insofar as his field of experience overlaps that of the author of the printed text. The old cliché, "You can take from a book only what you bring to it," is, in essence, true. The reader learns from a book only if he is able to understand the printed symbols and rearrange them into vicarious experiences in his mind. His ability to think, to reason, and to conceptualize makes it possible for him to receive new ideas from a printed page without actually experiencing the new idea, *but he must have experienced each symbol that helps make up the new idea!*

This is illustrated by an incident in a typical first-grade room. A city child told of a trip he took in the summer to an animal farm, where, among other things, he saw a kangaroo. None of the other city children had ever seen a kangaroo. Ideally, the teacher would show a picture of a kangaroo and, through discussion, build the understandings necessary to give children a correct visual image of a kangaroo. But there was no picture available at the moment, so the teacher resorted to the use of word symbols. She printed the idea on the board:

> Tommy went to the game farm.
> He saw a kangaroo.

Because of the unusual shape of the word "kangaroo" children memorized it quickly, but they learned nothing until the word took on

---

[4] Sylvia Ashton-Warner, *Spinster* (New York: Simon and Schuster, 1959).
[5] Sylvia Ashton-Warner, *Teacher* (New York: Bantam Books, 1964).

meaning. The teacher gave the word meaning by using the children's past experiences. Every child in the room had experienced size and variances in height, so when Tommy said, "The kangaroo is as tall as my Daddy," an image formed in each child's mind. If the children did not know Tommy's daddy, this image varied among them as they compared it to their own daddies. In the early part of the year, a rabbit had been brought to the classroom, so each child had experienced "hopping," "softness," and various concepts about the rabbit. Consequently, when the teacher added, "The kangaroo is soft. He hops. His back legs are much bigger than his forelegs," the children projected their past experiences into the new experience and gradually the blurred image of the kangaroo became more clear. Experience combined with the power of imagery made it possible for the children to gain new understandings, concepts, and learnings from their reading of the new word.

The sentence below may or may not communicate meaning:

John drove into the megalopolis each Saturday and took a class in origami.

Immediately we know that John went somewhere and took a course in something. But only those who have experienced and labeled a city or chain of cities as a megalopolis, and only those who have seen the art of Japansese paper-folding and have used the label "origami" to define it, will know the entire meaning of the sentence.

Read the sentences below:

1. The sentinent walked down the street with a pogo.
2. The coult walked down the street with a jeliet in his hand. Along came a magpiet.
3. The sentinent barep denred his oastes.

In each of these situations, you can probably read each sentence perfectly. But can you? Can you read or can you simply figure out sounds and words? Your knowledge of phonics and the skills in attacking new words which you learned in grade school have all been summoned up and put to use—but to what avail? Do you yet know the meaning of the sentences? You may be able to guess the meaning of numbers 1 and 2, but with number 3 you are completely lost. This is so because number 3 contains so many words unrelated to your field of experience that all your reading skills are still not adequate to give meaning to the sentence. It is beyond your reading level because it is beyond your experience level (both direct and symbolic).

Think back on how you read these sentences. You probably sounded out the unfamiliar words or associated them with similar words in order to put sense into the sentence. Look at sentence 1. What is a sentinent? You probably are thinking, "A guard or a soldier." What is a pogo? You are probably thinking, "A pogo stick." Why did you think that? You are trying very hard to put sense into the sentence—to tie it in with your experience, which was your first criterion in reading it. Then you used other criteria, but all directed toward the first: *to make it make sense!* Here are some of the things you probably did:

1. You sounded out the unfamiliar words and said them two or three different ways, trying to associate them with some spoken symbol within your own experience. *Children learning to read do this also. They try to apply phonics skills to new words and then associate them with some word in their oral vocabulary.*

2. You probably then associated the word *sentinent* with the word *sentinel* because they look alike and the sentence makes sense when you use this particular word. *In learning to read, children, too, associate words with other, familiar words in their visual vocabulary if they make sense.*

3. You probably then related the word *pogo* to a *pogo stick* because it, too, *looks like* the word pogo and it, too, *makes some sense. Children, in learning to read, learn meanings of words by the way they are used in context.*

In sentence 2 you probably thought of *coult* as a young horse because you associated it with the word *colt.* The word *jeliet* probably was difficult because, even though you could pronounce it, you could associate it with no word looking like it that could be effectively substituted in this particular context to give it meaning. Then you came to the word *hand,* and the meaning you had been able to build up in the sentence to this point was immediately shattered because young horses do not have hands. You hastened on to try to find a context clue but did not get much help. You probably read the last sentence as, "Along came a bird," associating *magpiet* with *magpie.*

Sentence 3 is completely lost to you; it is no more than jargon. Can you, then, read the sentence? No, you can not. Because reading is not word-calling; it is getting the meaning of the printed word from the page. The teaching of reading means simply helping children acquire those skills needed to get the meaning of the printed word from the page. But we have seen that the acquisition of all the skills is of little or no value without the ingredient basic to all reading— experience with the words to make them meaningful.

Now it is easy to understand why young children, before they can really learn to read, must have a wide range of experiences to which they have attached a multitude of oral symbols. We can see, too, why the primary program in reading must be loaded with experiences to which children and teachers apply symbolic expression. Thus the children are constantly building up new words in their speaking vocabulary so that they will be able to read them.

Reading is the ability to recognize, say, and understand the printed symbols on a page. Reading is a skill or tool which helps an author communicate with the reader. Children read because they want to know what is on the page. The reading itself is not sacred. It is what the reading *tells* the child that is important. Reading is an important means of communication but it is not the only one, nor is it the best. To insure the development of a good primary reading program children must have: (1) a large background of experiences, (2) the ability to listen well, and (3) a good oral vocabulary which labels their experiences meaningfully. With this background almost every child can be taught to read, provided, of course, he also has the required intelligence and has no serious physical, social, or emotional problem.

Teaching reading as a subject rather than a means for communication can be deadly for children. No one reads *reading*. He reads *something*—letters, books, poems, stories, newspapers—and he reads with a purpose. Each reading experience with children should have meaningful content, a purpose obvious to the child, and pleasant associations.

Not all children are ready to read at the same time. The wide socioeconomic and experiential backgrounds of children, combined with their physical development and intellectual ability, will determine the points at which children are able to begin the formal reading process effectively. Children often reach this stage at the first-grade level; therefore the formal reading program should generally begin in the first grade, when the average child has a mental age of about six and one-half years. The first-grade teacher is responsible for the continued development of the child as a whole, and to deprive him of a rich variety of experiences so that he may spend time reading from books is the quickest way to insure reading difficulty among children, both in ability and attitude. School personnel have been guilty of spending long hours having children read laboriously from good books which the children soon come to hate. The biology of the child is violated in long, tedious, uncomfortable sitting periods, in tiresome repetition, and in meaningless or dull stories.

When a first-grade teacher sees the teaching of reading as her major objective and consumes a major part of the child's day with reading, she is capitalizing on the excellent experiences the home and the kindergarten have provided for the child. For, after all, these give meaning to his reading stories, which, at the first-grade level, are based on his first-hand home and school experiences. She may flatter herself on the excellent reading ability of her children and be smug in her knowledge that she can teach any child to read! What she fails to realize is this: unless she continues to provide suitable additional experiences in social studies, community contacts, literature, music, and so forth, she is depriving succeeding teachers of their privilege of doing a good job in teaching reading. This explains why, too often, children start out as good readers but experience reading difficulty by the time they reach third grade. They lose meaning in their reading because planned background experience stops when formal reading begins.

A little girl in the first grade came home from school one day and announced to her parents that the children were to have two friends in school, and she named the two main characters in a popular reading series. For the next few days the child was enthusiastic over the motivation the teacher was giving them for the basic preprimers. Little by little, however, the enthusiasm died and the two characters were not mentioned for quite some time. Finally, one evening her father asked her what had become of the friends she used to talk so much about. At this, the six-year-old exploded, "Don't ever mention them to me again. All day long, that's all we hear—*Babs and Jim, Babs and Jim,* how I hate them!" Then picking up a book she opened to the page the children were reading and said, "Listen, Daddy!" and she read:

> Run *Babs*
> Run *Jim*
> Run *Rover*
> Run *Fluffy*
> Run, run, run!

Closing the book with an emphatic bang she looked up at her father and said disgustedly, "That's what we read today. Now, Daddy, I ask you, isn't that the dumbest story you ever heard!"

To children of the Space Age, who have radio, television, automobiles, fine recordings, and lovely books, such stories must seem insipid and cannot be expected to hold their attention long. Their real first interest in reading lies in their joy at discovering they *can* read. To exploit this joy, and to use it for needless repetition, means to soon destroy the only motivation the child has. The subject-matter of a primer does not hold the child; we cannot, as a rule, expect him to be interested in these first "stories" for long. In the average classroom, the child not only hears these stories read and reread by every member of his group; he has heard them read dozens of times by preceding and succeeding groups working at various ability levels.

How Does a Child Learn to Read?

To understand how a child learns to read means first to understand how he learns anything, especially how he learns to apply symbols to the world around him. It is a well-known fact that children the world over are born with the same physical equipment for producing sound. M. M. Lewis[6] has shown that all children make the same initial sounds in crying, babbling and gurgling. But children in different cultures *hear* different sounds; at a very early age the child begins to listen and to imitate those sounds which he hears or is able to reproduce and which meet his personal needs. The first sounds he is able to make require little tongue or lip agility and no teeth; they are made largely by blowing air through the lips with variance in the force of the air and differences in the shape of the lips. Thus "mama," "papa," and "nana" (for grandmother) are often among the first sounds American babies imitate.

Soon the child repeats other sounds, and then, with the development of the tongue, lips, and teeth, and with repeated experience, the child realizes that all objects in his life can be identified with a verbal label. He soon learns that all actions also can be labeled, and before

[6] M. M. Lewis, *How Children Learn to Speak* (New York: Basic Books, Inc., 1959).

long he is chattering words over and over—testing his ability to label those things with which he is familiar.

The child must memorize a word for every object in his environment and for every action he performs, and he must also learn the words that tie actions and objects together to make sensible sentences. This means he must recognize actions (such as walk, dance, run, jump, and crawl) and label them. It also means he must learn the shape of every object in his environment and remember it so he can label it. He must remember what a chair looks like, what a stove looks like, what a spoon looks like. Recognizing the shape, he can say the symbol that identifies it.

Children speak several verbal symbols on the conceptual level from the first time they are uttered. The word "table" is not only a label for a specific table; it is a concept because it is a generalization from several experiences with many different kinds of tables. In the illustration given in Book II of this series, *Creative Teaching of the Language Arts in the Elementary School,* we can see how the word "table" is already a concept in the mind of the child by the time he speaks it. He has learned that tables are objects with a flat top and four legs, which look somewhat alike, although there can be variances in size and shape.

In a college class the author recently attended, several different kinds of tables were set about the room. A four-year-old from the campus nursery school was brought in to visit. Each time she was asked to identify one of the tables by the question, "What is this?" she said, "Table," even though the tables varied in size, shape, and adornment. The next day, when she was returned to the room. the tables were dismantled—legs had been removed, cloths folded up, and the parts set about on the floor. When asked what each object was, she said, "Iron," "Wood," "Tablecloth," "A stick," "A plank" (for a piece of the picnic bench), "A board," and "A leg, I think." When asked if she knew what they could make, she suggested many things— but not a table.

A metal chair belonging to a kindergarten class had been left outdoors and was run over by a truck. When the chair was brought into the room, it was interesting to see that one child said, "What is that?" while another in the same room said, "What happened to the chair?" One child was able to visualize the original shape of the smashed chair, but to the other child, once it lost its shape, it lost its identity. So it was with the four-year-old from the nursery school. And so it is with most little children—a table is only a table when it is assembled as such; when ripped apart it is something else.

Children learn to recognize the symbols for objects in the same way they memorize the object—by its shape. At the beginning of the learning experience the word "table" is easily read because of its shape. Children do not need to know the phonetic sounds of the letters or the names of the letters themselves. To introduce these skills may slow the beginning reading power of some children, because then they have many things to learn and apply, and they do not need some of these things yet. Just as they learned to identify the table by seeing its shape, they will learn to read "table" most quickly by recognizing its shape. Most children pick up a wealth of words by recognizing their shapes ("sight" vocabulary).

Acquiring a sight vocabulary has its complexities. So many words are so nearly alike in shape that they become confusing, especially if they are also rather abstract in meaning. Study the words below:

1. on   no
2. saw   was
3. then   there
4. grandmother
5. hippopotamus
6. submarine

It is easy to see how a child can become very confused by the first three sets of words in this group. They are much alike in shape. A beginning reader often has difficulty developing a left-to-right concept because he has learned to recognize objects whether he sees them frontwards or backwards; he does not always look at a word from left to right and often calls *on, no* and *no, on.* Simple words, therefore, often create more reading difficulty in a child than the more complex words 4, 5 and 6, above. Each of these words has an unusual shape, as well as emotional or physical associations. Grandmother is very dear to most children, and the smaller word "mother" may be familiar to them. Therefore the word "grandmother" has many pleasant associations and is easily remembered. All the circles (o's) in hippopotamus may help the child remember it is about the big, fat animal the teacher showed them in a film. The shape of the word "submarine" even looks like a submarine, which may enable some child to remember the word after very few exposures to it.

A child learns to read his first words mainly by recognizing their shapes. After he is using many words fluently in his speech (sound images) and has many words in his sight vocabulary (visual images), skills are developed from these sight *and* sound images which help him to read all other words as well as to read independently. These skills include phonetic application, word analysis, and structural analysis.

Stages of Reading Development

There are basically four recognizable stages in the normal development of reading:[7]

1. The readiness stage.
2. The beginning reading stage.
3. The stage of rapid growth.
4. The stage of reading power.

The first three stages generally constitute the normal growth pattern of the primary-grade child. The stage of reading power is developed, as a rule, in the intermediate grades. The first three stages, when broadened, indicate the instructional tasks of the primary teacher.

The primary teacher is faced with six major instructional tasks:

1. Providing a good reading readiness program.
2. Developing a beginning program in reading—developing a basic sight vocabulary.
3. Developing good reading habits (eye movement, etc.)
4. Developing reading skills—work with words, phonetic analysis, structural analysis, speed, and comprehension.
5. Developing independent reading.
6. Developing creativity.

Each of the stages and tasks of the primary teacher will be considered on the following pages.

The Readiness Stage

In order for children to be able to read, certain conditions must be present.

[7] Paul McKee, *The Teaching of Reading in the Elementary School* (New York: Houghton Mifflin Co., 1948), p. 138.

First, the child must have a wide *experiential* background. Reading is the visual presentation of an oral vocabulary derived from experience. As stated above, to be able to understand the visual symbols, the child must have a direct or vicarious experience to back them up.

Second, the child must be developmentally ready to read. This means he must be physically, socially, and emotionally mature enough to read. Physical readiness means that his eyes must be developed enough so that they can focus properly on print about 12 inches from his face. It means that he must be able to hold a book and sit fairly quiet, and his attention span must be long enough so that he can concentrate for ten or fifteen minutes on a single thing. Physical readiness means that he has enough eye-hand coordination to react to printed symbols and handle reading materials automatically. His fine finger muscles must have matured to the point where he is not clumsy in his use of reading materials. And he must have developed certain physical skills, such as auditory and visual discrimination ability (see page 115).

Social and emotional maturity mean the child must be psychologically ready—he must have the correct attitude toward reading. He must feel emotionally secure and socially at ease, that he has status as an accepted member of a congenial group. Emotional disorders can provide blocks in the reading process. The child must feel accepted by his teacher and be comfortably at ease with reading materials. He must also feel challenged and motivated by the reading experience.

Third, the child must be intellectually ready to read. He must be able to conceptualize, to recognize symbols, and to understand the meaning of reading. Although very intelligent children may be ready at an earlier age than normal children, early studies showed that most children were physically, psychologically, emotionally, socially, and intellectually ready to read at the mental age of 6.5.[8] Since intelligence and reading ability are highly correlated, there will be vast differences in the reading abilities of children within any given grade.

Setting Conditions for Reading Through Skill Readiness

In addition to experiential, psychological, and intellectual readiness, there are certain skills which must be developed in each child before he is able to read.

[8] M. V. Morphett and C. Washburne, "When Should Children Begin to Read?" *Elementary School Journal*, XXXI (1931), pp. 496–503.

Developing the ability to listen and follow directions.

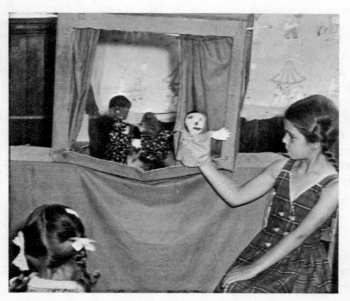

Developing a good oral vocabulary and good listening ability.

Developing good visual discrimination: manipulating shapes.

Developing comprehension abilities and visual acuity.

1. He must have a desire to read.
2. He must develop the ability to listen.
3. He must develop a good oral vocabulary.
4. He must develop the left-to-right progression concept and the ability to read on a line.
5. He must develop audio acuity.
6. He must develop a keen sense of visual discrimination.
7. He must develop the ability to comprehend.
8. He must develop skill in oral communication (speech).
9. He must develop skill in concept formation.
10. He must develop a knowledge of the alphabet.
11. He must learn how to handle books.

The Beginning Program in Reading

The beginning reading program is concerned with:

1. Developing a sight vocabulary.
2. Developing good eye movement across the page.
3. Developing a comfortable rate of speed in each child.
4. Making sure the child understands what he reads.
5. Introducing him to books within his range of ability.
6. Beginning to develop a phonetic sense in seeing likenesses and differences in words, both in sound and shape.
7. Beginning to help each child read some materials independently.

How does a teacher know when a child is ready for a formal reading program? Basically, when he begins to read! A child brings material to the teacher to read. He may pick out phrases or words with his fingers and read them. He seems to have a high motivation toward figuring out the printed symbols. He sees differences in words and shapes. He has a good sense of audio discrimination. He talks freely and expresses himself well. He is physically mature. And at this psychological time, he should be taught to read. Grade level has nothing to do with it.

There are many ways a teacher may determine whether or not a child is ready for formal reading. Careful observation is the first. As the children work and play at kindergarten and first-grade activities, the observing teacher notes that George cannot put simple puzzles together; he has no concept of the relatedness of shapes. At clean-up time Ellen persistently tries to put a long block back on a short shelf. Alice tries to shove a large doll carriage through a smaller doorway. Marcia cannot tell one note from another. Jerry cannot sit with the group for a discussion.

None of these children is ready to read. George, Ellen, and Alice need more direct experience in developing visual acuity; Marcia needs more direct experience in audio discrimination; Jerry is too immature to concentrate. The teacher will provide more direct experiences for these children to prepare them to read. In observing each child, the teacher may note countless clues that will indicate whether or not the child is ready to read.

Many check lists are available to help teachers determine the child's readiness. Check lists serve the purpose of directing the teacher's observation to specific acts in the child's daily routine which indicate whether or not he has mastered certain readiness skills.

Reading readiness tests may also be given to help a teacher determine whether her interpretation of the child's behavior is logical. Has he mastered the fundamentals prerequisite for success in formal reading?

Many readiness workbooks are geared to checking this readiness, but a wise and observant teacher can tell many of these things without printed devices, which do not appeal to all children. Workbooks used as a check for readiness are justifiable, but, when used as instructional material at this stage, they often create more problems than they solve. Overuse of the workbook may mean that children are not getting the meaningful experience background necessary to understand the material to which they will later be exposed. Workbooks can deal only with various sorts of printed symbols; they do not replace direct experience in any way.

The teaching of reading must be individualized. While much reading can be taught by group work, time should be allotted each day for personal instruction for those children who need it. Often the whole class may read together, as illustrated by the lesson in Chapter I. But no teacher can teach a child to read without knowing a great deal about him, his likes, dislikes, home life, neighborhood experiences, and the level of experiences he has from day to day.

The best teaching of reading requires both group and individual work in the classroom. Each child is ready to read at a different time, and because each child is unique he may need a different approach or different techniques when he reaches the formal reading stage. The large classes confronting elementary teachers in our classrooms today prohibit to some extent this kind of teaching, though more of it could be done. The use of groups has been developed, and children are organized into areas of "like" problems which facilitate the teaching of reading, or any other subject, for that matter. Some ideas concerning grouping and individual teaching will be discussed later in this book. (See page 73.)

Probably the first sign of a child's readiness to read is his ability to read pictures, which are often his first symbolic experiences. In our culture the use of picture symbolism has reached such proportions that we cannot conceive of a child who does not understand its use to some degree coming to school. Yet not so many years ago in a little rural school, a teacher showed a young child of Polish descent the picture of a cow and the child said: "What is that?" "Why, it's a cow," the surprised teacher said. And the child smiled wisely and answered, "Naw, this no cow! The cow—she's big, she's fat, she's round and soft . . ." and in his broken English he proceeded to describe the cow with the aid of his waving hands.

This child, of limited experience, could not identify the very first step in symbolism: the picture of the actual object. It is difficult for us to imagine children today with so little background and experience that they have never before seen a picture! Yet somewhere (incidentally, perhaps) but certainly at an early age, every child comes to recognize a picture of an object as his first understanding of the meaning of symbolic representation. It is another step, and sometimes a difficult one, for him to recognize the printed words as symbols representing the pictures. In our modern books, pictures provide a bridge for the gap in the understanding of written symbols. Many adults still find that pictures are easier to read than printed words, and many modern magazines capitalize on this knowledge and tell their stories in pictures to a wide reading audience.

The concept of symbolism develops within a child as he matures. At first it is difficult for him to associate the noisy, screaming, racy, bright red object that tears down the street with the dull, inactive symbol *fire engine*. As he learns that everything can be represented symbolically, and as he remembers best the names of unusual objects, he remembers best the unusual words. The shape and contour of a word helps the child to retain its visual image, as was shown on page 27.

Setting Conditions for Developing a Sight Vocabulary

Developing a sight vocabulary in children means exposing them to phrases and words used in many different contexts so that they remember their shapes and recognize them "at sight." The creative teacher will find many ways to do this.

The Experience Chart. The most common way to build a sight vocabulary is the experience chart. It is a sound, logical method because it follows what we know to be sound in the development of language. The teacher takes the children on a trip (common experience) to a farm. Here they talk about what they see (listening and then oral labeling). "What is the man riding, Miss Allen?" "It is a tractor, Bill." "What is that tall thing?" "That's a silo." "What is it for?" "They store ensilage in it," and so on. The teacher and children return to the classroom and record their experiences on a series of simple charts.

Our Trip

We went to the farm.
We saw a barn.
We saw a silo.
Ensilage was in the silo.
We saw the cows.
They ate the ensilage.
We like the farm.

First they learn to read the chart in whole sentences or phrases. The teacher helps them to recognize and remember the words by making a duplicate chart and cutting it into strips. Children match the sentence on the strips with the original chart by reconstructing the story on a pocket chart. The children may then have fun mixing the sentences and creating a new story with them.

Obviously, work with the first reading charts is largely memorization. Children have memorized whole stories long before they come to school. Every parent has had the experience of reading "The Three Bears" to his three- or four-year-old only to find that, in attempting to omit a line or two, he was prompted by the child who knew every word by heart.

The purpose of beginning reading charts must be kept clearly in mind: to memorize words and phrases to build a sight vocabulary. Memorization of the entire chart is necessary before memorization of the individual words is very logical.

After the teacher has developed a visual sensitivity to any particular chart, she can then cut it up into logical phrases and words, and the children can work with them in reconstructing the original story or creating new ones.

Caution must be exercised not to overuse a chart. As soon as the children seem to have memorized the phrases and words, more charts can appear using these words and introducing new ones. Charts can be embellished with pictures to make them more attractive.

* * *

Miss Holmes, in constructing her first reading chart with the children, had used the school bus as a common experience. The chart read like this:

Our School Bus

We have a school bus.
It is big.
It is yellow.
It is noisy.
It bounces.
We all ride it.
Mr. Ames is the driver.

The children memorized the story and had fun reconstructing it on a pocket chart. The day after the original chart had been made, Miss Holmes introduced the same words in a different context. On the pocket chart she had inserted a picture of a school bus clipped from a magazine cover. Under it she had printed on strips of cardboard:

What Is It?

It is big.
It is yellow.
It is noisy.
It bounces.
We all ride it.
What is it?

On the third day Miss Holmes introduced a new card, which said "Who is he?" Under it she constructed this story, using again the words from the old reading chart.

Who Is He?

He is a driver.
He drives a bus.
It is big.
It is noisy.

It is yellow.
It bounces.
We all ride with him.
Who is he?

Quickly the children learned to read about Mr. Ames. By this time they had memorized the words well enough so that Miss Holmes was able to construct another reading chart with the children at the next meeting of her beginning reading group.

*   *   *

Careful guidance in constructing reading charts is essential so that old words appear repeatedly in new context and new words are

Many "sight" words result when the creative teacher provides a series of creative, stimulating experiences.

introduced at a rate of speed commensurate with the child's ability to memorize them. Any defect in the use of reading charts is due largely to the inability of the teacher to find exciting, new, and interesting ways to use the constantly developing sight vocabulary of the children.

Charts need not all be *experience* charts—though they should obviously use words that children are using orally and which are based on their own experiences. As soon as a few words are known, they can be used in many ways on different kinds of charts. Thus children may have the opportunity to read them over and over in new situations.

Creative ideas for the development of reading charts are further developed in Chapter V.

The Use of the Basic Text

A creative teacher will make a careful study of the reading books she intends to use with her class so that she becomes very familiar with their content. The story about the element of discovery told on page 60 tells how the introduction of the preprimer can be a highly motivating experience if the teacher is so aware of the vocabulary the child will encounter there that she has helped him to learn many of the words in his experience charts beforehand. The introduction of any reading book should be an exciting experience for every child.

Once a child begins to read in books, his chart experiences should not cease. Chart-making may shift from story charts to those concerned with gleaning information, planning charts, vocabulary charts, evaluation charts, and such, but charts still play an important role in having the reading experiences of the young child grow out of his spoken experiences.

There are two points of view regarding the use of a basic text in developing a sound reading program. Some teachers avoid the use of the basic text until very late in the reading program because they feel it does not have meaning for many children. Basic texts present the lives of neither the subcultures nor of mixed racial groups. Nor do they represent children of low socioeconomic levels. Consequently, to some children these basic texts are as much outside the realm of their experiences as are the ancient fairy tales. Second, the teachers feel that the basic texts tend to give the impression that unless they are followed page by page the children will not develop good reading ability. Third, they believe the beginning stories in most basic texts are insipid and stupid, and consequently very disappointing to children after they have been making their own exciting charts. These teachers often use a basic text as a supplement to a well-developed reading program for the purpose of teaching skills, evaluating pupil growth, and securing material for a variety of purposes very quickly.

On the other hand, other teachers feel the basic text has been prepared by experts, and the step-by-step guidance offered in the teacher's manual is the most scientific way of teaching reading known to man.

Actually, a combination of the two points of view probably produces the best program in reading instruction. In teaching reading, as in all other teaching, the variable that makes the difference is the teacher. The creative teacher will use all materials and will make them work for her.

Often the child is introduced to books through the use of the "big book" used at the front of the room. This is a natural transition for him, because the big book resembles the charts his teacher has made. After the big book has been read by the class, each child will be happy to discover that he can read the small copy of the same material in his own hands.

Time should be taken at this point to help children understand the difference between the basic texts and the books they have been looking at and trying to read. If children understand clearly that a basic text is designed to help them learn to read, they will realize that it performs a different function for them than books of children's literature which they want to read. (See Chapters IV and VII.)

Some children develop such a rich sight vocabulary that they literally breeze through preprimers and primers. Contrary to popular belief, every page of a reader does not have to be covered. The one best guide for the development of a reading vocabulary is to listen to the words the children are *speaking* with meaning. If these words are the same as those used in the basic text, the children are ready for it. But the basic text should not constitute the total reading program of any classroom.

Easy Books for Beginners

Lately, the reading program of many classrooms has been enriched by the introduction of "easy beginning books" written especially for beginning readers. These books often do what the beginning readers do not. They tell a sensible, exciting story in a simple, direct way that rewards the children by making the reading of the story worthwhile.

Along with the easy beginning books has come much criticism as to their literary value. Literary value or not, they are far superior to the beginning stories in most basic text series. A visit to any classroom where these "easy books" are being used will show how eagerly they are accepted by children. Words are repeated over and over in such a way as to help the child develop a broad sight vocabulary. Various root words, beginning word sounds, word endings, prefixes, and suffixes are so simply introduced and so repeated that children often begin to use phonetic and word analysis skills to figure out the new words for themselves, thereby enabling the teacher to launch into a sound word-attack program at the time the child is most ready for it.

Many bright children have taught themselves to read with the "easy books," and many other children have delighted in their ability to read these books after one or two readings by the teacher.

Criticism or not, the "easy books" have made their way into the reading programs of most children, at least out of school, where parents have seen these books as one means to satisfy the hunger of the highly motivated beginning reader. The books can be put to profitable use within the school program if they are carefully integrated into the total reading program.

Developing Good Reading Habits

Good reading habits are developed at the onset of the reading experience if the teacher introduces reading to the children in the ways mentioned in previous sections of this chapter. Children develop good eye movement across a page because they are taught to see and read for ideas rather than words.

Physical conditions must be appropriate to develop good reading habits. The presence of books, bulletin boards, daily stories, and all the other motivational devices previously mentioned is necessary. One part of the room should be set aside for quiet reading time. Distractions should be removed. Simple rules for reading time should be established. Above all, reading should be enjoyable.

Reading is a tool or a skill to be used in many ways and for many purposes. Therefore, reading goes on all day—not just during a reading period. The children plan their day together and teacher prints their plans on the board. The children read these plans as soon as they are able, along with their individual notes and surprises. The teacher writes the news on the board when they "share and tell" and thus provides another chart. Billy and the others read their surprise charts to the group after the surprise is known; the class writes a chart of Billy's experience. Teacher reads stories to the children. Long-term plans for a puppet show are printed on a chart. A list of "Things We Want to Know" constitutes another chart of questions the class will ask on their train trip. And at some specified time during the day, teacher meets with groups or individuals for individual reading experiences or help in techniques.

Such a program shows the need for reading to the children and places reading in its proper place meaningfully. Children do not read just for the sake of reading; they do it to communicate, to hear what others have to say. Reading can be established as a habit for communicating when the skills taught during the reading period are put to use all during the school day.

Developing Reading Skills

As soon as a basic sight vocabulary has been learned and the reading habit has been established, and children are reading charts or books, the first-grade teacher must begin to build skills that will lead the child into independent reading ability. All these skills center around developing techniques in word recognition. These techniques may be listed as follows:

1. The use of picture clues to identify words.
2. The use of verbal context clues.
3. The use of word-form clues.
4. The use of phonetic analysis.
5. The use of structural analysis.

One instructional job of the teacher in developing independent reading skills is with the use of independent seat work. She must also be concerned with expanding the children's reading range through the introduction of new topics and supplementary reading materials.

Using Picture Clues to Identify Words

On page 34 an example of a child who had not learned to read pictures was given. This almost never occurs in our classroom today, when books, magazines, billboards, posters, television, and other forms of communication media introduce the children to their first basic printed symbol for a real life experience: the picture.

When children have had extensive work with pictures such as those suggested in Book II,[9] they develop the ability to study pictures closely and to be sensitive to many of their component parts. Ability to read a picture well will ultimately help a child to read the printed symbols that appear under it. In his desire to make his reading have sense, his eyes wander back to the picture to find the pictorial image of the word.

One picture in a primer shows two children pulling a third child in a red cart. The child reader does not have the word "cart" in his sight vocabulary. Being a rural child, he reads one of the sentences under the picture as follows: "Ted and Alice pull Sally in the wagon." "Wagon" is his word for the object in the picture as obviously the only word that makes sense.

The child's teacher will accept the word "wagon" until the child finishes the page, so as not to destroy the meaning of the story. As soon as the child finishes reading, she may ask him to look at the picture and the word for "wagon" and will ask if he knows another word that can be used as a substitute for wagon. If he does not, she introduces the word "cart" by printing it on the chalkboard. Often, 3 x 5 cards can help the child note the different configurations between the words "cart" and "wagon." The teacher cuts slits in the card with a razor blade so that only a word or phrase is exposed when the card is laid on a page of reading material. This has the advantage of blotting out the words immediately surrounding the troublesome word while allowing the child to see it used in context as soon as the card is removed.

Once the teacher is certain the word is in the child's vocabulary, she will correct it when he is reading to her if he mispronounces it. When children are reading so that their stories make sense, they are probably using picture clues to identify unknown words. Other skills

[9] James A. Smith, *Creative Teaching of the Language Arts in the Elementary School* (Boston: Allyn and Bacon, Inc., 1967), Chapter V.

will be needed to remedy these mistakes, but for the time being the child is using well the resources at his command.

Using Verbal Context Clues

While pictures may help children in reading many beginning stories, there are some instances when they do not. Here the child resorts to searching for clues in the context of the story itself. In the reading readiness program, he developed many verbal context skills in the work with audio discrimination, visual discrimination, listening, and oral expression.

Context clues, like picture clues, are often obtained by simply using the word in the sentence which makes sense. When the boy who read the word "cart" as "wagon" has more context clues at his command, he will look at the beginning letter of the new word and realize it could not be "wagon" because it begins with a "c" sound.

Suggestions for developing context clues follow in Chapter V, along with suggestions for the development of phonetic clues and word-structure clues.

Using Word-Form Clues

Word-form clues are those which deal with the outward appearance of the word. Recognizing likenesses and differences in words, recognizing beginning sounds and endings, and noting the lengths of words are the first kinds of word-form clues which a child uses to figure out the pronunciation of a word. The phonics program expands this ability and a program in structural analysis tends to complete it.

In developing a sight vocabulary, children build a base for skill in using word-form clues. Continued work in oral vocabulary building as described on pages 35 to 37 is necessary so that the spoken words of the child may be meaningfully recognized in print.

The Use of Phonetic Analysis

Phonics play an important part in the teaching of reading. In the reading readiness program, phonetic sounds are often used to refine audio discrimination. Children learn the consonant sounds such as "m" and the vowel sounds such as "a," the speech consonants and consonant blends such as "ch" and "br," and so on, less as a technique for teaching them to read than as a technique to help them hear and see minute differences in sounds and shapes. When these exercises are taught as games, or in meaningful ways, they are fun. It has been pointed out that children create sounds and use them in their speech and early writing. Teachers can capitalize on the "ch-ch-ch" for "train" and have the children reproduce this sound to accomplish the same ends as the more formal lessons in the manual. There is the "sh" sound when rocking baby to sleep; the "da-da-da-dat" sounds of playing at shooting machine guns, the "whrr-whrr" for the airplanes, the "z-z-z-z" sound of an automobile, and a multitude of others.

Learning sounds in the readiness stage of reading does not insure the child the ability to read phonetically, however, for that is not the purpose of sound consciousness at this stage. Many children do carry over this knowledge later into their reading but they should not necessarily be expected to. Most children learn to read initially by recognizing the *shapes* of words as they learn about people, animals, and things by *their* shapes. To a little child, all men may be classified as "Daddy" because they have a similar shape. Dogs soon become "bow-wow" regardless of size, because the shapes are similar; coffee tables, end tables, dining-room tables, and bridge tables are all "tables" at first due to their similarity of shape. It is later that the details of shapes within the shapes begin to make for discrimination. The child notices the unusual parts of objects and sees differences. Thus the tail of the dog, which is always moving, and the head, which is always barking, eating, or licking, come to his attention; differences are noted, and a more definite classification results. "Dog" becomes "cocker," "dalmatian," "collie." "Daddy" becomes "man," or "grandpa," or "Mr. Jones." "Table" becomes "coffee table" or "dining-room table."

So the child learns to identify words by shape and then the peculiarities within the words draw his attention. He sees wiggly "g's" and tall "T's," and when he notes differences within shapes he is also ready to notice they stand for the differences within the sounds he is making. This is the time when phonics should be taught as a reading aid and a step toward independent reading. Now the child needs techniques for attacking new words so he may eventually read independently. Again, the element of discovery can provide an excellent motivating force if the teacher teaches phonetics skillfully enough so the child discovers new words through sounds. Many teachers prefer to begin phonics, apart from the reading groups themselves, through word games. This is perhaps wise in that it does not interfere with the child's eye-span or slow up his reading when he is in the initial stages of establishing the reading habit. After a series of sound games have been played and the basic consonant and vowel sounds and consonant blends have been established, the teacher naturally makes the transfer to the reading situation by having the children sound some of the words they do not know in their reading books. This can be discovery, it can be fun, and children can spend time sounding out new words they meet daily.

Creative teaching of phonetic analysis. Douglas demonstrates a word beginning with the consonant blend "cl."

It must be remembered, however, that phonics is but one way to recognize new words and is no more important than a number of contextual clues.

The Use of Structural Analysis

Almost as soon as he begins to read, the pupil will find likenesses in words. First he will notice a familiar base word with a new consonant beginning, such as "night" and "sight." Often he will recognize small words in larger ones, as "mother" in "grandmother." When this begins to take place, children are capable of understanding the structure of words; now they may be taught the variations and deviations of words, which will help them in developing independent reading. A study of structure of words involves an ability to:

1. *Recognize base words in derived words.* A child reads: Helen was *reporting* to the class. He recognizes the word "port" and is able to apply his knowledge of prefixes and suffixes to "sound out" the word. Once he says the word to himself, he recognizes it as one he already uses orally and he has brought meaning to the sentence.
2. *Omit first or last letters to make a word.* The child substitutes a "p" for the "j" in jump, or drops the "e" from rote. He applies his knowledge of consonant sounds in the first instance, his knowledge of vowel sounds and their changes in the second instance.
3. *Recognize compound words.* Knowing the words "rain" and "fall," he quickly recognizes a new word, "rainfall."
4. *Find a little word in a longer word.* Discovering the word "let" in "letter" helps the child figure out the total word.
5. *Divide words into syllables.* Knowing that each syllable contains a vowel helps the child to properly pronounce the word "at-ten-tion."
6. *Recognize contractions.* (See Book II, *Creative Teaching of the Language Arts in the Elementary School,* Chapter VIII.)

Developing Independent Reading

The development of good reading habits and basic reading skills should place the child well along the road toward independent reading. Most children enter the stage of rapid growth in reading as soon as they begin to read independently. The main jobs of the teacher at this point are to continue to develop those skills which will give the child independent reading power and to supply a wealth of material geared to the reading ability level of each pupil. In addition to the reading act, there are certain mechanics of reading which greatly aid the child in the use of books and increase his power to work with books by himself.

Mechanics to Be Developed by the Primary Teacher for Independent Use of Books

1. Teach the alphabet names (very soon after the reading act is established).

2. Teach the order of the letters of the alphabet through:
   a. Arranging children's names in alphabetical order.
   b. Using the picture dictionary to find words they wish to use in sentence- or story-writing.
   c. Making a spelling booklet, using a page for each letter of the alphabet and then alphabetizing weekly lessons.
   d. Singing alphabet songs.
   e. Arranging in groups words with same initial blends, same vowel sounds, or same endings.
   f. Finding names in telephone books.
   g. Social studies words.
   h. Words where first and second letters are the same.

3. Teach the mechanical features of a book by:
   a. Using table of contents to—
      (1) Locate new stories.
      (2) Find stories children wish to reread.
      (3) Find material for research in Citizenship Education, Science, etc.
      (4) Select favorite story.
   b. Using title page.
   c. Using index to—
      (1) Locate specific things.
      (2) Locate songs.
   d. Recognizing statements, questions, and quotations.
   e. Understanding that the book is divided into units according to various topics such as animals, seasons, etc.
   f. Reading a double-column page through use of *Weekly Reader,* etc.

       g. Understanding relationship of page numbers to place in book (page 10 near front of book; page 150 in or near back of the book).

4. Teach care and handling of books.
5. Use alphabetical skills in other books such as:
       a. Dictionary (picture and others).
       b. Telephone book.
       c. Address books (make some).
       d. Reference materials in children's encyclopedias.
6. Develop an interest in authors and publishers.
7. Develop library skills by:
       a. Learning card catalogue in library a-b-c order.
       b. Learning that encyclopedias are in a-b-c order.
       c. Looking for pictures on given topic.
       d. Locating materials on library shelf.

These skills may be further developed through a variety of activities such as the following:

1. Organize a Reading Club, composed of children interested in helping locate books and caring for them. They meet once a week to locate books and stories about two or three topics of particular interest to the class and their studies.

2. Make booklets using table of contents, title page, etc., for Citizenship Education.

3. Put words on chalk tray and have children select words alphabetically.

4. Fish for words in alphabetical order.

5. Play various games whereby children put words in boxes with letters on them.

6. Make booklets in correlation with Citizenship Education, Science, etc., making use of these mechanical features.

7. Prepare cards upon which a number of related words are printed. In an envelope are placed smaller cards, which contain words to classify the groups. Child places word on card which is common to all words printed on card:

People

girl
man
boy

8. Use two sets of alphabet letters—one of capital letters and one of small letters. Mix them up and pass to class. Match pairs.

9. Each child will choose one word, and, when letters of his word are called, he will stand in position in an alphabetical line, with his word written in large letters.

10. Dividing alphabet into three parts (a-g) (h-p) (q-z). Drill is given in telling in which part of alphabet a certain word is found.

11. A reading tree:
   a. In the library corner have a reading tree where children can make their own creative symbols to put on the tree every time they read a book. A key to the symbols could be close by for quick interpretation. One could also have a reading league in the spring or summer. Baseball mitts cut from paper could hold the individual child's book record.

12. Refer to Book II,[10] Chapter VIII, for suggestions for the creative teaching of the above mechanics of reading.

The Intermediate Grade Program

The intermediate grade program in reading is often misunderstood or neglected because it is interpreted as a continuation of the primary program. The instructional tasks of the intermediate grade teacher may be the same as the primary teacher's, but they also go far and above those tasks developed in the primary grades.

Reading power is developed in the intermediate grades. When analyzed into its many parts, reading power is seen to come from the acquisition of many desirable and necessary skills. Developing these skills is the job of the intermediate grade teacher, who must concentrate on:

[10] *Ibid.*

1. The continued development and expansion of primary reading skills.
2. Continued independent reading.
3. Expanding the vocabulary and range of materials.
4. Developing more refined techniques of effective comprehension.
5. Developing the techniques of critical thinking.
6. Developing techniques for effective reading rates.
7. Developing the skill of reading carefully for directions and details.
8. Developing skill in oral or audience-type situations.
9. Developing more skilled approaches to word study and word attack skills, such as:
    a. Building word meanings.
    b. Mature techniques of word recognition.
    c. Advanced word-analysis skills.
    d. Skill in using the dictionary.
10. Teaching the efficient use of reference techniques:
    a. Ability to locate information.
    b. Note-taking.
    c. Outlining.
    d. Summarizing.
    e. Use of library resources.
11. Teaching how to apply reading skills in these ways:
    a. Dictionary skills.
    b. Book skills.
    c. Skills in locating information.
    d. Selecting main ideas.
    e. Skimming.
    f. Reading for beauty—interpretative and appreciative.
    g. Reading for detail.
    h. Reading dialects.
    i. Reading charts, maps, and graphs.
12. Developing organizational skills.

As children begin to utilize their word-attack skills and sight vocabulary by reading books on their own they generally enter a stage of rapid growth in reading. At this point, their interests and problems become so diversified that grouping by ability is likely to retard rather than help many children in the development of independent reading.

Something needs to be said about grouping and its direct relation to reading in the intermediate grades. One common conception of grouping is that the class is divided into three or four groups—the fast readers, the average readers, and the slow readers. This type of grouping implies that we are concerned with reading rate: the best (fastest and with greatest comprehension, generally above grade level); the average (about where they should be in terms of rate,

A creative way to check comprehension ability and the ability to follow directions.

comprehension, and grade level); and the poorest (slow reader, below grade level). Reading is concerned with much more than speed or rate. Comprehension or meaning (the acquisition of the thought the author is attempting to communicate) is much more important. Speed and comprehension are related, but both must be "taught." There are other important skills involved in the reading process which children will need help in developing. Vocabulary building is one. The ability to select the main ideas from different selections, to skim and to read differently for different material, to attack and discover meanings for new words, to summarize, to outline, to read for information, to read poetry—these and a host of other skills must be acquired by children if they are to be effective readers.

Teachers can discover who needs help in these areas and *group the children according to similar problems.* This is possible at any level once the reading act has been efficiently established. It has already been shown how vocabulary building may be developed (see Chapter I, page 3) with any group regardless of speed in reading. In a like manner the creative teacher can work up a series of lessons to help children gain skill in selecting the main ideas from stories or paragraphs regardless of their reading ability level. She may, for instance, run off on a ditto machine a story aimed at the poorest reader; her purpose is to teach a skill, not to worry over the reading matter itself. Everyone reads the story, and through discussion they select the main ideas and may even outline the story on the board. The teacher then gives the child a book to read on his own reading level, and he practices with a story from the book. There are advantages in this heterogeneous grouping in that children who read well can help those who do not. Good social relationships are developed in this process and the "sights" are raised for the slow child while the quick child gains status in the group. The slower child also stands a stronger chance of responding to and discovering answers so that he, too, gains status in the group.

Ability grouping is necessary to some extent. The problem the teacher confronts here is raising the ability in reading, if possible. But this is not the only reason for grouping. It is important that teachers remember that the best way to help children become better readers is to teach them the skills that will help them read independently. Fast readers as well as slow ones often have difficulty selecting main ideas, attacking new words, or understanding what they have read. When children are grouped to work on problems, the groups constantly change, and the stigma attached to a slow reading group dissolves. Real ability grouping implies flexibility. The grouping described above is really "content" grouping although it is often misnamed "ability" grouping.

Another logical way to keep children reading independently at the peak point of their ability level is through the personalized reading program described on page 74. In this type of reading program the major portion of the child's time is spent reading as an individual, not as a member of a reading group. Inasmuch as this is the way most people read in life, it seems to be a rewarding and practical way to teach children to read.

Success in obtaining independence in reading is based largely on the conditions set in each classroom for making reading an integrated, useful skill to be used throughout the school day. When children are successful in applying skills, they hunger to master more skills to attain more success. Success at each step of reading development is necessary to produce the psychological atmosphere where achievement can develop.

An example of the way grouping for reading can be developed

as part of a total school day will be found in Book V,[11] Chapter VII. Suggestions and illustrations for the creative teaching of the above reading skills will be developed in Part Two of this volume.

Summary

In order to understand how the basic principles of creative teaching may be applied to the teaching of reading, it is essential that the process of reading be understood and the various skills to be developed are known. This chapter has explained the process involved in the reading act and has defined the skills that must be developed in order to produce good readers. In the next chapter the new methods and organization plans for teaching reading which are currently popular in our elementary schools will be discussed, and each will be evaluated in terms of its adaptation to the principles of creative teaching.

TO THE COLLEGE STUDENT

1. This chapter has given you an overall picture of the reading process and some ways you might teach this process. You will need to read in more detail about other reading topics. Some are listed below. Assign them to various classmates and plan for them to report to the class. The bibliography at the end of this chapter will be of help to you.

1. The Pre-School Reading Readiness Program.
2. Remedial Reading and Corrective Reading.
3. Evaluation in Primary Reading.
4. The Role of the Reading Consultant in the Elementary School.
5. The Place of Workbooks in the Primary Reading Program: Can They Be Used Creatively?
6. Worthwhile Independent Reading Activities.
7. The Diagnosis of Reading Difficulties.
8. Establishing an Individualized Reading Program.
9. Organizational Plans for Teaching Reading.
10. A Study of the State of Reading in the United States Today Compared to Fifty Years Ago.
11. Supplementary Reading Materials.
12. Reading Tests.

[11] James A. Smith, *Creative Teaching of the Social Studies in the Elementary School* (Boston: Allyn and Bacon, Inc., 1967).

2. Using what you have read in this chapter defend or refute this statement: Television harms children's reading habits.

3. Make a list of all the creative ways you can think of to motivate children to read for a variety of purposes.

4. Take any reading manual you have available in your classroom and rewrite several of the lessons to present a more creative approach to the lessons than the one used in the manual.

5. Take some children to the library and allow them to choose any book they like. Make note of the range in interests and abilities. Discuss ways to meet the difference in interests and abilities in the classroom.

6. There are many suggestions as to how to motivate children to books given in Chapter VII. After you read that chapter, come back and review this one with this thought in mind: How does a good program in literature fit into the primary reading program?

7. Visit the poorest socioeconomic level of your community. Then examine the reading texts in the schools that the children from this section of town attend. Do these stories reflect the experiences of the children you visited? How might a teacher in such a section begin to teach reading?

TO THE CLASSROOM TEACHER

Examine your own reading program in respect to these questions:

1. Is my reading program a challenge to each child?
2. Do I have a plan for grouping that makes it possible for me to meet the individual needs of each child?
3. Are the books in my classroom and in the school library being constantly used by my children?
4. Does every child know why he comes to meet with a reading group each time we meet?
5. Do I use the manual and textbook as an *aid* or do I follow it slavishly?

If the answer to any one of these questions is no, you have an indicator that tells that a part of your program needs strengthening. Try one new thing each day to improve your reading program.

TO THE COLLEGE STUDENT AND
THE CLASSROOM TEACHER

In his book, *The Teaching of Reading in the Elementary School,*[12] Paul McKee presents an interesting approach to reading by using a strange alphabet to introduce his readers to the act of reading. See pages 23–38 of his book. How well can you read his primer by use of the sight method?

SELECTED BIBLIOGRAPHY

ADAMS, BESS PORTER. *About Books and Children.* New York: Henry Holt and Co., 1953.

ANDERSON, IRVING H. and WALTER F. DEARBORN. *The Psychology of Teaching Reading.* New York: The Ronald Press Company, 1952.

AUSTIN, MARY and COLEMAN MORRISON. *The First R.* New York: The Macmillan Company, 1963.

BETTS, EMMETT A. *Foundations of Reading Instruction. Part IV.* New York: American Book Company, 1957.

BOND, GUY and EVA BOND WAGNER. *Teaching the Child to Read.* New York: The Macmillan Company, 1966.

BROGAN, PEGGY and LORENE FOX. *Helping Children Read.* New York: Holt, Rinehart and Winston, Inc., 1961.

DeBOER, J. and M. DALLMAN. *The Teaching of Reading.* New York: Holt, Rinehart and Winston, Inc., 1960.

DECHANT, EMERALD V. *Improving the Teaching of Reading.* Englewood Cliffs, N.J.: Prentice-Hall, Inc., 1964.

DURKIN, DOLORES. *Phonics and the Teaching of Reading.* New York: Bureau of Publications, Teachers College, Columbia, 1962.

DURRELL, DONALD D. *Improving Reading Instruction.* New York: Harcourt, Brace & World, 1966.

FRANK, JOSETTE. *Your Child's Reading Today.* New York: Doubleday & Company, Inc., 1960.

GANS, ROMA. *Common Sense in Teaching Reading.* New York: Bobbs-Merrill Co., 1963.

HEILMAN, ARTHUR. *Teaching Reading.* Columbus, Ohio: Charles E. Merrill Co., 1961.

HESTER, KATHLEEN B. *Teaching Every Child to Read* (2nd ed.). New York: Harper & Row, 1964.

LEE, DORRIS M. and R. V. ALLEN. *Learning to Read Through Experience.* New York: Appleton-Century-Crofts, 1963.

[12] Paul McKee, *The Teaching of Reading in the Elementary School* (New York: Houghton Mifflin Co., 1948), pp. 23–38.

LeFevre, Carl A. *Linguistics and the Teaching of Reading.* New York: McGraw-Hill Book Company, 1964.

Monroe, Marion. *Growing Into Reading.* New York: Scott, Foresman and Co., 1951.

McKee, Paul. *The Teaching of Reading.* New York: Houghton Mifflin Company, 1948.

McKee, Paul and William K. Durr. *Reading: A Program of Instruction for the Elementary School.* New York: Houghton Mifflin Co., 1966.

McKim, Margaret G. and Helen Caskey. *Guiding Growth in Reading.* New York: The Macmillan Company, 1963.

Newton, J. Roy. *Reading in Your School.* New York: McGraw-Hill Book Company, Inc., 1960.

Norvell, George. *What Boys and Girls Like to Read.* Morristown, N.J.: Silver Burdett Co., 1959.

Russell, David H. and Etta E. Karp. *Reading Aids Through the Grades.* Columbia University: Teachers College Bureau of Publications, 1951.

Smith, Henry P. and Emerald V. Dechant. *Psychology in Teaching Reading.* Englewood Cliffs, N.J.: Prentice-Hall, Inc., 1961.

Smith, Nila Banton. *Graded Selections for Informal Reading Diagnosis: Grades 1 Through 3.* New York: New York University Press, 1959.

Spache, George D. *Reading in the Elementary School.* Boston: Allyn and Bacon, Inc., 1964.

Tinker, Miles and Constance McCullough. *Teaching Elementary Reading.* New York: Appleton-Century-Crofts, Inc., 1962.

Veatch, Jeanette. *Individualizing Your Reading Program.* New York: G. P. Putnam's Sons, 1959.

———. *Reading in the Elementary School.* New York: The Ronald Press Company, 1966.

Creativity and the Reading Process

Great progress has been made in developing helpful techniques and materials for teaching reading, but no packaged process will ever meet the wide variety of personalities faced by teachers in classrooms and looked after by parents at home. This is especially true if we approach children with a respect for their eagerness to learn and if we honor the integrity of their taste. Then, instead of teaching young people as if we were feeding them packaged prescriptions, we inspire them and challenge them to invest their efforts and ideas in learning to read.[1]

ROMA GANS

TO THE READER

Before you read this chapter, think of all the systems or methods of teaching reading with which you are familiar and ask yourself, "Through which of these methods could creativity be developed?" Also review any organizational plans for teaching reading with which you are familiar. Do some of these plans make the development of creativity an impossibility? An organizational plan sets conditions for the development of creativity and thus is very important in considering the creative teaching of reading.

Introduction

The teaching of reading *can* be a process by which creativity is developed in children. It certainly need not be as dull as it has become in many of our schools! The perceptive passages from Sylvia Ashton-Warner's book quoted at the beginning of Chapters I and II indicate how teachers can make the process of teaching reading a creative one.

In the reading act, a child has the opportunity to put his own experiences into new ideas and dream the dreams of others. He is able to explore and discover new words and new word combinations. He has a world of meanings to manipulate and rearrange. He has the

[1] Roma Gans, *Common Sense in the Teaching of Reading* (New York: The Bobbs-Merrill Company, Inc., 1963), p. vi.

opportunity to see his own experiences transcribed into a written or printed system of communication. Reading, when efficient and enjoyable, is an exciting adventure for each child. It *never* has to be dull, not if teachers understand what reading is, what creativity is, and what creative teaching is—and can put them all together.

The divergent thinking processes that underlie the creative development of children consist of many specific skills, each of which must be developed either separately or together, when possible. Many of these skills are developed in current reading programs. Those that are generally taught as part of the reading program as necessary to creative development are:

1. Visual acuity.
2. The ability to organize.
3. Independence.
4. The ability to redefine.
5. Associational fluency.
6. Expressional fluency.
7. Word fluency.
8. Ideational fluency.
9. The ability to elaborate.
10. Evaluation abilities.
11. Sensitivity to problems.
12. Ability to analyze and abstract.
13. Ability to synthesize.
14. Ability to think abstractly.
15. The ability to retain.
16. The ability to identify.
17. The ability to concentrate.
18. The possession of a wide range of information.
19. An openness to experience.
20. High perception ability.

Research has shown that creative children have developed these skills to a more refined degree than have noncreative children. Teachers will recognize many of the above characteristics as objectives already stated in many teaching manuals. While they are developing these particular skills they are contributing to the development of many component parts of the creative act. Add these objectives to others that develop creativity and we can see how the teaching of reading contributes strongly to creative development.

The Creative Teaching of Reading

When a creative instructional program is added to the inherent ability and personality of each child, reading can become a day-by-day experience in creative development.

Many barriers to the creative teaching of reading have risen in the past twenty years. Among them are:

1. Patterns of grouping for reading which do not meet individual needs in children and which often destroy the ego-concept of a child so that he loses his desire to read because reading is associated with unpleasantness.
2. The pseudoscientific concept that all children can be taught to read in the same manner.
3. The slavish dedication to commercial textbooks and workbooks which contain a reading program supposedly arranged in scientific sequence.
4. The lack of consideration of the socioeconomic level or racial background of the children in the school when selecting reading materials.
5. The extreme pressure placed on children to read due to the recent criticism of the public schools.
6. The lack of understanding on the part of teachers as to the exact place of reading in the school program, as well as a lack of understanding as to the total reading act.
7. The excessive emphasis placed on reading "periods" rather than an emphasis on reading as a skill to be used all day.
8. The inability of many schools to keep reading on a personalized or individual level.
9. The lack of recognition of the change in emphasis and need for reading in the space age.
10. The inability of textbooks and reading programs to produce material within the child's range of interest and experience.
11. Some teachers' lack of understanding of the structure of the English language.

Each of these barriers will be further developed throughout the following pages.

The assumptions behind these practices cannot be qualified in terms of sound education. If the learning process is creativity itself, then the teaching of reading must be an individual process taught by teachers who care enough about each child to make sure that he assembles his known experiences into new concepts each day and discovers or creates new skills which open new vistas to him.

In considering the normal developmental characteristics of children, we must not forget the importance of the element of discovery to the child. One of the greatest fallacies of educational practice is the constant attempt of the over-ambitious teacher to cover her material so quickly that the children have little time to discover things for themselves. At a very early age the child secures great delight in discovering. As soon as he is able to crawl and walk, he opens doors and closets, and explores and investigates to his heart's content. He observes very quickly how his parents and siblings do things, and he attempts to imitate. The joy in his voice shows his delight in self-accomplishment when he says, "Look, I did it all by myself!" This is the desire for independence that goes on within him continually. At first he may master simple accomplishments—pouring a glass of milk, filling a sand bucket, or buttoning his clothes. In any event, it is a creative achievement and another step in his growth, and the child recognizes it as such. He loves to learn, he wants to create—he wants to know! And he is delighted to discover that he has learned! Thus his inherent drive to create and learn is the greatest motivational device a teacher or parent has in working with children, yet in our rush to "get them told" we so often kill this joy of discovery—the fun the child has in learning by himself. The job of the teacher is to facilitate the learning process by setting conditions that lead the child to new discoveries rather than to tell him about everything he meets without giving him a chance to find out for himself. Teaching is not telling. In reading, as in everything else, children must have frequent opportunities to discover their own abilities. Discovery is part of the process of creativity.

*   *   *

The author was visiting a small rural school not long ago. It was a bright fall day and the children were having a play period out-of-doors. The school itself was a beehive of activity, and the classroom environment was rich with the results of many experiences the group had had together. In one corner there was a live rabbit, and there were charts on "How to Care for Our Rabbit," "Stories on Our Rabbit," and "Fluffy, Our Rabbit," as well as poems about rabbits and the like. On an attractive reading table the teacher had arranged a great many preprimers. She had also torn up old readers and primers and had stapled between covers of brightly colored construction paper stories that pertained to the many activities going on in the room. On many there were pictures of rabbits, and lettered below them were the same words that appeared on the reading charts.

While the adults were talking, a first-grader left the rabbit cage, went over to the reading table, and selected a picture book. The teacher's watchful eye observed him carefully. Finally he put down the picture book and noticed the books the teacher had made. Picking one up, he came to her and asked, "Miss Ellis, is this a book about rabbits?" "Yes, it is, Peter," she replied. "Wish I could read it," Peter said as he flipped the pages. "I bet you can," said Miss Ellis. "Aw, Miss Ellis," he grinned, "I can't read a *book!*" "Why don't you try?" she encouraged.

Peter opened the book to the first page. He looked at the picture and the line printed below it and he read, "I am a rabbit."

His eyes widened and he turned the page. Again he read, "I am white." The next pages went faster and faster, and his face and body became more and more animated as he read page after page. With eyes wide and starry he clutched the finished book to his breast, looked up at the teacher and said, "Why, I can read!"

She answered calmly, "Why, of course you can!" but he did not hear. He walked slowly to the doll bed in the housekeeping corner, sat on the bed, opened the book, and again reread the pages. After he had completed the booklet this time, he held it close to him and laughingly said to himself over and over as he rocked back and forth, "I can read! I can read! I can read!"

Teacher said, "Peter has begun to read."

When the children came in at her call, she assembled all the grades together and said, "We have a surprise today—something exciting has happened. Peter, do you want to tell them what you discovered you could do?"

So Peter shared his new ability with the group. Immediately four other first-graders wanted to know if they could read the books. Soon all the books were shared, and four more children "discovered" they could read. The older children were loud in their praise, and the whole afternoon passed in their hearing each other read. The books went home with the children, who departed eagerly, exclaiming, "I'm going to show my mother how I can read," or "Wait till Daddy hears I can read."

*   *   *

The masterful handling of this situation is impressive. How skillfully the teacher had paved the way for discovery, how well she had utilized the discovery to further motivate the children! All her hours of preparation, vocabulary-building, and chart-making had been repaid in this moment and the wise and skillful manner in which she waited for the children to discover books is an example of the type of teaching we should be doing to build attitudes and a love of reading.

Children are often plunged into reading texts before this kind of wise and careful preparation. So many school systems have become "manual-bound" that results in reading are often measured by achievement tests, with little attention to enthusiasm and general attitude and the degree to which these are used. None of this can be measured by an achievement test. Actually, one of the best evaluations of a good reading program might justifiably be empty library shelves.

Because they are prepared by experts, manuals can be of invaluable help in planning creative reading lessons. The following illustration shows how one teacher used the material in the reading manual but adapted it to her own particular group. She operated on the premise that there are at least three basic ways to motivate children: through (1) meeting their immediate needs and interests, (2) content which is appealing, and (3) technique. This particular teacher made reading exciting by an excellent "technique" motivation.

In the reading series she was using is a story of a surprise. Uncle Tim comes to visit. He has a surprise but it must wait until after dinner. But amazing things happen during the dinner. The dog asks for food, the roast turkey on the table shouts when it is about to be cut, and events in general become most confusing. In the end, of course, it turns out that Uncle Tim is a ventriloquist, and the surprise in his bag is a puppet.

In the manual, this story, like scores of others, is introduced by having the teacher put the new words on the board. The teacher and children discuss the words. An introduction to the story is printed verbatim for teacher to read. Next the children discuss the pictures. Teacher asks questions printed in the manual. Then they read laboriously, page by page, to find the answers to the questions. In one school this delightful story was taught to one second grade by a veteran teacher as routine. A few children were interested; the rest gazed around the room, fidgeted, yawned, and were scolded because they did not pay attention. Their entire approach to the reading group was one of apathy. Another teacher taught the same story to a group in the following manner:

During the planning period she placed before the class a suitcase with a paper saying "SURPRISE" on it. "What is this word?" she asked. When the children told her she said, "Yes, and in the suitcase is a surprise. But we won't be able to find out what it is until Timmy's reading group meets—but let's put it in our plans." So she scheduled a surprise on the board for eleven o'clock.

At the appointed time the children gathered eagerly to find out the surprise. Each guessed what it might be—and each word was printed on the board. After each child had offered a suggestion, teacher said, "No one has guessed it yet. I'm going to give you some clues. Let's see if you're good detectives." Little by little, she gave an introduction to the story similar to the one in the manual. As she talked, the new words were brought into the conversation and lettered on the board. Finally she said, "Our last clue is in the reading book. Johnny and Mary get the same surprise as we are to have. Let's read their story. Let's look at these words on the board, too, because Johnny and Mary used many of these words in trying to find out their surprise."

So the story was read and the suitcase was opened. When the puppet was taken out each child had the opportunity to speak through it, telling how he liked the story. The group then dramatized the story simply, inviting other children to observe and using the books for their speaking lines.

In terms of the objectives of modern education, instructional materials cannot be effective if they emphasize any one area of the child's growth over another. They must not, for instance, do the child's thinking for him if he is to be taught to think for himself; they must in no sense be used to "fill in" time if he is to develop a worthwhile use of leisure time; they must have purpose if he is to gain knowledge and skills; they must not create mental blocks within him but must encourage learning if he is to have sound mental and physical health. If individual differences are to be met, the same books, workbooks, and materials cannot be used solely in the same class. If we are to develop responsibility, independence, and cooperation, instructional materials must be designed for individual problems, as well as for mass education.

A teacher must realize that she herself knows best the problems and abilities of her group. She must come to know that it is the children she is teaching—not the book. She must realize that her years of training give her the privilege of knowing how to teach better than the

Reading: a creative process and a creative product.

average layman, and that even an intelligent layman could teach reading if the only process involved was reading a book (the manual) and doing what it said. As a professional person, it becomes her duty to invent and create new ways of teaching reading so that each child learns to read and *a remedial program is unnecessary*—corrective programs perhaps, but not remedial. She must learn to teach as individually as possible, and if this is prohibited by the large number of children, she must teach well by groups or by some personalized program.

Teachers who understand the development of children will use each child's language experiences at any given point to develop new uses for language. These experiences will be reassembled into new learnings integrated with the life activity and the creative drive of each child. His reading development can be the most creative of his experiences if he approaches the threshold of children's literature with a drive to read and a body of skills he knows how to use.

An Historical Perspective of the Teaching of Reading

Great controversies have been waged over the methods of introducing formal reading to children. Forty years ago reading was taught almost entirely by a very complicated, and often unrealistic, phonetic system. This system did not produce efficient, enthusiastic readers among many average and below-average children, so a break was made and the "sight" method of teaching became popular. Under the old phonics method, reading was introduced through a memorization of the alphabet and its basic sounds, a study of phonics, and word analysis. Advocates of the sight method of teaching beginning reading pointed up these advantages:

Reading is a skill and a tool. Children do not read for reading's sake. They want their reading to tell them something. They should begin to read at once, and the sight method permits this.

Motivation is very important to reading. The best motivation for a child in reading is to discover that he *can* read. A child can begin to read very simple stories immediately through the sight method. It is true that he probably cannot figure out new words at the very beginning of his reading experience, but the job of the teacher is to see to it that the words he knows are used over and over in new context and that his sight vocabulary grows a little every day.

With the sight method children learn more quickly because they have only one thing to remember: the shape of the word and the sound for it. In a phonetic approach to reading, the child is burdened by many things to remember: the names of consonants and their sounds, the names of vowels and their many varied sounds, the sounds for speech consonants and consonant blends, and for unusual letter combinations, and the fusion of this variety of sounds into a sensible word symbol.

The phonetic approach to beginning reading must resort eventually to the memorization of many "sight" words because of the many exceptions to all rules of phonetics. Also, some authorities say that from 15 to 25 percent of the language is nonphonetic or is dubiously so. This often creates great confusion in a child. Take the sound "ough," for instance. A child reading along comes to the sentence, "The bird sat on the bough." He looks at the picture for a clue to the new word and reads, "The bird sat on the branch." The teacher immediately corrects him and tells him the sound for "ough" is like "ow." A while later the young reader comes to the sentence, "The meat was tough," and reads it, "The meat was t-ow." The teacher explains that "ough" also says "uff" and that he must remember both sounds. Later he reads, "Billy looked as though he could sing," and he reads it, "Billy looks as th-uff he could sing." Again he must learn a new sound for "ough." And then he encounters the word "thought."

He must choose from all these sounds the one that gives the sentence proper meaning. It would be just as easy for him and would facilitate his reading if he memorized each of these words rather than take the time to interrupt his reading to sound them all out.

The phonetic approach to beginning reading requires a carefully controlled vocabulary development program. Often this forces a teacher to slavish dedication to a commercial reading series. Much of the creative work of the children cannot be or is not used because it does not fit into the highly developed sequential acquisition of skills. If the context of the commercial text being used is not about the life experiences of the child, he soon loses his motivation for reading.

Spoken language is learned through imitation. The child uses language as communication years before he is able to identify nouns and verbs and long before he is able to analyze the structure of language. These skills come after oral facility with language has been established. A child learns to read many words naturally from television, from his book, from billboards, and so forth, without ever having to know the alphabet or the phonetic sounds of the alphabet. Whole words have meaning; to distort them means to remove much of this meaning. Just as the kindergartener on page 26 did not recognize the crumpled chair and the nursery-school child on page 26 did not recognize the dismantled tables, so do many children not recognize common words when they are syllabicated or broken up phonetically. The study of the structure of words is more sophisticated than the memorizing of shapes and not totally necessary for the recognition of words.

Skills in reading do not consist entirely of being able to call out words. Habits of good reading must be established from the onset of the formal reading program, or the child may be hampered a great deal in his reading development. Good eye movement is essential from the start. Good readers read for ideas. This often means they read groups of words much the same as they read one idea. Children, too, can be taught to read this way. "In the box," "to school," "around the corner," "said Billy" are good examples of phrases which can be read as one word because they contain one idea. Reading by ideas helps the child to obtain speed and better comprehension in reading. A good reader has about three fixation points across a line of the printed page. An overdose of phonics may cause the child to stop unnecessarily to look at parts of words rather than to read for ideas.

This simple device which has appeared in many magazines recently illustrates the above concept. Read the idea in quickly.

```
   /\              /\              /\
  /  \            /  \            /  \
 /Paris\         /Once \         / Bird \
/In The \       /In A   \       /In The  \
/The Spring\   /A Lifetime\    /The Hand   \
------------   ------------    -------------
```

Each phrase is so familiar that it is read as one word. Only by careful examination can the reader notice that there are double articles used in each phrase. Good readers would not notice them at a glance. Only plodding, slow "word" readers would be aware of the double articles at a first reading. Even beginning reading can be taught by thought units.

There are so many exceptions to word-attack rules (such as those centered around the use of a double vowel) that children learn them best after *they have learned to pronounce a word from memory.* The sight reader is handicapped temporarily by not being able to recognize new words, especially if they are out of the realm of his experience. Consequently, as soon as the habit of reading has been established and the child is reading smoothly and with good comprehension, this handicap is overcome by using the reading vocabulary he has now acquired to teach word recognition skills and to develop reading skills.

Since the early controversies over sight versus phonics teaching, much research in the total area of language and linguistics has added to our understanding of the teaching of reading. Some important new concepts have been added.

Part of the communicative power of language lies in its rhythm, pitch, tonal quality, and the intonation of language. A baby has no understanding of words as such yet he very often cries at a loud noise or if someone shouts angrily at him. Conversely, he smiles, coos, and gurgles at the soft, comforting words of his mother. His reaction here is to the *music* of language, not the language itself. Linguists tell us that this musical quality is a major part of communication and should never be omitted in instruction in any of the language skills, reading included. The child who reads, "Paul—went—down—the—street," with every word sounding exactly the same has been handicapped in reading development because too much concentration has been placed on words rather than meaning and intonation. The children might as well be reading words in a list rather than words arranged in a sentence for the purpose of communicating an idea.

This implies that the rhythm of language is important to the understanding of language. Although this is especially true in oral reading, it is also true in silent reading. While reading silently, a child does not *hear* intonation but he thinks it.[2]

Linguists are telling us also that

no one can get meaning from the printed page without taking in whole language patterns at the sentence level, because these are the minimal meaning-bearing structures of most written communications.[3]

This minimum requirement from the linguist's point of view tends to reinforce one of the viewpoints of the advocates of the sight method—that children be taught to read by thought units.

Reading should be taught in connection with the other skills of language. This was illustrated by the lesson described in Chapter I.

Our concept of the reading process has been expanded. Horn points out that the author of a book

. . . does not really convey ideas to the reader: he merely stimulates him to construct them out of his own experiences. If the concept is . . . new to the reader, its construction more nearly approaches problem solving than simple association.[4]

Reading, then, encompasses mechanical processes and mental processes, and teaching must be directed to the development of both of these processes.

To comprehend printed material, the reader must perceive entire language structures as whole—as unitary meaning-bearing patterns. Meaning-bearing language structures can be taught to children as a base to the reading process.

Although the basic philosophy of the linguistic approach to reading focuses on letters and words as the most significant units in methodology, LeFevre says

. . . in my approach to reading instruction the word is treated as a minor language unit for many reasons. Some of these reasons are linguistic, others are pedagogical. In English the word is an unstable element,

2 Carl A. LeFevre, *Linguistics and the Teaching of Reading* (New York: McGraw-Hill, Inc., 1964).

3 *Ibid.,* p. vii.

4 Ernest Horn, *Methods of Instruction in the Social Studies* (New York: Charles Scribner's Sons, 1937).

whether it is taken as a semantic or as a structural unit. The most significant structures in English are intonation patterns, grammatical and syntactical word groups, clauses, and sentences.

Single words, analyzed and spoken in isolation, assume the intonation contours of whole utterances. Single words thus lose the characteristic pitch and stress they normally carry in the *larger constructions that comprise the flow of speech and bear meaning.* This automatic upgrading of words may lead many learners to "read" word by word, or by pattern fragments, without regard for whole structural patterns that carry meaning. This upgrading may thus contribute to the frequency and extent of serious reading disability among pupils of all ages. So far, little has been done to develop reading of American English by its known structures instead of by its vocabulary.[5]

LeFevre, a linguist, proposes a sentence method of teaching reading which applies a linguistic description of American English utterances at the sentence level to their graphic counterparts, written and printed sentences. He bases his method on fourteen assumptions gleaned from the knowledge of linguistics. His assumptions include some of those mentioned above: that children should learn to read and write the language they speak and understand, that they develop a consciousness of pertinent language processes and their interrelationships with graphics, that analytical slicing of larger language segments into smaller segments should be done only to the extent that the reading process requires it, that the child learning to read should practice reading entire meaning-bearing language patterns at the sentence level, that all aspects of the language arts program should be coordinated.

We tend to be extremists in educational practice. We tend to throw out one system of reading and adopt another one because all children are not reading as well as we wish. We do not seem to learn by experience. Many schools threw out the sight method of teaching and went back to the phonics method, forgetting that the reason the phonics method was discarded in the first place was because *it* was not producing the kind of readers we hoped for. It is like throwing out the child with the bath water. Many schools today, because of this policy, are actually *creating reading disability* among many children. The current situation regarding remedial reading bears out the truth of this statement.

Each system of reading has contributed to our understanding of

[5] Carl A. LeFevre, *Linguistics and the Teaching of Reading* (New York: McGraw-Hill, Inc., 1964), pp. xvii–xviii.

the total reading process, and each has had inherent in it many ideas that have helped in teaching the majority of children to read. But no *one* system has yet solved the multitude of reading problems in any *one* school. Modern trends tend to be more sensible in that they realize the value of each of the many systems and adapt their strong points to some new reading plan. But no *one* system is ever going to work with *every* child and the only sound philosophy a school can possibly have is this: Any system of reading is justifiable if it teaches all children to read up to their ability, but no *one* system ever is!

Dechant has made an excellent summary of numerous fallacies concerning reading methods and gives the following pertinent examples:

1. Learning the letters of the alphabet is a handicap to successful learning of reading.
2. Learning to read and reading by a mature individual are the same process and involve the same factors. Because the letter is not the meaningful unit of perception in reading, it therefore cannot be the initial step in learning to read.
3. With the right method *every* child can learn to read. And there is but *one* right method of teaching reading.
4. Every phonically-trained child is necessarily a word-caller. Indeed the child of very low IQ may become a word-caller because it is easier for him to learn to pronounce words than to learn and remember word meanings.
5. The reading readiness program exists *only* because present methods of teaching reading are so slow and so unsuccessful that we must justify our delaying of formal reading instruction until the child can be more successful with it. And it protects the teacher when certain children make no progress through the first grade.
6. Whenever our "favorite" method doesn't work, it must have been taught improperly.
7. The phonics approach interferes with the child's ability to take meaning to and from the printed page and keeps him from thinking with the material.
8. Phonics is best taught incidentally. It should be introduced only after the child has learned a certain number of words by sight to help him to read words with which he has difficulty.
9. The phonics approach is wrong because phonically-trained children do not read as rapidly nor as fluently as analytically-trained children. This may be true of beginning readers, but does drilling children to handle very rapidly a small, controlled vocabulary in grade one necessarily guarantee that they will be able to handle longer and less-controlled vocabularies in sixth grade?
10. The whole word method is completely visual, and the phonic method is completely auditory.

11. Drill in phonics will cause children to dislike reading.
12. Children learning to read by the sight method will develop a permanent interest in reading.
13. The developmental reading method prohibits children exploring and broadening their interests. (The individualized reading program is thought to allow children this opportunity.)
14. The so-called "contextual reader" is the best reader . . .
15. Practice alone will help the pupil to improve. Some proponents of the individualized approach seem to be falling into this error . . .
16. The controlled vocabulary in the basal series is more insipid than the vocabulary used in phonic materials.[6]

Many of these fallacies exist because of lack of understanding of the reading process, but most of them are due to the fact that educators have tried to defend systems of teaching which they were using. Each can be true or not true, depending on the teacher. The creative teacher will recognize all of these fallacies of thinking as possible outcomes of poor teaching. She will not close her eyes to the fact that each of these statements may be a truth (especially one such as No. 11) when the teaching of reading is a mechanical process that is imposed on a child rather than an organic process which grows from within him.

Current Methods and Plans of Teaching Reading

Confusion often exists between reading methods and plans for organization. The Initial Teaching Alphabet concept is a new *method* for teaching reading, but Individualized Reading is an *organizational plan* for teaching reading. New methods result from deeper understandings gleaned from research in the areas of methodology, linguistics, communications, language, and so forth. New plans of organization are simply ways to arrange a teaching day so the methods can be most effectively employed. The Individualized Reading concept offers no new method of teaching: it simply offers a plan for organizing a school day so we may best put to use those methods with which we are already familiar. Every new method and organizational plan is a creative idea that has contributed to our understanding of the reading process or how reading might be taught. But none is the answer to all problems everywhere. A summary of methods and plans may help in the understanding of how creative teaching can be developed.

[6] Emerald V. Dechant, *Improving the Teaching of Reading* (Englewood Cliffs, N.J.: Prentice-Hall, Inc., 1964), pp. 77–78.

Methods of Teaching Reading

A review of the most common current practices in the teaching of reading will serve the purpose of evaluating each as it relates to the creative development of children.

Phonic approach. This is a system that develops efficiency in word recognition by employing the speech sounds of the English language in a sequential pattern. It utilizes the forty-four most frequently used speech sounds in English. It begins with the teaching of short sounds of five vowels and progresses to the study of the ten most frequently used consonants. Consonants are soon blended with vowels in pronouncing units or syllables. The system develops from the known to the unknown, from simple to complex, and left-to-right eye progression is assured because children always attach new words at their beginnings.

Phonics supplies the child with a reading vocabulary approximately equal to his speaking vocabulary. It is designed for use in *all* basal reading series and integrates the total language arts program.

Basal reading texts. This approach to reading provides a series of basal materials that is supposed to provide for a systematic and sequential development of all the skills, understandings, and abilities necessary in interpreting written symbols (the total reading act). The materials are designed as a base of operations, however, not as a scientific exposition of the reading process. They can only be considered as part of the total reading program.

Language experience approach. This method recognizes that an oral language background and an experience background are basic to vocabulary development and word recognition throughout the elementary grades. It pays homage to the logical sequence of development of language mentioned previously in this chapter. The language experience approach has three aspects: (1) it extends experiences to include words that express the experiences through oral and written communication, (2) it makes a study of the English language and develops a form of personal expression, and (3) it relates ideas of authors to personal experiences through using a wealth of materials to build reading skills. The lesson taught in Chapter I is basically a sample of this approach to reading, which has much in common with the recent linguistic approach advocated by LeFevre.[7]

[7] Carl A. LeFevre, *Linguistics and the Teaching of Reading* (New York: McGraw-Hill, Inc., 1964).

Initial teaching alphabet. This medium, commonly known as the ITA, has broken down the English language into forty-four new characters that provide each major phoneme of English with its own symbol. This eliminates the complicated process, often so confusing to children, of associating inconsistent character-to-symbol relationships as they appear in current spelling forms. This new alphabet, with its spellings, provides the learner with a consistent alphabet code. It is designed to facilitate transition to the traditional alphabet once reading fluency is reached with the ITA alphabet. This method claims to make the reading process simpler, quicker, and more successful. Sir James Pitman of London, England, has promoted this system and claims it is a medium, not a method. But, because of the definition of method suggested above, it is classified as a method here.

Words in color. The most important contribution of this approach is its full and rapid extension of the linguistic capacities of the learners. The power of reading, writing, and spelling with meaning all language already owned as meaningful speech is developed as a unity. Color is used to help solve quickly and easily the problems created by the ambiguous graphene-phoneme relationship of English without affecting the usual spelling. The many spellings of each sound occur in the same color, and each of the many sounds of one spelling occurs in a different color.

The linguistic approach. This approach to reading stresses four features: (1) Beginning reading material is based on sentence patterns that contain words that the child knows. The child must recognize the written words in the sentence structure as words he already speaks. (2) As a basic requirement for beginning reading, the child must know the alphabet and identify by name the individual letters. He must be able to determine immediately whether two sequences of two or three letters are alike or different in respect to both the individual letters and their order. (3) Early in the reading process independent "extensions" of the word matrices are created to build the pupil's ability to read hundreds of words he has never seen written before. (4) Reading for meaning requires the building of situation meanings out of words and sentences. Therefore, books without pictures force pupils to read for meaning rather than guess by using picture clues.

More recent advocates of the linguistic method have stressed the importance of teaching reading more in a thought structure (such as the sentence), and have also emphasized the importance of intonation in the understanding of implied meanings, as in LeFevre's work quoted above.

Current Patterns of Organization for the Teaching of Reading

Personalized or individualized reading. Because reading ability is closely related to intelligence and other factors, such as emotional and social adjustment, the reading level and ability of each child will vary greatly. Any personalized approach to reading is beneficial to children. A total personalized or individualized reading program, where each child develops at his own rate of speed and in accord with his own interests, *is* possible.[8, 9] In such a program none of the stages in reading development are skipped, nor is the methodology for teaching reading greatly altered. The difference is largely in the organization of the classroom program.

In organizing a class for individualized reading instruction, the commonly accepted pattern of grouping children according to reading ability or in relation to reading problems is unnecessary. Each child selects his own reading materials, and the teacher so organizes the day that she may spend time hearing each child read.

Because the program is one of self-selection, the individual interests and purposes of the children can be realized and abilities developed as rapidly or slowly as the child's inherent growth pattern permits.

Individualized instruction in reading does not mean that children never meet in groups. They often do because some reading is taught best in groups. Also, in developing an individualized reading program, teachers discover that small groups of children have similar problems or need help in similar skills, so they group these children together.

The individualized reading program recognizes the simple fact that no grouping eliminates individual differences. Almost no two children read at the same level or read the same material at the same time. The teaching of reading as individually as possible gives each child the opportunity for reading without interference, competition, or distraction from other members of a group who may be reading faster or slower than he. In addition to his right to proceed at his own rate, he learns many skills in the self-selection of materials.

[8] Jeannette Veatch, *Individualizing Your Reading Program* (New York: G. P. Putnam's Sons, 1959).

[9] Peggy Brogan and Lorene K. Fox, *Helping Children Read* (New York: Holt, Rinehart and Winston, Inc., 1961).

Creative teachers have had the success that might well be expected from such a reading program. The number of books children read under the guidance of these teachers has skyrocketed. Interest in reading and associated skills has developed to unexpected proportions, and the skills of reading seem to have developed as much.

Multilevel reading instruction. This approach to reading is designed to meet the individual differences that occur in each child's reading process, developmental growth, and ability to learn. The SRA laboratories worked out materials to aid the teachers in developing each of these strands of development.

The learning laboratory process is introduced to the class, and the teacher supervises it individually. The materials can be used in a variety of combinations, so that a great deal of self-learning is fostered and the teacher is free to help those who need it. The pupil learns the names and sounds of the ordinary English alphabet, its phonic and structural sight-sound combinations, and linguistic word patterning as units of thought. He then proceeds to decoding meanings from more complex units. This type of organizational plan generally leads into an individualized reading program. Actually it contributes no "new" way of teaching; it is simply a plan whereby the teaching of known methods may be employed more individually.

The ungraded reading program. This organizational plan grew out of the concept of the ungraded school and is often used by schools as a step toward complete ungradedness. As such it is actually a misconception of ungradedness and is practically the same plan of organization employed by what was once labeled the Joplin Plan. In essence the purpose of ungraded reading programs is to regroup children in schools where there are several grades on each level so that all teachers do not have too many reading groups in each classroom. Teachers share the children during reading times—one teacher may work with a slow ability group, one with an average ability group, and so forth. The theory is that each teacher, having a narrower range of reading ability with which to deal, can devote more time and help to the individual student. Many variations of this plan are now in use in many of our schools.

Departmentalized reading. The concept of departmentalization as practiced in the high schools and junior high schools has been projected into the elementary schools. Children go from teacher to teacher for each subject. During reading period the children are grouped by ability levels, and the wide range of reading within any one group is reduced, thus making more individual help possible for each child.

Ability grouping. Children are homogenized according to ability to diminish range in reading ability and to provide more individual attention for each child. In the ungraded reading and departmentalized programs, this plan is prevalent in one form or another.

Grouping within the classroom. This plan has been popular for many years and still is considered the most sensible by many educators. The children are grouped by the teachers for reading instruction during various times of the day. Groups are flexible, and children may be shifted from group to group as their reading problems change. Children are basically under the guidance of one teacher, and she is responsible for helping each child. The groups are built around common problems of the group members. Many schools use a variety of basal texts under this plan so that the various groups work with different materials yet all the materials are geared to the ability level of the group.

Team-teaching plans. In some schools the above plans are often called "team-teaching plans" because teachers share students and do some planning together. However, they are responsible largely to one or two reading groups, the core of which may or may not be the students in their own home rooms. So-called team-teaching reading plans are often unjustifiably named, for true team-teaching means that teachers are willing to subject their methodology to the scrutiny and evaluation of their peers. Under a *real* team-teaching plan this element is essential. One teacher may teach a reading skill while others watch and then, in conference, evaluate the lesson, so that lessons continually improve. Planning sessions are an integral part of team-teaching. Some days one teacher takes a large group, while on other days these groups are broken down into smaller groups. Thus all teachers are teaching at a given time. The basic philosophy behind this plan is to make instruction ever more effective and to meet the individual needs of students as much as possible.

Method and Creativity

In Chapter I the principles of creative teaching and the basic principles of creativity were stated. Which of the above systems and plans for organization contribute to the development of creativity, and which do not? Both systems *and* plans must be considered, for creativity is a *process* and a *product* and the process of creativity is made possible by the conditions set for it in the schoolroom. The organizational plan of the classroom constitutes one of the major conditions for hindering or developing creativity.

Reading can be creative in both process and product. It may seem at first that, since reading is the recognition of words whose patterns are already formed, it is largely a convergent thinking exercise and allows for little creative development. But, as stated above, reading is more than a set of skills; it is a *problem-solving* situation. The reader must choose from all his experiences those meanings which the author intends to convey by the particular choice of a word. He must evaluate, make decisions, pass judgment, think critically—sometimes creatively. He must at times be spontaneous in his reactions, flexible in his interpretations, original in his thinking. All of these skills are concerned with the development of divergent thinking processes. When reading lessons are designed to develop these skills, creativity is being developed in children.

In learning to read, creativity may also be developed through the process. At times the total process as described by Marksberry (see Book I of this series, *Setting Conditions for Creative Teaching in the Elementary School,* Chapter VI) may be noted, as in the reading lesson described in Chapter I of this book. At other times, only certain skills of creative growth are developed in the process. When reading is creatively taught, problems are posed to children who become involved with them and struggle through the problem to the time when "insight" (or discovery) comes. The example of discovery cited above is an excellent sample of the way children can develop creative thinking processes through the learning of the reading process. The teaching of each reading skill—even those which often appear to be uncreative—can be utilized to this purpose.

*   *   *

Note how Miss Rogers taught the application of beginning consonants through the use of discovery.

The first-grade class had been collecting pictures that illustrated all the sounds of the beginning consonants and pasting them on large charts around the room. They had played many games with beginning consonants and knew them well. Miss Rogers next wanted these children to see how the application of these consonants could create new words.

One day David spilled some ink. He cleaned it up and later, when the class made their customary reading chart of a summary of the day's work, the children put this sentence on the chart: *David spilled the ink*.

After the chart had been read, Miss Rogers said, "I'd like to come back to one word in our story and have some fun with it." She wrote "ink" on the chalkboard. "What is this word?" she asked.

The children told her. "Now look at our charts around the room," said Miss Rogers. "We know most of the sounds of those letters. Can any of you put some of those sounds with this word and discover a whole new word?"

In a second, Jerry had caught on. "Pink," he said.

"Very good," encouraged Miss Rogers, "any others?"

Soon the words were flowing from the group. Miss Rogers printed each word on the chalkboard.

Jennifer raised her hand, "Miss Rogers, could we do that with other words, too?"

"Well," asked Miss Rogers, "could we?"

"Yes," said Jennifer, "we have the word 'art' on the chart and I could make 'cart' from it."

In a few minutes the children were trying to make new words from all of those on their charts. Josie made another discovery. "When you say the words together it makes poetry." So they discussed how rhyming words sounded alike at the end.

"They look alike, too," said Alice.

"What part looks alike?" asked Miss Rogers, pointing out that rhyming words sounded and looked alike at the *end*.

"I have an idea," said Miss Rogers. "I will give each of you a large piece of white construction paper. You will put any small word you can think of at the top of the paper and put below it all the words you can make from it. Then we'll put all our charts on the bulletin board so we can share what we have learned. Maybe some of you can take them home and have your brothers and sisters think of words that can be made like this. And there's something else. I'll bet after you make them some of you can use them at the end of sentences to make a poem!"

The next morning the bulletin board was covered with the charts as children shared their words. About half of them had tried them out in poems. This was David's:

David's Yink

I have a yink.
My yink likes to sink and
    slink and drink.
What he likes to drink
    is pink ink.
So if you have lots of pink ink
    You should get a yink, I think.

*   *   *

The *process* of teaching reading skills can be creative. It can produce some creative products as well when it is kept in its logical sequential developmental place in the child's learning experience.

Creative teaching *could* be applied to each of the above systems of teaching reading. In all truth, however, it must be observed that none of these systems is designed to develop creativity, *and if most of them are followed in the form advocated by their creators, they tend to limit creativity rather than develop it.*

The phonics approach is very limiting in this respect. This author feels that primary reading especially must follow the language sequence development. It is true that some children learn to read words without saying them first, but this is an exception, and all children *think* the words if they do not say them. If a teacher is to build a meaningful understanding of phonetic analysis, she can do it only on the material with which she is provided: the speaking vocabularies of her pupils. The alphabet of sound is learned before the alphabet of letters. And some sounds are more prevalent than others in different cultures and in different towns and in different schools within each town. These are the sounds that should be taught first.

Bobbie, who lives in a railroad town, comes in to the classroom saying, "Choo-choo-chug-chug," as he imitates a train; the teacher shows the children how Bobbie's sound would look in print—and they *discover* the "ch" speech consonant at the beginning of the words. On the other hand, Mike, who lives near the airport, brings in an airplane and says, "Whirr, whirr—swish, swish, swish," as he flies his toy plane through the air. His teacher has material for working on other sounds. A rigid, preconceived program in developing sounds is even more difficult for children to comprehend than a rigid, preconceived development of words. Neither contributes much to the development of creativity.

Advocates of the phonics approach to *beginning* reading feel that there are too many words to memorize by sight, so teaching the components of words is a more logical approach. This logic can be challenged when we consider that every word consists of many components and that these components are less meaningful to the child than the whole word. It is no more difficult to memorize a host of words than it is to memorize a host of meaningless sounds for each letter in the word or for groups of letters in the words.

The sound elements in the phonics approach are reduced to forty-four, but in application there are many more combinations a child must learn. Phonics strives to bring out the consistencies in the language, yet many of the rules it advocates are not consistent. One of the most common rules given to children at an early age is the one defining the use of a double vowel in a word—that when two vowels appear together the first one usually says its name and the second one is silent. A recent study by Theodore Clymer reported in *The Reading Teacher*[10] shows that this rule is applicable in only 45 percent of the English language. Is it, then, a rule? Clymer found that, of all the so-called "rules of language" that we give children to figure out new words, only 20 percent were applicable 100 percent of the time. Some are applicable only 10 percent of the time. Unless a rule is applicable *almost all* the time it is not a rule—it is an exception and learning it as a rule is an example of how we force the full use of language into disuse in the unconscious mind. Creativity is limited in its development when these approaches to reading skills development are used.

Clymer's work supports the fact that the English language (at least that portion of it used for the teaching of reading in the primary grades) is only about 80 percent phonetic.

The basal reading text program has already been discussed. When adapted to the children's use, it can provide a medium for developing creativity and for promoting creative teaching. But when it is followed rigidly page by page it can contribute little or nothing to creative development.

The language experience approach is the one from which illustrations in this book have been most commonly selected. It offers unlimited opportunity for creative development in teachers and children.

The initial teaching alphabet is sound in many respects and allows a flexibility in using the consistent alphabet code. But it is also very limiting in that it restricts written communication to the group

[10] Theodore Clymer, "The Utility of Phonic Generalizations in the Primary Grades," *The Reading Teacher,* XVI (January 1963), pp. 252–58.

exposed to ITA. One of the strongest criticisms against ITA is that it distorts the visual image of the true shape and spelling of English words. Because so much emphasis is being currently placed on the *image* of the word for correct spelling purposes, critics of the plan agree that while children may read sooner and better, there will be problems when they come to transfer to the regular traditional spelling of words. Supporters of the plan claim this is not the case, and one piece of research has supported their claim. Because the ITA is comparatively new in this country, judgment on its contribution to creative development must be withheld.

The words in color approach to reading does not distort the traditional spellings—in fact, it emphasizes the problem areas of words so children may fix them better in their minds. This method of teaching, when used judiciously, could lead to extensive creative development.

The linguistic approach, in its early stages of development, was limiting in some ways yet creative in others. It was limiting in that Bloomfield's[11, 12] first program for the teaching of reading through the linguistic approach was very detailed and demanded excessive conformity to carry out the program. It was creative in that children could explore and invent new words. Sounds were used in new word forms in Bloomfield's materials whether they made a *real* word or not. Criticism was leveled against this technique because some educators felt that young children, with limited experience and limited vocabularies, were confused because they could not tell the nonsense words from the words they did not yet know. Their desire to make sense out of their reading was challenged. Recent approaches (such as that advocated by LeFevre and mentioned above) can contribute a great deal to creative development in teachers and children.

Some of the *plans of organization* mentioned above set conditions so the creative process can be enhanced. Among these is the *individualized reading plan,* which, if properly carried out, can provide a highly creative, efficient, and individual reading program. The SRA materials are designed for individual use and can do a great deal to help children develop their own reading skills. As a self-learning device, either can be a springboard for much creative development providing it is used discreetly and with other reading activities.

[11] Leonard Bloomfield, *Language* (New York: Holt, Rinehart and Winston, Inc., 1933).

[12] Leonard Bloomfield and Clarence L. Barnhart, *Let's Read: A Linguistic Approach* (Detroit: Wayne State University Press, 1961).

The ungraded reading program, if isolated from a total ungraded school situation, is not conducive to the development of the creative process. Reading is isolated from the other language skills; the experiences of the children do not provide a base for the development of language, and often children do not know the teacher well—nor she them. It has been stated that a prerequisite to teaching reading is that teachers must know their children and their experiential background. This organizational plan seems to violate most of the necessary conditions for creative development. Some teachers manage to teach creatively and develop creativity with this plan, but it is very constricting at best.

Departmentalized reading and *ability grouping* plans have the same drawbacks as the ungraded primary reading plans. Obviously, a truly creative teacher may make her lessons with these groups very creative, and some aspects of creative development may be realized, but the consistent, planned program in creative development cannot be carried out when so much preplanned material is shoved at the children, especially if there is little carry-over into the other areas of the curriculum.

Grouping within the self-contained classroom has tremendous potential for creative teaching and creative development. In this situation, the teacher and children know each other well, reading can be an integral part of the total curriculum, the teacher can contrive experiences throughout the day to be used in the reading time, flexibility of scheduling is possible, progress in creative development can be more carefully evaluated, language arts can be taught as coordinated units, interests of the children can be utilized in developing vocabulary and reading skills, flexibility of grouping is possible, and the teacher can give help to children throughout the day.

In the true concept of the nongraded school as advocated by Goodlad and Anderson,[13] these aspects of the total school program would also apply to fostering creative development through the teaching of reading.

Team-teaching plans obviously can contribute to developing the creative process when they are *real* team-teaching plans as described above. When they are team-teaching in name only, the limitations in developing creativity are the same as those mentioned above under *departmentalized reading.*

---

[13] John I. Goodlad and Robert H. Anderson, *The Nongraded Elementary School* (New York: Harcourt, Brace & World, Inc., 1963).

Creative Teaching and Reading Materials

Very few current reading materials are constructed to develop creative processes in children. In fact, one of the most devastating blows to the creative process comes in the slavish adherence to exercises in many of the workbooks. Workbooks can make a contribution to creative teaching, but few of them do at present.

In developing creativity, we strive for a new product, for uniqueness and difference. Yet countless exercises in workbooks have children drawing an object to resemble a pattern already placed on the page. "Color it like this." "Make it red." "Draw three balloons like this one." These directions may be a check on reading comprehension but, because of their excessive repetitiveness, they are fatal to creative development. If creative development is to be one of the major objectives of the elementary school, we cannot negate what we do at one time of the school day by the materials we use at another time. It doesn't have to be like this. Look at these exercises:

On this page there are four boxes. In each box draw something that you saw on the way to school this morning.

The word "red" is printed at the top of this page. In the first box draw three red things you have at home; in the second box draw two red things you have in your room; in the third box. . . .

Make a picture of your favorite friends and then put the number of friends you have drawn in this box.

Such exercises check reading comprehension and the same concepts as the ones stated in the workbook above. But such a difference. One removes patterns, challenges the child's imagination, stimulates his flow of ideas, encourages originality; the other flattens it into a prescribed answer. In assigned seat work and in exercises designed to build reading skills, creative products can be encouraged, divergent as well as convergent thinking processes may be put to work, open-ended situations may be utilized, individuality can be stressed, new knowledges and skills may be applied, problem-solving processes rather than busy work may be employed, the individual component skills of creativity can be practiced, all areas of the curriculum may be correlated, and *every* activity can be meaningful and productive. These are the essentials of creative development listed in Chapter I.

Many reading materials are adaptable to the development of creativity in children. Others, such as the teaching machines, concentrate on convergent thought processes in the teaching of skills and are not. One of the most needed commodities in the elementary school today is a rich variety of independent reading activities geared to developing the creative process. It is hoped a start has been made by the suggestions in this and the other volumes of this series.

Summary

Creativity *can* be developed in the teacher and the student through the teaching of reading. Some of the systems for teaching reading currently used in our schools provide little chance for creative development, while some appear to provide countless opportunities for it. Some plans of classroom organization deny the full development of teacher and student to their creative potentials; others seem to promote it. Almost no independent reading materials currently used in our schools consistently provide for creative development. A careful scrutiny of teaching plans, organizational plans, and teaching materials must be made if the teaching of reading in any school is to promote creative teaching among its teachers and creative thinking among its pupils.

TO THE COLLEGE STUDENT

1. At the beginning of this chapter you were asked to review methods and organizational plans for the teaching of reading and check them in terms of developing creativity. Did your analysis agree with the author's viewpoint?

2. Check your own reading ability. If a reading clinic is available on your campus, ask the director to speak to your class about reading disability in college students and give a demonstration reading diagnostic test. How do you account for your own reading disabilities?

3. College students often complain that the large numbers of readings required from them for each course makes it almost impossible for them to read what they want to read. Do you feel you would read more or less under a freer reading plan than now exists

in your college? Think of all the plans you could use, if you were a college instructor, to motivate your students to free reading and then suggest ways such plans could be initiated. Perhaps your college instructor may permit you to work one or more of these plans on a trial basis.

4. Examine the material you have read this week in terms of *how* you read it. Which assignments did you read quickly? Which did you read slowly? Which did you read over? Which did you enjoy? Was your rate of reading faster for some than others? Do you read material you like quickly or slowly? What generalizations can you make from this examination?

TO THE CLASSROOM TEACHER

1. What "method" of teaching reading are you currently using? What organizational plan are you currently using? Make a conscientious list of the ways your method and your organizational plan hinders or encourages the development of creativity.

2. Examine Dechant's list of fallacies regarding reading as reported on pages 70–71. Are some of these fallacies ones in which you have believed? Submit yourself to some critical and creative thinking and determine why they are fallacies.

3. How can you turn the heterogeneous grouping of children in a classroom into an asset in the teaching of reading creatively?

4. Think of all the ways by which you can teach phonics creatively.

5. Using Clymer's report as a basis (see page 80), determine which vowel rules should be taught as rules rising from generalizations and which are really exceptions to the generalization. Then determine more creative ways to teach the exceptions than those advocated by your basal series.

6. Your author's first teaching was in a one-room rural school containing all eight grades. On his arrival at the schoolhouse, he discovered he had *no* beginning reading books. There were five children in the first grade. How would *you* go about teaching reading in this situation?

TO THE COLLEGE STUDENT AND
THE CLASSROOM TEACHER

1. Make a list of the conditions you must set in order to teach reading creatively. A review of Chapters VII and VIII in Book I of this series, *Setting Conditions for Creative Teaching in the Elementary School,* may serve as a guide.

2. Following is a list of statements collected by the author from faculty meetings and discussion meetings he has attended. Analyze each comment and discuss the fallacies of the thinking behind each:

Our principal insists each child read two preprimers, two primers and two first-grade readers before we are allowed to promote the child to the second grade.

We must work harder at teaching reading because half of our children were below grade level on the achievement test.

We don't begin social studies until the third grade because reading is so important we spend most of our time on it.

We are going to ungrade our reading program and I'm glad. It will make it so much easier for the teachers.

3. Using material from the preceding chapters, plan a program for teaching adult illiterates (of average or above-average intelligence) how to read.

4. Make a list of as many situations as possible where reading skills may be developed without small group meetings.

5. Refer to the lesson at the beginning of Chapter I. Plan a good reading lesson for culturally-deprived, average-intelligence children which will attain the same objectives as the lesson described in Chapter I and where it will be unnecessary to group the children (that is, individual differences will be met within the total class group).

6. Design some independent reading activities that will develop creativity in children. Take stock of some of the independent activities you are already using and evaluate them in terms of their value in creative development.

SELECTED BIBLIOGRAPHY

ANDERSON, H. E. (ed.). *Creativity and Its Cultivation.* New York: Harper & Row, Publishers, Inc., 1959. Chap. 2.

BAKER, S. S. *Your Key to Creative Thinking.* New York: Harper & Row, Publishers, Inc., 1962.

BRICKELL, HENRY M. *Commissioners 1961 Catalogue.* Albany, N.Y.: State Department of Education, 1961.

————. *Organizing for Educational Change.* Albany, N.Y.: University of State of New York, State Department of Education, 1960.

BROGAN, PEGGY and LORENE FOX. *Helping Children Read.* New York: Holt, Rinehart and Winston, Inc., 1961.

BRYSON, L. "Training for Creativity," *School Arts,* LX (September 1960), 5–8.

BULLETIN OF BUREAU OF SCHOOL SERVICE. *Creativity in Its Classroom Context,* XXXVI, No. 4. Lexington, Ky.: College of Education, University of Kentucky, 1963.

BURKHART, R. C. *Spontaneous and Deliberate Ways of Learning.* Scranton, Pa.: International Textbook, 1962.

CARLSON, RUTH K. "Stimulating Creativity in Children and Youth," *Elementary English,* XXXIX (1961), 165–169.

DALE, EDGAR. "Education for Creativity," *The News Letter,* XXX, No. 3 (December 1964).

EISNER, ELLIOTT. *Think With Me About Creativity: Ten Essays on Creativity.* Dansville, New York: F. A. Owen Publishing Co., 1964.

GANS, ROMA. *Common Sense in Teaching Reading.* New York: Bobbs-Merrill Co., Inc., 1963.

GETZELS, JACOB W. and PHILIP W. JACKSON. *Creativity and Intelligence.* New York: John Wiley & Sons, Inc., 1962.

GOODLAD, JOHN and ROBERT H. ANDERSON. *The Nongraded Elementary School.* New York: Harcourt, Brace & World, Inc., 1963.

GUILFORD, J. P. "The Structure of Intellect," *Psychological Bulletin,* LII (1956), 277–295.

HARRISON, MAURICE. *The Story of the Initial Teaching Alphabet.* New York: Pitman Publishing Corporation, 1964.

LEE, DORRIS M. and R. V. ALLEN. *Learning to Read Through Experience.* New York: Appleton-Century-Crofts, Inc., 1963.

MACKINNON, DONALD W. "What Makes a Person Creative?" *Saturday Review,* X (February 1962).

MIEL, ALICE, ed. *Creativity in Teaching: Invitations and Instances.* Belmont, California: Wadsworth Publishing Company, Inc., 1961.

OSBORN, ALEX F. *Applied Imagination* (3rd ed.). New York: Charles Scribner's Sons, 1963.

————. *Your Creative Power.* New York: Charles Scribner's Sons, 1948.

PARNES, S. J. "Can Creativity Be Increased?" *Art Education,* III, No. 1 (Fall 1961), 39–46.

PARNES, S. J. and H. F. HARDING (eds.). *A Source Book for Creative Teaching.* New York: Charles Scribner's Sons, 1962.

RUGG, HAROLD. *Imagination: An Inquiry into the Sources and Conditions That Stimulate Creativity.* New York: Harper & Row, Publishers, Inc., 1963.

RUSSELL, DAVID E. *Children's Thinking.* New York: Ginn and Co., 1956.

SMITH, JAMES A. *Creativity: Its Nature and Nurture.* Syracuse, N.Y.: School of Education, Syracuse University, 1964.

STEIN, MORRIS I. and SHIRLEY HEINZE. *Creativity and the Individual.* Glencoe, Illinois: The Free Press, 1960.

STERN, CATHERINE and TONI S. GOULD. *Children Discover Reading.* New York: Random House, Inc., 1965.

STRANG, RUTH and DONALD M. LINDQUIST. *The Administrator and the Improvement of Reading.* New York: Appleton-Century-Crofts, Inc., 1960.

TORRANCE, E. PAUL. *Education and the Creative Potential.* Minneapolis: University of Minnesota Press, 1963, 103–118.

———. *Gifted Children in the Classroom.* New York: Macmillan Company, 1965, Chapter 7.

———. *Guiding Creative Talent.* Englewood Cliffs, New Jersey: Prentice-Hall, Inc., 1962.

———. *Rewarding Creative Behavior.* Englewood Cliffs, New Jersey: Prentice-Hall, Inc., 1965.

VEATCH, JEANETTE. *Reading in the Elementary School.* New York: The Ronald Press Company, 1966.

WALSH, FRANCES. *That Eager Zest.* New York: J. B. Lippincott Company, 1961.

WERTHEIMER, M. *Productive Thinking.* New York: Harper & Row, Publishers, Inc., 1954.

ZIRBES, LAURA. *Guidelines to Developmental Teaching.* Columbus, Ohio: The Bureau of Educational Research and Service, Ohio State University, 1961.

Literature and the Reading Program

Childhood will have no difficulty with literature if it has a chance to develop its own native gifts in language. This, of course, is not the whole story, but it is one of its most important chapters.[1]

HUGHES MEARNS

TO THE READER

Before you read this chapter, look at the bibliography on page 100. Find one of the anthologies of children's literature in the library and enjoy some children's stories and poems. Also, you will enjoy this chapter more if you spend some time browsing through a children's library first.

Introduction

The skill-building program described in the first three chapters of this book constitutes one half of a good reading program; the other half is a rich program in children's literature. Reading skills are learned so that children may be able to read the literature written for them. A good school library is essential, therefore, in developing a well-rounded reading program.

Children's literature makes definite contributions toward creative development in boys and girls and offers many opportunities for creative teaching. Literature is the creative product of the minds of creative people. As a painting serves to fire the imagination, so does a fine story, a well-composed poem, or a good book. Children who write their own literature are always eager to see what others write. True literature stimulates the imagination and contributes to the children's concept of the use of imagination in creating. The creative teaching of literature can contribute to creative development in many ways:

[1] Hughes Mearns, *Creative Power: The Education of Youth in the Creative Arts* (New York: Dover Publications, Inc., 1958), p. 75.

1. It can stimulate children to write for themselves.
2. It can provide a means of therapy for troubled children.
3. It can help children build skills in expression, in defining, and in elaboration.
4. It can help build a colorful vocabulary that will assist each child to express himself better.
5. It can serve as the basis for constructive daydreaming and complete identification with a problem (so necessary for creative problem-solving).
6. It can make children more discreet in passing judgment and making choices, especially in the use of words.
7. It can be the perpetual source of creative stimulation for every child.
8. It can develop a sensitivity to places, sights, sounds, words, life problems and people.
9. It helps children build a set of standards and values regarding creative writing.

Careful plans made through use of charts.

Careful plans made through the use of charts culminate in an original play.

Literature should not be "taught"; it should only be *read* and *enjoyed*. The teacher's job in sharing a story or a poem with children is a simple one: she is an intermediary between the author and his audience, and her major duty is to try to put across the author's ideas as though she were a substitute for him.

Through literature the child develops his tastes in reading for pleasure. If he experiences satisfaction in the stories the teacher reads, he will seek out this satisfaction in other stories. Satisfaction, happiness, contentment, fun, joy, positive release, pleasure: all of these feelings should accompany the literature period in the classroom.

Literature fulfills a need in the modern school which does not confine it to the language arts alone. It touches on every aspect of living and therefore should become an integral part of the entire school program. At least once every day, and in some instances many more times than this, a teacher should read a poem or story to the children regardless of age range or grade placement. The wealth of available material gives her resources for every occasion.

Although literature is often classified among the fine arts, in the elementary school it can be combined with any area of the school curriculum. Social studies books can only be, at best, a summary of facts about a country or a period in history. They cannot consume space to give to children the feeling for the way of life in any given country or any period of time. Without the "feeling" element facts cannot help children understand life in a time or place different from their own. Reading about Switzerland in a social studies book is one thing and reading *Heidi* is another. Facts about the Revolutionary War cannot impart to children the terror, the suspense, the fear, the bravery, the courage, the compassion, or the hatred which war arouses in the hearts of men, but reading *The Matchlock Gun* or *Drums Along the Mohawk* can. Social studies books reach the minds of children, but literature reaches their hearts.

Good literature recaptures the *mood* rather than the *facts* of life. The life of a by-gone period of time is reconstructed, a strange place comes alive, or a feeling or mood saturates the listener to the extent that the author is able to communicate in an imaginative manner. It is not the *story* of Tom Sawyer and Huckleberry Finn that makes *The Adventures of Tom Sawyer* a delightful book—it is the author's unique ability to make every boy today feel a kinship with Tom because he understands Tom through the genius of the author's communicative power. Tom makes fires glow in the hearts of fathers, bringing back the carefree adventurous feeling of their own boyhoods; he evokes nostalgic memories through the magic grouping of words. So literature can transplant us to another world or another period of time; it can create an emotional situation, a mood or tone, a feeling. We experience sadness, love, joy, disgust, hatred, sympathy. This we do through empathy, our ability to project ourselves into the situation and live within the consciousness of the characters created by the author.

The therapeutic value of literature must be recognized. Creative writing provides emotional release, and, in reading the writings of others, many children are able to project themselves so that they receive help with their own problems. They come to understand human nature by learning that their problems are not unique.

The field of literature, then, belongs in the area of the creative arts for the aesthetic values it has; it belongs to the field of language arts, for it is the most perfected use of symbolic communicative tools; it belongs to the area of the social sciences for the knowledge and understanding it develops. More intimately than any other subject-matter area, literature, as children write it and read it, goes hand-in-hand with goals of the modern school. It *is* communication through creative experiences.

Criteria for Choosing Literature for Children

Literature is concerned more with the telling of the story than the plot. It is the raising of the commonplace to the beautiful by caring enough to choose exactly the right word for the right place. Leland Jacobs[2] gives five criteria for the selection of literature to read to children:

1. The story should have a fresh well-paced plot.
2. It must have unique individuality.
3. It should contain plausible, direct conversation.
4. It must have well-delineated characters.
5. The story must have authentic outcomes.

Jacobs also feels that good children's literature must be free from obvious sentimentality while rich in honest sentiment; it must be

---

[2] Leland B. Jacobs, "Children's Experiences in Literature," in *Children and the Language Arts,* ed. Virgil E. Herrick and Leland B. Jacobs (Englewood Cliffs, N.J.: Prentice-Hall, Inc., 1955), p. 194.

free from direct moralizing but rooted in genuine spiritual and moral values; it must be free from cuteness and triteness but vigorously unhackneyed and distinctive; it must be free from talking down or misunderstanding of children's abilities. He feels good literature has "memory" value—there is a residue of meaning after time lapses.

There have been many surveys[3] developed to assist the teacher in the selection of appropriate literature at various age levels. These surveys show that children tend to have specific interests at different ages, but with the changing interests there remain some persistent overall ones. Children tend to maintain an interest in machines, nature, everyday experiences, holidays, love, fun stories and poems, and in make-believe.[4]

Young children prefer literature that has one main plot. They want to be able to anticipate the outcome of the story. They like literature that sets a mood and they like "direct" conversation. They enjoy colorful "tongue-tickling" words and prefer simple, natural climaxes in their stories. They like stories developed around one main character, and generally they prefer one acceptable boy or girl hero, although sometimes an animal hero will act as an acceptable substitute. And they like literature with illustrations that also tell the story.[5]

As children grow older, they develop a keener interest in animals, especially specific animals, such as horses or cats. Older children like folk literature and stories of American folk heroes. They like modern magic, stories about contemporary experiences, historical fiction, regional fiction, and intergroup fiction. They enjoy reading about child life in other countries and like biographies and books about science. They also like stories built around such themes as sports, games, religion, arts, crafts, heroes, humor, mystery, travel, nature, or about children with their own characteristics and problems.[6]

In choosing books for children's reading, or in guiding children in the selection of their own reading, teachers will keep in mind the following sources: contemporary literature, great stories and classics, realistic tales, fanciful tales, stories of fiction, stories of information,

[3] George Norvell, *What Boys and Girls Like to Read* (Morristown, N.J.: Silver Burdett Co., 1959).

[4] Leland B. Jacobs, "Children's Experiences in Literature," in *Children and the Language Arts,* ed. Virgil E. Herrick and Leland B. Jacobs (Englewood Cliffs, N.J.: Prentice-Hall, Inc., 1955), pp. 196–198.

[5] *Ibid.,* p. 198.

[6] *Ibid.,* pp. 200–204.

current material in periodicals, popular materials and distinctively literary reading matter, anthropologies, and inexpensive books on children's literature.

Creative Teaching of Literature

A good story or a good poem will stand by itself; it needs no embellishment. Because this statement is obviously true, librarians and teachers sometimes frown on any activity that detracts from the story or poem being read to the children.

While the basic criterion for using any piece of literature *is* that it communicate effectively and beautifully, much can be done to develop children's taste in literature. Today's children are exposed to much cheap, yet often impressive, writing. They become confused when no attempt is made to help distinguish the difference between good and poor literature. Children are not born with a set of standards and values. These they develop as a result of the understandings they glean from their experiences. Setting conditions for the creative teaching of literature means that the teacher provides experiences that help each child to become more selective in his reading, more critical of the type of material he reads, and more sensitive to good writing.

Inasmuch as empathy is necessary in order to experience literature, and the ability to project oneself into any situation is dependent on one's own related experiences and feelings, it is not enough that children hear good literature in the classroom—they must *experience* it. This means that while sometimes the reading of a poem or story will suffice in itself, in most instances conditions must be set so the children can experience or live the material being read. It is this additional attention paid to the "good" stories and poems that makes children realize they are special. By living and feeling the story with the characters, and by learning to express their own feelings in carefully chosen words, they come to see the skill of the author—and to appreciate the quality of the work. Through classroom experiences with literature, they build their own values and standards, and learn to evaluate the writing of others.

In setting conditions for developing a love and appreciation for literature there are a few hints a teacher might follow:

1. *Remember that it is not only the plot that makes the story*

a good one; it is the way it is told. Encourage the children to use the author's words as much as possible. Be sure that the Elephant's Child does not look only for the crocodile but for "the great grey greasy Limpapo River all set around by fever trees."

2. *Children can interpret the author's words only in light of their own experiences.* Do not try to force your interpretation of a story on them. Let them dramatize or retell it in their way. Although their interpretation may not be the same as yours, the retelling does give you an opportunity to correct gross misconceptions.

3. *Enjoyment of the piece of work, not perfection of performance, should be the goal.* Should some child's or some group's contribution be exceptionally well-received, the class may work on it to "polish it up" for other classes or for parents. This should only happen occasionally, for polished performances take too long to prepare. Children should receive enjoyment from experiences with literature every day.

4. *Continually draw attention to phrases or words in the writing that make it unique or give special delight.* All over America children love to chant:

> He meant what he said
> And he said what he meant
> And an elephant's faithful
> One hundred percent.

or

> Listen, my children, and you shall hear
> Of the midnight ride of Paul Revere—

and

> "The time has come," the Walrus said—

and

> Speak for yourself, John

and

> Fourscore and seven years ago

Phrases lifted from literature are as much a part of life as learning itself. To know them is part of the children's rightful heritage.

The teaching of reading and the enjoyment of literature go hand-in-hand. In skill-building reading periods, children learn the tools needed to unlock the joys concealed in the world of books. Children come to school with a reservoir of literature of some kind in their background. Much of this can be used to teach reading. Miss George, for instance, printed the favorite phrases of her children on a chart before the room, and these children learned to read them as they learned to read an experience chart.

The first reading chart composed by the class may well be their first experience at composing literature. A sensitive teacher will make certain that these first charts *are* good literature, simple as they may be. A good program in the enjoyment of literature and poetry may grow out of the first compositions of the children. The account of the stories composed by the slow first grade in Chapter I shows how a lead is provided for the teacher to read *The Fir Tree* and other related stories. The chart composed by the teacher in Chapter III about the bus driver was her cue for reading *The Little Red Automobile* and other stories. As soon as children write their own stories, the stories may be placed on charts and read and enjoyed by other children. Every topic suggests a work of literature or a poem that will help children understand the power of effective communication. An understanding and appreciation of good literature develops most readily when children write their own and then discover that others enjoy the power of expression through words.

Summary

No reading program is complete without a planned parallel program for the enjoyment of literature. All the language arts become meshed in a final product when children write their own literature and read the effective writing of others. All the teaching of listening, speech, oral expression, reading, and handwriting skill is directed to this end. None of the teaching of any of these skills of communication is of any substantial value unless it all results in the application of the skills in effective writing for oneself and enjoyment of the writings of others.

TO THE COLLEGE STUDENT

1. Using the criteria stated in this chapter for good children's literature, bring a collection of children's books to class and evaluate them. Which books do you feel are especially creative or contribute to children's creative development?

2. Discuss the following problems in class:
   a. What part do picture books play in a literature program? Are picture books good literature?
   b. How does television contribute to an appreciation of good literature in children?
   c. What makes a classic in children's literature?
   d. What authors do you remember from your childhood? What authors do children currently enjoy?
   e. How can literature develop creative components of the intellect?

3. Plan a social studies unit which you could teach in its entirety through children's literature.

4. Read *Island of Blue Dolphins,* by Scott O'Dell, a Newberry Award book, and discuss all the ways you can think of in which it could be used in the classroom in connection with various areas of the curriculum.

5. Design and illustrate a children's story or book. Try it out on children and note their reactions.

6. Set aside a short period of time in class, and ask one student each session to read a child's book or story. Rediscover for yourself the delightful world of children's literature.

7. Have each student make a list of the books he remembers from his childhood. Make a composite and note which books were enjoyed most by the members of the class. Check your favorite books against the favorite books of children today. How well has your choice withstood the element of time?

8. Assign some members of the class to select passages from current literature, both good and poor. Have each member read a

selection from his choice but do not tell the origin of the writing. Ask the class members to rate the passages on the following basis:

    a. Excellent piece of writing (good literature).

    b. Good piece of writing (fair as literature).

    c. Fair piece of writing.

    d. Poor writing (poor literature).

After all passages have been read and rated, expose the origins. Can you identify good literature?

TO THE CLASSROOM TEACHER

1. Examine your daily program for the past week and notice the amount of time you spent on children's literature. Do you have a well-balanced reading program?

2. Examine your classroom and note the stimuli you have provided for interesting children in literature. Are you doing enough? How can you do more? How can you get the children to help? Have you provided materials on many reading ability levels?

3. Observe the books your children cherish. What clues does this observation give you for creative teaching in your classroom?

4. Outline a plan for teaching the history of the United States through the use of children's literature.

5. Think of all the ways you can to teach art through the use of children's literature.

6. Collect specific stories from children's literature that lend themselves to: (a) the building of values, (b) the solution of children's problems, (c) the development of appreciations, and (d) the development of empathy.

TO THE COLLEGE STUDENT AND THE CLASSROOM TEACHER

1. Collect specific stories from children's literature which lend themselves to interpretation through puppetry, dramatization, dance, pantomime, shadow plays, and music.

2. Discuss these problems and statements together:

    a. To what degree should a teacher impose her standards for good literature on children?

    b. By what techniques can a teacher develop good taste in children for literature?

    c. The filming of children's classics often destroys the joy of reading the classic by children.

    d. The violence on television is no greater than that to which children have been exposed in such stories as *The Red Shoes, Hansel and Gretel, Grimm's Fairy Tales,* and *Red Riding Hood.*

    e. Children today do not seem to have much use for poetry. Boys, in particular, regard the reading of poetry as "sissy." How might this specific characteristic be identified with creativity?

    f. The lack of an appreciation of poetry by elementary school children is caused by the fact that it is not a part of the general school curriculum in most schools today.

3. Some literature written for children is appreciated more by adults. Can you find such books? How do you explain their popularity among adults? Read some to children and note their reactions.

4. Make a list of all the children's books or stories you remember which you did *not* like as a child. Why did you *not* like them? Check them against the criteria for good literature stated in this chapter and decide whether or not they could be classified as good literature. Reread some of these stories now and see if you still feel the same.

SELECTED BIBLIOGRAPHY

ADAMS, BESS PORTER. *About Books and Children.* New York: Henry Holt and Company, 1953.

ARBUTHNOT, MAY HILL (compiler). *The Arbuthnot Anthology of Children's Literature.* Chicago: Scott, Foresman and Co., 1953.

———. *Children and Books.* New York: Henry Holt and Company, 1953.

EAKIN, MARY K. *Good Books for Children.* Chicago: The University of Chicago Press, 1959.

EMRICH, MARION V. *The Child's Book of Folklore.* New York: The Dial Press, Inc., 1947.

FENNER, PHYLLIS. *The Proof of the Pudding: What Children Read.* New York: The John Day Company, 1957.

FERRIS, HELEN. *Favorite Poems Old and New.* Garden City, New York: Doubleday & Company, Inc., 1957.

FRYATT, NORMA R. *A Horn Book Sampler.* Boston: The Horn Book, Inc., 1959.

GRUENBERG, SIDONIE M. *More Favorite Stories Old and New for Boys and Girls.* Garden City, New York: Doubleday & Company, Inc., 1948.

HUBER, MIRIAM BLANTON (ed.). *Story and Verse for Children.* New York: The Macmillan Company, 1940.

HUGHES, ROSALIND and G. N. EDWARDS (eds.). *Let's Enjoy Poetry.* Boston: Houghton Mifflin Company, 1958.

JOHNSON, EDNA, EVELYN R. SICKELS and FRANCES CLARKE SAYERS. *Anthology of Children's Literature.* Boston: Houghton Mifflin Company, 1960.

LARRICK, NANCY. *A Teacher's Guide to Children's Books.* Columbus, Ohio: Charles E. Merrill Books, Inc., 1960.

MARTIGNONI, MARGARET (ed.). *The Illustrated Treasury of Children's Literature.* New York: Grosset & Dunlap, Inc., 1955.

STRANG, RUTH, ETHLYNE PHELPS and DOROTHY WITHROW. *Gateways to Readable Books.* New York: The H. W. Wilson Company, 1948.

TOOZE, RUTH. *Storytelling.* Englewood Cliffs, N.J.: Prentice-Hall Inc., 1959.

Part Two

The Nurture of Creativity Through Reading and Literature

An Overview

Excessive conformity serves as an anticatalyst to the development of creativity. I recognize that many of the skills necessary for effective reading mentioned in Part One of this volume must be taught through conforming, convergent thinking processes. But I also feel that the conformity suggested by our current reading programs has been exploited to excess with the damaging result that children have suffered in attitudes toward reading and in acquiring the necessary skills for reading. I am convinced that intelligent teachers could find more creative methods of teaching these skills to children and have more rewarding results if they were not inclined to follow preconceived methods so religiously.

It is with this conviction in mind that the material for Part Two of this book has been chosen. This material does not suggest a step-by-step development of a reading program. Because of space limitations I have attempted to show instead how several of the creative teachers I have observed have taken the teaching of some of these common skills and have developed them well in children through their own creative abilities.

I have chosen to include, as much as possible, those illustrations which demonstrate one or more of the principles of creative teaching outlined in Chapter I. These illustrations are concerned not only with the development of necessary reading skills, but also with the development of divergent thinking processes—and consequently the development of creative powers in our boys and girls.

V
The Creative Teaching of Reading in the Primary Grades

. . . A molehill can be a mountain to a sparrow. . . .[1]

RUMER GODDEN

TO THE READER

If you have been under the impression that the teaching of reading skills must be a very conforming, rigid sort of experience, read the following books by John Ciardi: The Reason for the Pelican[2] *and* I Met a Man.[3] *Then ask yourself this question: How could I teach phonics with these poems? Discuss this with other people and you will begin to see that your impressions were incorrect.*

Introduction

Mr. Cline's purposes became clear as he developed his lesson in the first-grade class I was observing. I listed them in my notebook as follows:

1. To develop the concepts of the words "wonderful" and "beautiful."
2. To build a sight vocabulary.
3. To extend skills in phonics by stressing rhyming words.
4. To develop creative writing in his group.
5. To integrate the language arts into a meaningful experience.
6. To develop a meaningful audience type situation.
7. To check the children's ability to recognize learned words in new context.
8. To provide materials and experiences for each individual in his room so that all might share a common language arts experience.

---

[1] Rumer Godden, *An Episode of Sparrows* (New York: The Viking Press, 1955), p. 204.

[2] John Ciardi, *The Reason for the Pelican* (New York: J. P. Lippincott Company, 1959).

[3] John Ciardi, *I Met a Man* (Boston: Houghton Mifflin Company, 1961).

Mr. Cline had set conditions for his reading class by setting up a tape recorder. He had also placed on the chalkboard tray two cardboard book covers, one in bright green and one in bright red. Each was hinged along the left border with masking tape so that it opened easily like a big book and was clamped to a cardboard of the same size which served as a back cover. Neither book contained any pages. On the cover of the red book he had printed the words "BEAUTI-FUL, BEAUTIFUL" and on the cover of the green book he had printed "WONDERFUL, WONDERFUL." Several large sheets of chart paper were taped to the chalkboard above the books. The children, returning from lunch, were eager to know what they were going to do with the materials at the front of the room.

Mr. Cline held up the book covers. "Today we are going to work with two words and I have printed them on the covers of these two books. Can anyone read them?"

Some children could. So the words were read and a discussion held about their meaning. Many children told of beautiful things and wonderful things they had experienced. At the close of the discussion Mr. Cline said, "Let's make a list of all the beautiful things we have discussed and put the words on this chart paper."

The list read like this: mother's roses, a sunset, my puppy, my mother, our school, my doll, a kaleidoscope, trees, flowers, paint, colors, baby sister, baby brother, my church, stained glass windows, music, bubbles, a rainbow.

A similar list was made of the wonderful things children had experienced. Mr. Cline then continued, "I thought it would be a good idea if we had some beautiful and wonderful experiences together this afternoon, and I have brought in some things I want to share with you. First of all let's look at this picture."

Mr. Cline set a beautiful painting of a rural scene on the chalkboard, and the children talked about it. When Mr. Cline asked for words to describe the painting, the children offered many ideas, which he printed on the vocabulary chart.

"Now let's think about the word 'wonderful,'" he said. "I have here three bags. Each has in it something wonderful to feel. I will pass the bags around and each of you may feel what's in them. Tell me how it feels and what you think it is but do not peek at it."

The bags were passed around, and each child responded to Mr. Cline's directions. Words such as "fuzzy," "warm," "soft," "cuddly," "tickly," appeared on the chart along with such words as "kitty," "toy dog," "mouse," "fur," "hair," "rabbit," as the children guessed the objects in the bag.

Next Mr. Cline asked the children to put their heads down on their desks and close their eyes. "There are wonderful things to smell," he said. "Breathe deeply and tell me what you think you smell or what the smell reminds you of." At this point he sprayed pine-scented air spray around the room.

"Perfume," "mother's roses," "deodorant," "flowers," "shaving lotion," "the woods," "Christmas trees," "cologne" and other words appeared on the chart. There were also phrases such as, "It smells like my Daddy when he is all dressed up to go out with my Mother."

Finally Mr. Cline said, "Keep your heads on your desks and open one hand. I will put something in your hand. Eat it but do not look at it." He dropped a jelly bean in each upturned palm, and again a flood of words issued as to what it was and how it tasted.

"Candy," "jelly beans," "sweet," "like perfume," "good," "sugar," "sticky," "crunchy," "smooth," "delicious."

The children watched Mr. Cline print these words on the vocabulary chart.

"I am going to print a sentence at the top of each of these four pieces of chart paper here on the chalkboard," he said. "See if you can read them."

On each of the four pieces of paper he printed the following sentences:

> There are beautiful things to see!
> There are wonderful things to feel!
> There are beautiful things to smell!
> There are wonderful things to taste!

"Now, let's look at all these words we have used today and see if we can write a story or poem under each of these titles. We may want to use other words besides the ones we have put on our vocabulary chart, and we may want to rhyme some of our stories. Think for a while and then share your ideas with all of us."

Soon the four stories were composed: two of them appear below:

There Are Beautiful Things To See

Mother's roses yellow and red,
Baby sister in her bed.
A rainbow in the sky,

A puppy running by.
Bubbles in the air,
The ribbon in Mary's hair.

.   *There Are Wonderful Things To Smell*

Shaving lotion.
Mother's flowers.
Perfume.
Fires burning.
Cakes baking.
The woods.

Mr. Cline then read the stories to the children, using a liner. They then read the stories together and put them on the tape recorder. During the playback the children read silently from the originals.

A discussion of new words followed. Compound words like "sunset" were utilized to develop the concept of compound words. The rhyming words "red" and "bed," "shy" and "by," "air" and "hair" were analyzed for phonetic development and the application of initial consonant sounds to common endings.

"I wonder how many of you have learned to read some of these words—especially the new ones," Mr. Cline continued. "I have used many of these words and some others to make up new stories you have not read before. I shall pass them out and you will read them silently. There is a beautiful or wonderful picture to go with each story. If you have trouble reading any of the words, raise your hand and I will come to help you. As soon as each one of you can read your story you will show the picture and read the story to the rest of us."

Mr. Cline had pasted attractive pictures from magazines and books to large cardboards. He had printed a story to go with each picture; some had very simple words and sentences, some had complex ones so that every child, from the lowest ability reader to the highest, would have a story to read. Each story contained either the word "beautiful" or "wonderful."

The simplest stories were one-line ideas that accompanied a lovely picture and said simply "Beautiful baby!" or "Beautiful tree!" The next most difficult was a beautiful picture of a piece of colored burlap. The story read, "Cloth is beautiful." The third was a picture of a United States Marine in full-dress uniform, and the story said, "He feels wonderful!" A colored picture of the Chicago skyline was accompanied by the phrase, "Beautiful, wonderful city!" One picture of a sunrise was accompanied by, "Beautiful light! Beautiful sight! Good-bye night!" A picture of a tree in a farmyard in the early morning had a poem that went:

> Look, it is morning
> And all I can see
> Is a beautiful house
> And a beautiful tree.

More difficult stories went with pictures of a sunrise and read as follows:

> This is a beautiful shining day.
> It is before breakfast.
> The rooster is not up.
> The children are not up.
> Mother is not up.
> Get up, rooster!
> Call the children!
> Call Mother!
> Tell them to see the beautiful, shining day!

The children enjoyed reading the stories to each other. Then Mr. Cline drew their attention back to the two books with which he had introduced the afternoon's work.

"You will notice," he said, "that these books have no pages in them. I have pages ready that will fit the books, but they're all blank. I am going to give each of you two pages. On one make something beautiful or wonderful with your crayons. On the other page write a story about the thing you drew. Then we will read them to each other and put them between the book covers. Use as many words as you want from our list on the vocabulary chart. I will help you with words that are not there. You may want to make poems or stories—do it any way you like—go!"

The children who finished first were asked to read a new sentence which Mr. Cline had printed on the board. It said, "There are beautiful and wonderful things to *hear!*" Then they were challenged to draw pictures and write stories for this concept.

This lesson is the essence of creative teaching. It breaks away from stereotyped methods of teaching vocabulary, word recognition, word-attack skills, structural analysis skills, phonetic analysis skills, and the typical sequence of manual-type teaching.

Mr. Cline's plan blasts the theory that children of differing abilities must meet in small groups or other individualized grouping plans every day for reading instruction. Reading in Mr. Cline's room is taught through the natural sequence of language development; children and their spoken vocabularies come first in the process—and individual differences are met through the adaptation of the *materials to the children,* not the children to the materials, as so many of our current reading systems demand.

A review of Mr. Cline's objectives as I wrote them in my notebook shows that *each* was met, and met well. An integration of the teaching of language skills makes possible the meeting of multiple objectives so often *not* accomplished when reading experiences are isolated from other language experiences.

A check with Chapter I will show how Mr. Cline's afternoon with the children followed the basic principles of creative teaching. His teaching considered individuals, and he accepted all individual contributions. Individual and unique products resulted from his work. Divergent thinking processes were balanced with convergent thinking processes. Open-ended situations were utilized. At times during the lesson children faced the unknown and they created. The process of reading, writing, and teaching elicited the creative products from the group and from individuals within the group. The experiences were success-oriented, problem-solving techniques were employed, skills were developed, words and objects were manipulated and explored, and democratic processes were used. The special methods of expansion and substitution, association, suggestion, adaptation and modification were utilized.

The lesson was evaluated by the performance of the children, by their obvious enthusiasm for their work, by the creative products in the group work, and in the pages each made for the two books.

The material that follows contains ideas which may provide some motivation for the teaching of reading in ways as creative as those used by Mr. Cline.

The Readiness Stages

In Chapter II the various stages in learning to read and the instructional tasks of the teacher were defined. The components of each stage were discussed. These stages are elaborated in the material below.

Children Must Have a Desire to Read

The teacher sets conditions for all reading by making clear to the children the *need* for reading and the joy which comes from being able to read. Some ways teachers have done this follow:

1. Read to the children every day for enjoyment. Let them experience the fun in books.

2. Use books frequently to look up material for them. When children see the teacher use books to identify objects or to find out about them, they will want to learn how to use them too.

3. Keep many picture and simple story books around the room where they will be easily available to the children.

4. Keep bulletin board exhibits, displays and other exhibits, book jackets, and peg-board exhibits of good books in your classroom all the time. (See Chapter VII.)

5. Use books and stories as the basis for puppet shows, dramatizations, shadow plays, roll movies, and various other activities, as described in Chapter VII.

6. Make simple books of children's experiences. They can contain paintings, magazine pictures, and simple stories or sentences.

7. Letter notes and messages to the class on the board. List on the board questions children ask. Even though the children cannot read them, the teacher can read these questions to the children and they will come to recognize the value of reading and writing as a method of keeping records.

8. Utilize the immediate school environment fully. Take children on simple trips to observe the fall foliage, to hear the sounds on the playground, to observe the play equipment and possible science resources in the school yard. Use these trips as an experiential background for making simple picture books when the class returns to the schoolroom.

The first step in the creative process is creating such strong motivational drives in children that they are almost driven by a passion to learn. When reading is regarded as problem-solving, and teachers consider the building of a strong desire to read as a motivational-involvement process, they are accomplishing the first step in all good learning, especially creative learning. The desire to read can fire a child to explore the reading process and the structure of language so that creative teaching can follow.

Children Must Develop the Ability to Listen

See Book II of this series, *Creative Teaching of the Language Arts in the Elementary School,* Chapter IV, for ideas of creative ways to help children to learn to listen.

Children Must Develop a Large Oral Vocabulary

Refer to Book II, Chapter V, for creative ways to develop a large oral vocabulary.

Creative children are fluent in verbal expression. One way to develop creativity in children through the teaching of reading is to develop this oral fluency in all children. A summary of some of the ways previously suggested to bring this about appears below.

Kindergarten and primary grades.

1. Tell stories about pictures, experiences, news items, original drawings, and so forth.

2. Retell stories (vary them by having one child tell part of a story, another child continue it, still another finish the story).

3. Listen to stories and poems.

4. Plan activities together (trips, parties, and so forth).

5. Hold class discussions (science, nature study, and such).

6. Encourage children to dictate stories about pictures, experiences, and so forth.

7. Encourage children to report on facts—something new learned.

8. Converse in groups.

9. Note and tell "number" stories.

10. Provide first-hand experiences ("scuffle in leaves"). Think of words to describe this.

11. Make lists of various schoolroom activities.

12. Make up and answer riddles.

13. Encourage children to use different words that mean the same thing (nice day, lovely day).

14. Learn opposites (night, day; come, go) and make charts.

15. Sing songs.

16. Listen to records, songs, stories and poems.

17. View movies and film strips.

18. Praise children when they use good descriptive words. *Example:* Peter said, "The milkweed seed is fuzzy." Fuzzy is a good word.

19. Display posters about coming events.

20. Encourage children to label some pictures and books for exhibit.

21. Change the end of a story they have heard. Attempt to motivate their creativeness in making a new ending.

22. Start an original story and have children think of an ending.

23. Confront children with problem situations for which the solution involves real life experience or activities.

24. Introduce games with speaking parts.

25. Compose "thank you" notes and "invitations."

26. Use finger plays.

27. Record experiences of trip taken.

28. Have "Show and Tell" periods.

29. Have children dictate stories about their own pictures, experiences, or interests.

30. Read bulletin board announcements, notices, labels, captions, titles of books, signs, action words to children.

31. Make charts of all kinds:

    a. Word charts (words from projects, books, T.V., films, conversation, etc.).

    b. Phonetic charts.

    c. Picture charts.

    d. Color charts.

    e. Experience charts.

    f. Weather charts.

    g. Our helpers, and so forth.

32. Make individual picture and word booklets.

33. Make a picture dictionary and a card catalogue.

34. Learn to recognize known words in different context through diversified activities.

35. Tell news.

36. Dramatize and pantomime stories.

37. Imagine experiences. (How does a small chicken feel when you touch it? Soft, fluffy, warm, cuddly.)

38. Discuss current events, holidays, things observed in newspapers, magazines, environment, and such.

39. Exchange gift boxes with children in other parts of our country. (Florida—gifts sent back: coral, conch shell, coconut shell.)

40. Associate words with pictures.

41. Learn words having more than one meaning.

42. Use many word associations, such as, "If you were near a pond what might you see?" (duck, tall grass, trees) "What might you hear?" (rippling water, frogs croaking).

43. List beginning, middle, and end of words, and find likenesses and differences.

Children Must Have Developed the Left-to-Right Concept

Children do not easily acquire this skill. In observing objects for the first six years of their lives, they study them from every angle and learn to recognize and name an object such as a chair from the front, the side, the back, from underneath or over the top. Then they are presented with reading material and must always remember to look at it one way: from left to right. Many ways of helping children develop this concept can be employed. Some children will have no difficulty with this skill, while others will need a great deal of practice.

1. Show children picture stories of four or five pictures in a sequence, placed from left to right. Have them tell the story by moving along from picture to picture. Point out to the children that reading words is similar to this plan—we go from left to right to get the story.

2. Comic strips use this technique and can be effectively employed in some instances for the same purposes. Comic strips with little or no reading are especially effective for this purpose.

3. The teacher should take particular care to write or print on the board, or on cards or charts, from left to right so that children will develop this concept through imitation.

4. After picture stories have been read, the teacher can scramble the pictures and children may rearrange them in the correct order.

5. Draw simple devices on dittoed sheets where children begin at the left of the paper and proceed to the right. For example, the picture of a mouse appears on the left side, the picture of a piece of cheese on the right. The teacher tells the children to take the mouse to the cheese with their eyes. Similar ideas would be to take the baby to the rattle, the dog to the bone, the kitten to the milk, the block to the shelf.

6. Many primary reading-readiness texts and manuals provide

interesting ways to develop this concept. Refer to the teacher's manual to locate such material. This is one way manuals can be of great value.

Children Must Develop Audio Acuity

In order to be able to read, each child must develop a sensitivity to sounds. An infant recognizes gross sounds such as the clanging of a bell, the honking of a horn, or the barking of a dog. As his sense of listening develops, he is soon able to hum, showing he can differentiate pitch. His hearing skill must be developed until he becomes sensitive to sounds in words that are very much alike—"men" and "man," "catch" and "ketch," "we're" and "were." Finally he must develop a good ear for phonetic training, a sensitivity to sounds themselves such as *m, n; pl, ch, ā, à,* and so forth. Many suggestions for developing listening skills may be found in Book II, Chapter IV.

1. Nursery rhymes may be effectively used to develop good listening, to improve speech, and as a beginning for choral speaking (see Book II, Chapter V). To improve audio acuity have children say certain nursery rhymes (especially those which are almost entirely direct conversation) in a variety of ways to indicate a mixture of emotions. For instance, say "Pussycat, pussycat, where have you been?" angrily and have the children give the next line with the proper emotional tone. Then try saying the same lines happily, sadly, coyly, fearfully, excitedly, timidly, and anxiously. Try this technique with other nursery rhymes, such as *Simple Simon* and *Where Are You Going, My Pretty Miss?*

2. Miss Frey used recordings a great deal to develop audio discrimination among her children. She encouraged them to note likenesses and differences in the music by:

    a. Pretending they were something tall whenever the music went high, and something short when the music went low. She would stop the music and say "freeze," and all children then held the high or low pose while the others guessed what they were.

    b. Encouraging the children to do rhythm patterns to the music. On fast music they could run, skip, fly. Other music suggested skipping, hopping, marching, jumping.

    c. Singing along with records (the children relate motions to voice interpretation).

    d. Encouraging children to listen to instrumental records (as soon as a child hears a violin he begins to make the motions of the violin).

    e. Encouraging children to reproduce the rhythm of the music by clapping, tapping, or snapping fingers, which can then be combined into a percussion rhythm without the record so the children can sense a definite beat.

    3. Miss Marcus often asked a question by singing it. The children answered by singing a response that completed the musical tune which Miss Marcus had begun. She took roll in this manner: she would sing, "Johnny Jones, Johnny Jones, are you here? Are you here?" to the tune of *Frère Jacques* and he would answer, "Yes, I am, Miss Marcus. Yes, I am, Miss Marcus, here I am, here I am." After the children had used known tunes this way, they made up original ones.

    4. Mr. Graves used singing finger plays with his children. Often the forefinger and the middle finger of each hand became the feet for imaginary dolls and children made up dance steps on the tops of their desks with these "finger feet" to go with recorded music. The children also did small dramatizations of other songs and stories in this manner.

    5. When children compose tunes on glasses, flower pots, or spikes of different lengths suspended from a board, it is easy for them to see that the longer the spike or the taller the glass, the higher the pitch. Experimentation with hitting all sorts of materials to determine the kind of sound it makes can lead to a classification chart and help children in refining their ability to recognize variances in pitch.

    6. One of the best ways to help develop audio acuity is to provide a music center in the room where children can experiment with instruments. Drums, bells, xylophones, rhythm instruments can all be played and classified for high, low, and in-between sounds. (See Book IV of this series, *Creative Teaching of the Creative Arts in the Elementary School.*)

    7. Miss Ames used many of the traditional patterns of clapping and tapping, such as having the children repeat a pattern of claps and taps which she produced, to develop audio acuity. But she carried this into more creative activity when she asked the children to listen to music, or to some sound outside the window, and to repeat this sound by clapping or tapping in as many ways as possible. When the rhythm of claps was established, the children used it as a basis for building a

clapping or tapping tune. Often various rhythms were combined to make a "clapping" band. At times various tempos were combined as well as rhythms. Children reproduced their rhythm by striking wood, glass, or plastic. Later these were combined to make percussion tunes.

8. Mr. Richardson taped sounds at home (the refrigerator, radio, telephone, shower), and the children had to guess what the sounds were. However, when a child recognized the sound he did not tell the others. He gave clues to help the others determine the sound ("It is in the kitchen." "You make this sound every morning.").

9. Miss Yager took her children on "listening" walks where the children listened to and listed all the sounds they could hear. A walk around the school made them sensitive to bird sounds, peepers, blowing wind, rustling leaves. A walk along the street made them aware of cars whizzing by, horns honking, brakes screeching, voices shouting. Even a walk down the school corridor made them alert to clocks ticking, typewriters clacking, dishes rattling, balls bouncing. The children made up listening games in the classroom by "discovering" all the ways they could make noises and then having guessing games to see how many noises they could recognize while blindfolded. These included opening and closing a desk drawer, closing a closet drawer, stamping a foot, tapping a bell, closing a book, winding a clock, bouncing a ball, and so on. Often these sounds were combined into a "sound" story (see Book II, *Creative Teaching of the Language Arts in the Elementary School,* Chapter IV). The words to describe these sounds were always placed on a chart before the room.

10. Stories and poems may be used effectively for accomplishing many of the hearing skills developed through music. While reading poems, the teacher can have the children clap in as many ways as possible to fit the rhythm of the poem—and the children can softly clap various patterns while the teacher reads the poem. Some stories lend themselves to soft noises spoken in rhythm as a background for the reading of the story. Dramatization of the stories helps the teacher to point up likenesses and differences and sequences in the story. Sequence can also be developed in determining who speaks first in the dramatization, who speaks next, and so on.

11. As soon as children are able to rhyme words and note the similarities and differences of initial beginning sounds, the children may use cards in a variety of ways. Use 3 x 5 cards or cards cut from chip board and have the children go through old magazines and catalogues to find pictures to paste on the cards. Beginning sounds

can then be matched with the cards. Each child takes ten cards. If the letter *d* is placed in the pocket chart, every child hunts through his cards to find words that begin with the *d* sound and they are placed in the pocket chart under the *d*.

Shopping at the Supermarket is a game children enjoy which adds variety to the above suggestion. Obtain a small shopping bag and have the children make picture cards as suggested above. Each child spreads his pictures out on his desk, which becomes the counter for which he is clerk. One child is chosen to be the shopper, and he takes the shopping bag. He says, "I am going to shop for all things that begin with a *b* sound." He goes from desk to desk, and as he sees a picture he says, "Mary, I would like the butter and some bread please." If the shopper does not take *all* the cards on Mary's desk which begin with *b* and Mary can catch him, he must give up the shopping bag and Mary takes over.

12. As soon as children can recognize the beginning sounds of their own names, have each make a chart of construction paper with the first letter of their names at the top and the names under it, and then either all the words or pictures they can find which begin with the same sound as their own names.

13. Chart-making to categorize sounds is a worthwhile activity. Such charts may be on the following topics: Words That End Alike; Words That Start Alike; Words That Have the Same Middle; Names That Sound Alike.

14. The rhyming exercises mentioned in Book II of this series are excellent in developing audio acuity. The teacher says, "What will I do if I spill the ink?" and a child must answer in a statement that rhymes, such as, "Wash your clothes out in the sink." Making original poems or rhymes, supplying missing rhyming words, making charts of rhyming words—all are good preparation for phonics exercises and all help children develop audio acuity.

15. *Barnyard Frolic.* Assemble two sets of word cards with the name of one animal commonly found on a farm on each, such as dog, duck, goat, cat, and chick. Print the word "barnyard" on one of the cards. The leader keeps a complete set of cards for himself and then distributes one card to each player. When the leader holds up a card with the word "dog" on it, the child who holds the matching card must "bow-wow" like a dog, and so on. When the leader holds up the card with "barnyard" on it, each child must respond with the sound made by the animal named on his card.

Children Must Develop a Keen Sense of Visual Discrimination

Research shows that creative children have a particularly keen sense of visual discrimination. Thus, in developing visual discrimination, teachers are also helping a child to develop his creative powers.

Children are called upon to note minute differences in word shapes and then in letter shapes in order to read. First a child recognizes shapes of objects about him: a drum, a ball, a swing, an automobile. Then he notices differences within objects of the same or similar shapes: dull or shiny, sad face or happy face, brother or sister. He also develops the concept of related shapes at a very early age: large and small, big and tiny, long and short. To read he must be taught to select the one shape that is different from the others, and eventually to see differences in word shapes, such as "mother" and "grandmother" and "on" and "no." In the end he must discriminate between little shapes that are very much alike, such as an *o* and an *a* or a *b* and a *d*.

In a sense all kindergarten activities are natural readiness experiences in visual perception. The work and play which children do with blocks gives them the necessary experience they need to work later with shapes and objects. From their work with paints, clay, cut paper, finger paint, doll furniture, dolls, miniature furniture, toys, and other materials, they gain the experience and concepts essential to the beginning reading program. In this sense the kindergarten program becomes a most important part of a child's formal schooling.

Conditions can be set for developing skills in visual discrimination in many creative ways:

1. Miss Martin often used her art period to develop a sensitivity to different shapes and the relationship among shapes. She saved all the odd pieces of colored construction paper from the children's art work. Several times a week she would give each child a piece of plain grey, buff, or white construction paper at the beginning of the day. Then she placed on it one of the unusual colored shapes from her scrap box. The children could then paste the shape on the plain paper and, using *any* medium, make something of it. Very creative and original ideas emerged from this activity.

2. As a variation of this activity, ask a clothier or clothing merchant to save his books of sample cloths for you. Tear out the swatches of sample cloth and use them the way Miss Martin used the

Puppetry needs a good story to put it across at all ages.

scrap pieces of construction paper. Some of the cloth samples will have the texture of fur or will be beaded or brocaded. The additional quality of texture adds to the motivation for creating new relationships.

3. Some games help develop visual acuity. In the Change-the-Face Game, the teacher draws a large face on the chalkboard and hands an eraser and chalk to a child telling him that he may go to the board and *change* or *add* one new feature to the picture drawn there. The child in turn passes the eraser and chalk along to another child. Each change or addition changes the picture and helps children focus attention on one specific part of the total shape much as they will later need to see that one line makes the difference between the printed *a* and *d*.

4. A variation in this game is to draw a scene on the board which is simply a background, perhaps a mountain and a tree. Each child must add something to the scene. In one class so much had

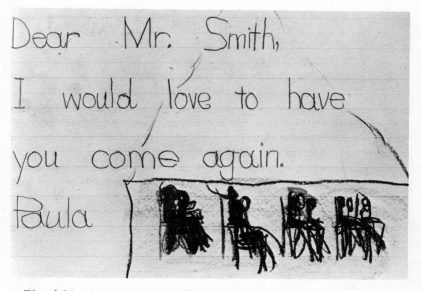

The children's own letters make excellent beginning reading material.

been added to the scene that the picture was nearly full, so one first-grader drew a tongue hanging from the dog's mouth—and the last six-year-old to draw in the scene drew a fly on the tongue.

This activity may be changed by having the children add to or change the scene as they did with the face in the preceding game.

The Change-the-Face Game.

5. Other games that children enjoy are these:
    a. Place several small familiar objects on a table and cover with a cloth or paper. Remove the cover, exposing the objects for a few seconds. Then replace the cover and ask the children to name as many objects as they can recall. Gradually increase the number of objects exposed. This game requires careful visual attention.
    b. Place several objects under the cover on the table. Expose these objects for a few seconds. Have the children close their eyes while one object is removed. Rearrange the remaining objects. Expose them again while the children try to recall which object is gone.
    c. Describe some object and have the children guess what it is. For example: I am thinking of something little and white with long ears and a short tail and pink eyes, and so forth. Have the children try to visualize while the object is being described. Describe the clothes and appearance of some child until the children can guess who is being described.
    d. Collages are excellent in helping children develop visual relationships. A box of junk (cloth, buttons, candy box papers, cellophane pieces, feathers, cotton, foil, pipe cleaners, and such) can be placed before primary children. From these they can make three-dimensional designs, thus focusing their attention on shapes and their relationships.

6. Walks to gather shapes may be taken as in the listening walk described above. Children collect leaves of various shapes, rocks, twigs, and so forth, mount them on charts, and study shapes. Pictures of objects in the community can be used to note likenesses and differences in shapes (mail boxes, traffic signals, fire alarm boxes, telephone poles). Duplicating various traffic signs is excellent for this, because children often learn to read the word painted on the sign by simply recognizing the shape of the sign.

7. Mr. Rhodes drew a triangle, a square, a rectangle, a circle, and a trapezoid at the top of a large piece of cardboard. The children then hunted for things in the room to fit these shapes. Under the circle they drew a picture of a clock, a thumb tack, a saucer, an ink bottle, a compass, and a telephone dial. Under the square they drew a window, a box of crayons, and a chalk box. Every day some child discovered a new shape to add to the chart.

8. Mr. Rhodes later handed out dittoed sheets covered with circles and asked the children to draw something in each circle which fit that shape in their classroom. The next day he again gave them a sheet of paper covered with circles and asked them to fill in as many things of that shape as they could think of at home; the next day they thought of round things out of doors, and so on. Dittoed sheets covered with squares, triangles, rectangles and other shapes were also given to the children. At the end of each day, the children shared their ideas.

9. Miss Ellis arranged a bulletin board twice a week on which she put pictures or a series of pictures that told a story; in each some details or one of the series was omitted. The sign at the top of the bulletin board said, "What is missing?" Children enjoyed searching for the missing details.

10. A variation of Miss Ellis' plan is to put into a series of pictures a foreign picture and ask, "Which one does not belong in this story?" Comic strips are excellent for this purpose.

11. Classification games are excellent to help develop visual discrimination and a relatedness of shapes and ideas. Children draw or paste pictures of animals or homes or many objects. The teacher (or a child) makes a series of charts such as "Found at the Zoo," "Found at My House," "Found at the Grocery Store," and the children match the object with the correct chart. Before children can read, a picture of an animal may be substituted for the word "zoo," a house for "home," a store for "grocery."

12. "Find me" games are realistic. The teacher simply starts the game by bringing a book or any object to the front of the room. She says, "Billy, find me a bigger book," and Billy does while the whole class checks. Other directions, such as "Find me a brighter colored book," "Find me a prettier book," and "Find me a thicker book," sharpen visual acuity and build concepts for difficult words.

13. Comparisons in visual form may be made by matching mother with baby on a flannel board, a chart, or a pocket chart. Many tiny ducks, chickens, rabbits, and other animals are cut from construction paper and distributed to children. The mother animals are placed before the class and children match the babies with the mother. A more creative situation results when children are encouraged to make up stories in which the babies are mixed up to begin with but eventually get home to mother. Such books as *Whose Mother Are You?* are very appropriate for reading at this time.

14. Miss Fred made oak tag vocabulary cards cut to the shape of word configurations:

look   Jane   cook

Words were compared for shape in terms of likenesses and differences.

15. *Finding likenesses or differences.* The teacher can make many sets of "twin" cards with dogs, clowns, houses, boys, girls, cats, and so on. The game is to match all the twins to "make them happy." The games of "Old Maid" and "Snap," where this kind of matching is developed, are excellent.

As a more complex step, the teacher can make many abstract designs with lines for children to increase ability to determine likenesses or differences. Again working from the simple to the more difficult, the first "set" of line cards may be made with the different one being a second color (two blue lines and one red). The difference could be in position, as three vertical lines and one slanted line. The difference could be in the number of lines in each group. These should be kept as "sets." A more creative element enters the game when children design their own sets, trying to create some that show differences in only one way, for example.

16. Mr. Good used plain pieces of colored construction paper, which he held before the group. One child would rise when the red sheet was held up and say, "My sweater is red," and another would say, "My bow is red," until all the red objects in the room had reported, and then another color was used.

17. Miss Farnsworth's group enjoyed a game called, "I Went to the Window." A designated child went to the window, looked out, faced his group, and said, "I went to the window and saw a tree." The next child then repeated what the first child had said but added another object. This continued until one row or one group of children all had an opportunity to go to the window. It is an excellent game for keeping a sequence and developing observation and listening powers.

18. Picture puzzles are always challenging and creative devices for building visual acuity. Enlist the aid of some children in the intermediate grades to make puzzles for the kindergarten. Appropriate magazine covers or pictures from calendars should be mounted on durable cardboard; tablet backs make good mounts. Paste should cover mount and then be weighted until dry. A number of pictures should be cut in two uneven parts and the matching pieces placed in

envelopes. Other pictures should be made into puzzles of three or four parts.

19. *Finding what goes together*. Set aside a box in which to put things that are used together. Encourage children to bring objects for this box. Pencil and tablet, plastic cup and saucer, doll's shoes and socks, can and can opener, hammer and nail, comb and brush will appear. The activity becomes more creative when unusual things are put together and the child is called upon to relate why. Jonathan put a picture of a cake and a dill pickle together "Because," he said, "they are my favorite foods."

20. A variation of the old fishing game may be adapted to many uses. Use a glass mixing bowl or fish bowl. The fish are made of construction paper; on them are mounted pictures that begin with different initial consonants. Place several staples on the heads of the fish. Make a pole with a stick or a pencil with a good magnet suspended from it. The game may be played with two children or a group. Take turns with the magnet to catch a fish. When a child catches the fish he names the picture that is mounted on it (for example, "ball"). If he can give another word that "begins just like it" (such as "bed"), he can keep the fish. If not, he returns the fish to the bowl. The one with the most fish is the winner.

21. *Wheel of Fortune Games*. Make a large cardboard circle or wheel on whose outside edge pictures (such as a mitten, baby, cake, door, and such) have been mounted. A spinner is placed in the center of the wheel.

Make small circles of colored paper or use kindergarten beads. Make a large chart of oak tag (12 x 18) on which pictures representing the same initial consonant sound but different from those on the wheel are mounted.

Procedure: Child spins the spinner on the wheel. He names the picture where the spinner stops, finds a picture on the chart that "begins just like it," and puts a circle or bead on it.

Suggestion: A more difficult step is to omit the chart and have the child give another word that "begins just like" the one where the spinner stopped. Keep score of how many he got right with a colored circle.

22. There is no technique that helps children hear and see ideas in sequence any more readily than a roll movie where favorite stories are discussed scene by scene. A child is assigned to draw each scene, and the whole thing is then pasted on a roll of shelf paper and retold

as a picture story. The retelling with the pictures helps children organize and remember details that went unnoticed with the first reading of the story.

Game approaches are especially useful with children who are under a great deal of stress, either from their environment or their own failures in reading. Throughout the program of instruction in reading, games tend to relieve stress in some children and free them to learn. In addition, game approaches such as those mentioned above develop creative growth by increasing awareness, helping children see things in a different way, encouraging exploration and manipulation of objects and words, and demanding flexibility of thinking.

Children Must Develop a Comprehension Ability

Research on the creative personality has shown that creative children are more sensitive to problems than noncreative children are. They like to redefine and rearrange, to bring order and understanding out of disorder and disorganization. They like to produce; they have strong intuition and identification ability. Since all of these skills are also part of the total concept of comprehension skills in reading, a teacher is also developing those aspects of creativity in children. The mastery of comprehension skill is closely linked to the child's intellectual development and his ability to listen, to conceptualize, and to organize well. Many general activities can be used to check the children's comprehension ability in kindergarten and first grade: interpreting the main idea of a story; retelling a story with some specific questions by the teacher to check depth of comprehension; encouraging children to react to a story; interpreting a picture story in sequence; finding missing details in pictures and stories; following directions; anticipating endings in stories and poems; finger plays; following sequence in games such as "Looby Loo"; and general discussions with children about material read to them.

Most of these activities are of the type that develop convergent thinking processes. Some that develop comprehension skills *and* creativity are: making roll movies, as mentioned above; developing stories or story endings after a fragment of the story has been read; dramatizing stories or poems; pantomiming stories or making puppet plays or shadow plays from them; interpreting the ideas in a story by reading a sequence of pictures; and using the stories as a basis for making pictures, murals, dioramas, and other art work.

It has already been pointed out that much of the material used in commercial workbooks tends to jeopardize the child's creative development by giving him too many patterns to trace or imitate. Excess use of this sort of activity should be avoided. Instead of using exercises that say, "Draw like this," check comprehension in more creative ways, such as the ones mentioned on page 83, and others, such as: Fold your paper into 4, number each box 1, 2, 3, 4. In Box 1 draw something that lives in a tree, in Box 2 draw the part of the story that was funny, etc. This gives the child the opportunity to apply his own creative powers and, at the same time, tells the teacher what she needs to know.

Some samples of creative ways of checking comprehension in the primary grades follow:

1. Mrs. Arthur would ask the children questions that were not in the context of the story but could be answered if the children really understood the story. The questions were such as these: What season was it? What time of day was it when Tom lost his cat? Did Mary and Tom have any relatives living near? Did they have any friends close by?

2. Many primary teachers have a discussion of important daily news from which a news chart is made on the chalkboard. This is an excellent beginning step in organizing material, choosing main ideas, recognizing proper sequence, and checking overall comprehension.

3. Miss Ellis printed a note for her boys and girls on the chalkboard each day. At first she used drawings to communicate, but as soon as the children knew any sight words they appeared on the chalkboard. One such note in the advanced stage said, "Dear Boys and Girls, Good morning. Today we go to the library. Please have your books ready."

4. Oral book reports, even from picture books, can help the teacher decide whether or not the child understands what he reads.

5. Miss Jones read stories to her children and then gave them dittoed sheets with three or four sentences about the story. The children put them in proper sequence.

6. Mr. Hayes cut out pictures and made a sentence to put under each one. Then he mixed up pictures and captions to see if the children could put them together correctly. *Example:* Picture of a grocery ·store. *Caption:* This is where Mary buys her bread.

7. *A picture to draw.* Make up a story and see if children can read it and then draw the picture. *Example:* Nancy likes the farm. The sun is shining and the birds are singing. She is playing ball with Joe. She has on a green dress and black shoes. Joe has on brown

pants and a yellow shirt. They also like to swing and go swimming in the pond. It's such fun on the farm.

8. Mr. Farmer played a short cartoon film and cut off the sound. The children had to tell the story from the pictures.

9. Film strips with no captions may be used in a similar manner to help build comprehension skills.

10. The construction of many kinds of experience charts helps children develop comprehension skills (see pages 35–37).

The upper primary grades. Activities in the upper primary grades which develop comprehension and creativity are many. A few examples follow:

1. Miss Isaacs, who was using the individualized reading plan, encouraged her children to draw a series of pictures about their book or story and show them to the rest of the class in a miniature roll movie, using facial tissue boxes or shoe boxes as the stage for the movies.

2. Miss Isaacs often checked comprehension by the following method. She divided a piece of oak tag into four parts. On each part she pasted a different picture. In an envelope she printed sentences that told something about each picture. She always included three or four sentences that did not pertain to the pictures. The children matched the sentences with the proper pictures and discarded those which were unrelated.

3. The "matching opposites" game is always enjoyed by children. Shoestrings may be attached to a game card by knotting the ends on the reverse side of a card and holding them in place with scotch tape. The shoestrings may then be threaded down to the correct answer.

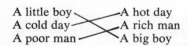

4. Actual reading comprehension can best be checked when reading communicates—and once again charts of various kinds can be an excellent check on comprehension (see pages 130–140, which follow).

Children Must Develop Skill in Oral Communication, Which Will Eventually Help in Their Oral Reading

Many suggestions for developing oral expression skills in a creative manner were made in Book II of this series, Chapter V.

Children Must Develop Skill in Concept Formation

The ability to understand concepts comes largely from experience with the use of words and their application to new situations. Many suggestions for concept development have been given in this book (such as the one at the beginning of this chapter). For other suggestions, see specifically Book II of this series, *Creative Teaching of the Language Arts in the Elementary School,* Chapters V, VI and VIII. In the research on creative personalities creative children were able to conceptualize better than noncreative children. Helping children to form concepts contributes to their reading skill and creative skill development.

Children Must Develop a Knowledge of the Alphabet

As soon as children begin to hear sounds of letters, the letter should be introduced as a symbol to represent the sound. Letters will be learned individually before they are learned in alphabetical sequence. The latter can be taught as soon as most of the children recognize and associate sounds with their letter symbols. Little use is made of the alphabetical sequence as such much before the upper primary or early intermediate grades, but the letters should be recognized early in the reading program.

Some suggestions for introducing letters may be found on pages 151–155 and 157 of this book and in Book II of the series, Chapters VII and VIII.

1. Following are some suggestions to help children see their letter sounds in printed symbol form. These may be used as first steps toward building an alphabet consciousness.

    a. Help each child learn the first sound and letter of his own first and last names.

    b. Write on the board *r, h, l, g, f, m, y, w, b,* and so forth, and have children point to and name the letter that stands for the sound heard at the beginning of a list of dictated words or the letter with which their own name begins.

    c. Make large capital letters on oak tag and have various children whose names begin with a capital shown stand and name the letter and sound.

    d. Use large pictures that have many objects beginning with the same sound. Identify the letters.

e. Find those words in spelling lists that sound alike at the beginning or end.

f. Make individual sound picture booklets.

g. Match (oral exercises—each child must say the sound and the word that begins with that sound):

h. Substitute initial consonant of words such as "Dick," "pick," "lick."

i. List initial sound or sounds on board and have children find as many words as possible for the sound or sounds listed from their related reading in science or from their spelling lesson.

j. Emphasize both likenesses and differences in words.

2. Many exciting alphabet books are currently available on the commercial market. These are excellent aids in helping the children *see* the alphabet over and over again.

The Beginning Formal Program

Building a Sight Vocabulary

From the accounts already given in this chapter and others in this book, the conclusion may be drawn that building a sight vocabulary can be a very creative process. Some further illustrations demonstrate the limitless possibilities for doing this in creative and meaningful ways.

1. Simple charts may be made on the chalkboard each day for several purposes. These charts repeat the words used to date in as many ways as possible. Drawings may be substituted for words unknown to the children. Mrs. Noyes introduced the words "paste," "scissors," and "brushes" on this chart:

Today's Helpers

Bobby will pass the milk.
John will pass the crackers.

Mary will pass the napkins.
Angie will pass the paper.
Peter will pass the paint.

Michael will pass the

Helen will pass the

George will pass the

Daily planning can be done on a chalkboard chart each day. Miss Farrell, a kindergarten teacher, saw evidences of reading readiness in a group of her children. She was concerned at the time with helping the children to plan. (An account of this appears in Book V of this series, *Creative Teaching of the Social Studies in the Elementary School,* Chapter V.) In brief, she selected magazine pictures of children engaged in schoolroom activities and pasted them on cardboards. As they planned the day together, she placed the pictures in logical sequence on the chalk tray, thus developing the readiness skill of logical sequence. Soon she began to add simple cards printed with these words, "We play," "We work," "We eat," "We dance." The children were told that these labels said what the children in the picture were doing. After a very short time, she saw children matching pictures and words. Finally she was able to use a pocket chart to plan the daily program. First she would plan the day with the pictures, then add the labels, and then allow the children who could do so to make up a program of duplicate labels on the pocket chart.

2. Charts for unusual days may be printed on the chalkboard:

Happy Birthday!

Today is Helen's birthday!
She is seven.
We will sing to Helen.
We will read to Helen.
We will have a party.
Happy birthday, Helen.

Look! Look!

Today is a good day.
Someone is coming.
Who is it?
It is Mr. Jones.
He will show us pictures.
They are pictures of our trip
to Mr. Jones's farm.

Christmas!

Today is for Christmas!
We will have our party!
We will have fun!
We will have popcorn!
We will have games.
We will have presents.
We will have a play.
We will sing.
Christmas is fun!

3. Daily news can be printed in chart form on the chalkboard in initial reading experiences to develop a sight vocabulary. Each morning, children who have some important news tell about it. The teacher helps in making simple sentences of this news on the board. Miss Martin's first news chart looked like this:

Our News

Today is Wednesday.
It is warm.
Bill is sick.
We will take a trip.
We will go to the park.
Today we have gym.

Later, after the children can print, master ditto papers can be lined lightly and one child each day can be assigned to copy the news from the board onto a master ditto paper. On Friday, all the dittoed copies can be run off on a duplicating machine so that each child has a copy of each day's news. These can be stapled between colored construction paper and a cover drawn so the child may take home his grade newspaper each week.

After the newspapers are assembled on Friday afternoon, they provide excellent material for reviewing the words learned during the week.

4. Reading from a variety of charts for directions helps children develop this skill independently. A sample of one such chart is called "Helping Hands." Each child traces his hand on a piece of oak tag. He cuts out what he has traced and writes his name on the "hand." An 18 x 24 sheet of oak tag is divided into as many sections as there are duties in the room. On each section a duty is written. These sections are either taped or fastened so that the "hand" slides in and out easily and can be readily seen.

The oak tag hands are changed every day or every week, as the children decide.

5. *Individualized reading through chalkboard and other charts.* Teaching children to read individually does not imply that each child is always on his own reading program. Common experiences give children common understandings and these can be employed for group work. Individual teaching does imply that certain individual needs, problems, and interests must be met, for each child may need extra help or attention at some time.

Some good examples of individual techniques for teaching beginning reading follow.

Mrs. Wallace's children come into the first-grade classroom in the morning. There are notes on some of the desks, and on the board are taped a few large sheets of paper with various children's names on them. One says:

> *Billy*
>
> Surprise, surprise,
> Billy has a surprise!
> What is it?

The teacher tells Billy to read what is under the paper. Billy lifts it up and printed under it on the board is:

> Go to the kitchen.

Billy goes to the kitchen and there on the table is a reading chart. It reads:

> Surprise!
> Today is Billy's birthday,

> This is a surprise,
> Billy will make a birthday cake.
> We will have it for lunch.
> Surprise us, Billy.
> Read the box. ·

Pasted on a box of cake mix on the table are directions printed in large letters.

> Pour flour in bowl.
> Add 1 cup milk.
> Stir.
> Call Miss Wallace.

If Billy cannot read all of this he gets help, but the words are largely those which have come from the vocabulary chart and the reading experiences the group has shared. Billy mixes the cake and calls Miss Wallace. She helps put it in the oven for that is dangerous for Billy to do alone. Miss Wallace and Billy plan to frost the cake and decorate it for the surprise for midmorning lunch.

Similar experiences are had by other children on their birthdays. The same charts can sometimes be used. Later, after the lopsided, irregularly frosted cake is served, the class makes a chart about Billy's surprise, and words are used in new context.

Other children read instructions for simple household duties and for treasure hunts—exciting, important experiences. Mary's note says:

> Mary may go to the library.
> Find a story.
> We will read it.

Sally's note says:

> Sally may water the plants.
> Sally may set the table.

Other charts on the board say:

> Surprise.
> Surprise for everyone.
> All may peek.
> See the surprise.

And under the paper on the board is a picture of some boys and girls giving a play. Under the picture is printed:

Today we will have a play.

Because Miss Wallace knows her children well, she is able to utilize their interests to develop personal sight vocabularies. Each week each child gets at least one personal note on the board. An example of one such chart said this:

Look, Don.
Look and see.
See your surprise!

When Don lifted the flap of paper he found this printed on the board:

Here is a surprise.
It is for you.
Show it to the boys and girls.
Show it at Show and Tell.

An arrow pointed to an envelope stuck to the board which was labeled "For Don." Inside the envelope was a stamp from France. Miss Wallace remembered that Don is a stamp collector when she received a recent letter from France.

Individualized reading charts can make reading very precious and truly communicative to children. The time a teacher spends after school each afternoon preparing for such reading experiences is very small in relation to the results obtained.

6. *Labeling*. Objects in the room may be labeled with cards and tags to make simple sentences. Signs such as "This Is the Reading Table" and "Our Library" help children to visualize many words over a period of time.

7. *Dramatizations*. Dramatizations can be used to develop reading skills. After the teacher reads a story, labels can begin to play a part in dramatizing it. The imaginary scenery can be labeled "This is a tree" or "Here is a house." Characters can be labeled "I am Dick" or "I am the mouse." Actions and sounds can sometimes be read from cards instead of being enacted.

8. *Vocabulary charts*. Occasionally a word or phrase that takes

on great importance to the children comes up in the classroom, and the teacher may print it on a vocabulary chart for future reference. Words that arise in an experience such as the Show and Tell period reported in Chapter V of Book II of this series is one such example. Words around holiday time may be printed out of context on a vocabulary chart and still have a great deal of meaning to the children. Vocabulary charts are excellent ways to keep the picture and the spelling of current words before the children and are of special value after children begin to write and can use the phrases and words in their stories and poems.

9. *Surprise charts.* Surprise charts are sprung on the children as new arrangements of words already learned. Surprise charts can serve many purposes.

    a. They can repeat words already learned in new and exciting forms.

    b. They can be constructed as riddles.

    c. They can be used as announcements such as the following:

Surprise! Surprise!

Today we have a surprise.
We will go to a play.
It is at 10 o'clock.
It is in Miss Jones's Room.
It is about Peter and the Wolf.
That is our surprise!

Look! Look!

We have a surprise!
It is in the room.
It is near the door.
It is something to look at.
Can you find it?

10. *Other charts:*

Charts can be devised for many purposes:

    a. To give directions:

Look, Look!

Here is some paper.
Fold it.

Make a book.
Draw pictures.
Tell us about it.

b. To make announcements:

Lunch Today

This is our lunch today—
Milk
Hamburger
Roll
Potato chips
Ice cream

c. For daily planning.
d. For long-term planning:

Our Plans for the Circus

1. We will go to the circus.
2. We will draw pictures.
3. We will act like animals.
4. We will have clowns.
5. We will read circus stories.
6. We will sing circus songs.
7. We will make a book.
8. We will have a circus.
9. We will make tickets.
10. We will invite mothers and fathers.

e. To use children's individual or group creative writing (see page 8).
f. To list children's questions for science or social studies. These may later be printed on a card so each child learns to read his one question—and is perhaps responsible for finding the one answer.
g. To evaluate classroom experiences:

What Makes a Good Report?

1. Speak clearly.
2. Think about what you are saying.
3. Look at the class.
4. Speak loudly.
5. Do not speak too long.

h. To use for reference purposes:

How To Write A Letter

Your letters should look like this:

> Penfield School
> Penfield, N.Y.
> October 26, 1967

Dear Mother,
    We are going to have a play. Can you come? We will have the play on _____ at _____ o'clock in Room _____.

> With love,
>
> _____

i. *The letter chart.* Often the children in the initial reading stages compose letters of thanks on the chalkboard which the teacher (or some capable child) sends to the deserving person. Letters of invitation, announcements, and trip permission slips may also be developed in this manner. At times it is appropriate for the teacher to coach the recipient of the letter to answer the children with a letter printed in simple chart form. All people do not possess the skill of writing proper manuscript, but a letter printed in this style with large lettering, which can be placed on the bulletin board for all to read, is a thrilling experience for the children and a rich experience in communication.

Here is a sample of one such letter written by a father (who was a teacher) to a group of first-grade children who sent him a Christmas gift because he had made them a reading table for their room.

Dear boys and girls,
  Christmas was coming!
  I had a gift under the tree!
  It was from you.
  I could hardly wait.
  But I did.
  I waited and waited.
  Finally Christmas came.
  I ran downstairs,
  I opened my gift,
  I saw the tie-holder—

It was wonderful.
It was just what I needed.
I was happy.
Thank you.
This is how I looked when I opened my gift.

your friend,
Mr. Smith.

11. *The surprise box.* The surprise box fulfills the same purpose as a surprise chart except that it makes possible the use of three-dimensional objects in building vocabulary. A large box is cut open at one side so as to produce a "flap" effect. This flap enables the children to raise the front of the box and look inside. On the flap are printed words similar to these:

> Surprise, surprise!
> Look and see.
> See the surprise inside!

On opening the flap the children find an object with printed symbols to describe it. A slit in the top of the box in the back makes it possible for the teacher to print these cards and to drop them in the box easily.

Mrs. Hodges used the box often to introduce new materials to the children. One day, on lifting the box, the children found a lump of clay. On the back wall of the box was printed:

> *Surprise!*
>
> Today we have clay.
> We will play with it.

> Look for it.
> Find it.
> Play with it.

On another day she introduced the new reading books through the use of the box. Sitting in the box was a book. Behind it was printed this card:

> *Look!*
>
> A new book!
> We will read it.
> We will each read it.
> We will read it at 10 o'clock.

Miss Swengle used a surprise box to stimulate creative writing. She put a music box in the box one day and behind it she printed:

> Look!
> Listen!
> Hear me!
> What do I say?
> We will write about me today!

One day she put a beautiful fall picture in the box. Below it she printed:

> Tell about me.
> Tell about me at Show and Tell time.

Miss Swengle sometimes used the box to introduce letters and invitations.

Surprise boxes can serve a multitude of purposes as well as provide meaningful reading experiences. When placed on a table near the door, they are an excellent motivating device for children as they enter the classroom. Often children can be encouraged to provide a surprise and create a message to go with it after they begin to do manuscript writing.

Setting Conditions for Building a Sight Vocabulary
Through Various Individual Approaches

Reading can be made a personal experience from the start of the formal reading program. Inasmuch as some children are ready to read before others, the individualized reading program has much merit. Where a completely individualized reading program is impossible, attempts should be made to personalize the reading experience in as many ways as possible.

Conditions can be set so creative teaching of reading on a personalized level can take place. Examples of such conditions set up by creative teachers follow on the next few pages.

1. Miss Wallace (page 133) personalized her reading program for the children by making individual reading charts on the chalkboard.

2. Mrs. Lanning, who knew her first-graders had had an excellent readiness program in kindergarten, brought a camera to school and took a picture of each child on the first day of school. She and her husband were both amateur photographers. They developed many pictures (five of each child) and made thirty prints of the group picture. This was paid for by the parents, who were sent a letter explaining the project along with a routine request for other money the children would need for books, milk money, cafeteria money, and so forth.

Mrs. Lanning arranged her children in groups of five in the classroom. She dittoed these words near the bottom of thirty sheets of paper:

I am _____
I am in the first grade.

Room was left over the printing for each child's picture, which he pasted on the sheet. He then printed his name in the blank space, copying it from a model taped to his desk. During the next two days each child made five copies of this sheet—pasting his own picture and printing his own name on each copy. On the last day of the first week of school, the children swapped copies so that each child had five different pictures with five different names. Mrs. Lanning printed the words "My First Book" on the chalkboard, and the children drew the words on colored construction paper with crayons. They then drew a picture on the construction paper and stapled in the five pages. Each member of this class, at the end of the first week of school, had created his own reading book. Each page of the book repeated the same words except that on each page was a different name to which the picture gave the clue.

The next week a book was made of "My Friends," and this time the children at different tables swapped pictures. A new page was added at the end of this book. It was the picture of the class. Under it was dittoed:

> This is the first grade.
> They go to school.
> They are friends.

With the continued use of drawings and photographs Mrs. Lanning was able to help each child build a sizable library of his own reading books and, of course, a superb reservoir of sight words. The last book of the year was a class yearbook summarizing events of the first grade for the entire year.

3. In Miss Allison's first grade a sight vocabulary was introduced on a personal basis by having the children draw pictures of a trip taken soon after school began. Each child could draw as few or as many pictures as he wished. As soon as he finished his pictures he put them in a logical sequence and brought them to Miss Allison, who sat before a primary typewriter. Each child told about his pictures or told a story about his pictures, which Miss Allison typed on the primary typewriter, helping the child to put it into short phrases with meaningful vocabulary.

Miss Allison skipped several spaces between the stories about the individual pictures. When the dictation was complete, Miss Allison told each child to cut apart the story between the large spaces and paste the story to the proper picture. Each child then stapled his pictures between construction paper covers, and Miss Allison helped him print the name of his book.

Her first reading lessons were built around teaching each child to read the story in his own book. Soon the children were reading their books aloud to the class. Before long they were reading to each other by twos and threes (teaching each other, actually) and finally swapping books.

By the end of her first week of formal reading, Miss Allison had a homemade library of thirty-two books from which to draw. This was increased by thirty-two more the second week and for several weeks thereafter. Before long some children were typing, illustrating, and binding their own books to share with the class.

4. Miss Johns personalized her reading program by having the

children use a home experience the first day of school. The children drew two or three pictures of something that happened at home. Then Miss Johns printed the dictated story on the picture. These were bound in construction paper and shared with the rest of the children. This is Jimmy's:

PAGE 1

Baby Sister

PAGE 2

I HAVE A NEW BABY
SHE IS A GIRL
SHE IS MY SISTER
HER NAME IS LISA

Soon Miss Johns's children were also sharing books.

5. Miss Myers ran off dittoed drawings of the new schoolbuilding on the first day of school. Below the picture she printed "Our School." On the same day she took the children on a tour of the new school. When they returned to the room she had them draw pictures of their trip. She printed stories below the pictures and used these as a personal reading experience for each child.

6. Miss Maggio had each child draw an illustration on one cover of a manila folder. Then she helped the children print "My Stories" on the cover. Each day the children had an opportunity to come to Miss Maggio and tell her a story built around an assigned topic. The first day they told about themselves. The next day the topic was "My School." Then they made stories about "My Father,"

then "My Mother," then "My Pet." Miss Maggio printed each story on primary paper and put it in the folder. She used these stories to teach each child his own sight vocabulary. Each child in this room soon had a book of stories different from any other child's. They were encouraged to illustrate the stories, and soon the books were full enough to be bound. Children working in small groups read their stories to each other and swapped books, helping each other to learn the new words.

Developing Reading Skills

Once the act of reading is established and children have a large enough sight vocabulary from which to develop independent reading skills, attention must be focused on their known oral skills in order to develop the printed skills of word attack. Picture and context clues are natural steps leading to the more complex use of word-form clues and phonetic and structural analysis skills. Many of these more complex means of developing reading skill can be taught creatively. If the teacher will remember that creative teaching calls for strong tension-building motivational techniques, convergent and divergent thinking processes may be initiated by the motivation of *content* of high interest, a *technique* of high interest, or a *process* of high interest.

Many of the following illustrations and suggestions have been included for developing convergent (as well as divergent) thinking processes because of their high motivational interest to children. Others enhance specific phases of creative development, such as substitution, expansion, minimization, or elaboration of ideas. Others were included because they develop affiliated skills necessary to creative development, such as making judgments, developing relationships, and evaluating and making decisions, all of which were demonstrated in Mr. Cline's lesson at the beginning of this chapter.

Developing Verbal Context Clues

The manner in which a word is used in a sentence or phrase often gives the child a clue as to its pronunciation and meaning. Each phonetic skill he acquires makes him more certain of the word as he works to decipher it. Lacking phonetic skills he will often guess at the meaning and continue reading if his guess makes sense to him. Phonetic analysis, structural analysis, and other forms of word attack are taught simultaneously and are meaningful to the degree that they are taught in the situation where the child encounters the problem.

Some general suggestions for teaching verbal context clues follow:

1. Choose the best word out of a group of words to best express a thought.

2. Draw attention to specific words by asking such questions as: Find the word on this page which means *a small house* [cottage].

3. Begin a notebook where new words are listed alphabetically under various classifications such as travel, music, art, homes, and so on.

4. Make charts that classify words for use in creative writing and reading such as emotion words, fun words, and elephant words (see Chapter V, Book II of this series).

5. Find irrelevant words in a story.

6. List descriptive words for creative writing (see the illustrations on pages 106 and 176).

7. Think of all the possible descriptive words for a certain object, picture, or action. Put them on a chart.

8. Find words of opposite meaning and list them.

9. Learn words that have more than one meaning.

> *Example:* Mother *set* my hair.
> A hen will *set*.
> We have a *set* of dishes.

Note that these words *look* and *sound* the same although they have different meanings.

10. Find irrelevant words in a classified list.

11. Encourage use of unusual words, note unusual shapes.

12. Rewrite thoughts using different words with the same meaning.

> *Example:* Mary *got* a letter.
> Mary *received* a letter.

Note the differences in shapes of words.

13. Have children suggest sentences for a group story, thank-you note, invitation, experience charts, and so forth, and then have them select the ones they like best.

14. Make a picture dictionary; correlate with other subjects to enrich the vocabulary.

15. Introduce a primary commercial dictionary.

16. Make cards containing sentences or paragraphs which contain a strange word that cannot be determined from the sentence alone. This puts the child in the position of using whatever skills he has to determine the pronunciation of the word.

> *Examples:* Peter bought some *bread* at the grocery store.
> Mary *ran* the sweeper every Saturday.
> We cut the bread with a *knife.*

17. Put on cards or on the chalkboard sentences that have an obvious word omitted. Children fill in the word demonstrating how the context gives clues to the word.

18. Compare opposites. Write lists of words and have children dictate opposites. These may be put on cards so that children may try independently to "match opposites."

19. Develop the concept of synonyms by using words from children's stories. For example, a child mentions or writes about a "fright." A synonym may be a "scare." Collect these on charts or cards.

20. Refer to the materials for developing audio and visual discrimination (pages 115–126) for other suggestions for developing verbal-context skills.

21. Adapt the fishing game on page 125 to context clues by using on the fish phrases containing new words as well as single words.

22. Print or type a simple paragraph using the children's sight vocabulary but omitting the key line. After it is read, have children dictate the key line. This makes an interesting and diverse type of reading chart.

> *Example:* I am yellow
> Mr. Ames drives me.
> I go to school every day.
> Boys and girls ride me.

23. Reverse the above suggestion by making riddles. These exercises help the children see the need for total comprehension, the importance of context, and the necessity for the correct reading of key words.

24. Make charts or ditto sheets leaving blanks where one word will make sense:

Mary had a _____ doll.
She put on its _____ hat.
She put on its _____ coat.
She put it in its _____ carriage.

The word can be "small," "tiny," "big," "pretty," or one of several others. Put the same word in each blank and then try substitutes that will make the story more interesting to read. This is a good way to show the use of synonyms in context.

25. Children enjoy simple games which help them in using the context to recognize words.

a. *Color Game*. Write a list of objects (such as snow, apple, carrot, grass) on oak tag and leave a space after each one. Then put a list of color cards in a separate envelope. The child who matches the greatest number wins. *Example:* apple—red; snow—white.

b. *The Stores*. On oak tag write headings (such as grocery store, bakery, hardware, drug store, and furniture store). Under each store list several things you could buy in it. Then cut the lists apart and put them in an envelope by themselves. The headings should also be in a separate envelope. The object is to see if the child can put the right article under the correct store heading.

c. *Stock Car Race*. Make a race track and divide it into sections. Make words or phrases and put them in a box. The children can make their own cars and cut them out. Each child is allowed to move one space on the track for every correct word or phrase he can read.

d. *Phrase Cards*. On one set of cards (oak tag or shirt cardboards) print phrases such as "I can see my —" or "I have the —"; on another set have illustrations of objects. The children put them together to make a sentence. Some number names can be used, as they are introduced functionally in the classroom situation.

Developing Skills in Word-Form Recognition

Word form clues are developed in many general ways:

1. Look at words—note the length, tall and short letters, ones

that go below the line, and such. A box can be built around the word to note its shape as well as similar or dissimilar parts.

2. Word-form clues are used more effectively by children when they learn certain phonetic skills. Some of the phonetic skills that are needed at the time are:

    a. Look at beginning letter and recognize sound or consonant blend.

    b. Recognize root words to which prefixes and suffixes have been added (colored chalk appeals to children).

farm	*read*	*slow*
farmer	reread	slowly
farming	rereading	

    c. Recognize long and short vowel sounds.

    d. Know and use the main rules for sounds of vowels.

    e. Final "e" dropped before adding endings (rope, roping).

    f. "E" at the end of a one-syllable word makes the vowel long (name, cone).

    g. When two vowels are found together in a word, the first vowel is long, the second silent (moan, seat).

    h. "R" is a vowel controller.

    i. In a two- or three-letter word having one vowel, the vowel sound is usually short (at, can).

3. Know and use the main rules for consonants.

    a. Recognize silent consonants (pneumonia, knife).

    b. The consonant at the end of the word is doubled when certain endings are added (run, running, hit, hitting).

(See pages 151–162 for suggestions for teaching these basic phonetic attacks and for cautions to be considered in applying them. Some more creative techniques for developing word-form clues follow.)

    c. *Page Mask.* Cut from a discarded book the page that is to be used as a sample. Cut a piece of paper to fit the page. Hinge the paper with mending tape or gummed labels. Holding the page against a window, draw little boxes on the paper around the words that the children found difficult. Cut out the boxes and expose the words. This is a way to let the children analyze the words that they have been having trouble with. The teacher can work with them on the difficult words using the mask, and then the children can work in groups, helping each other.

d. *Charades.* On the pocket chart place action words such as "angry," "temper," "generous," "flying." A pupil is then chosen to go to a corner of the room and blindfold himself. Then the teacher will point to one of the words on the board. Someone in the class is chosen to come to the front of the room and perform the action indicated by the word. The child who is blindfolded will then uncover his eyes. By watching the actions of the person in the front of the room, he will try to guess the word that is being acted out. He must then find the card that gives the word.

e. *Lollipop Game.*

> I'm selling lollipops, I'm selling lollipops,
> Fresh sugar candy from the candy shop.
> I'm selling lollipops, I'm selling lollipops
> No one knows where I shall stop.

Leader says above words as he walks around the room holding paper lollipops on which are written words. When leader says "Stop!" he pauses by a child and shows him the word. If the pupil knows the word, he is given one of the paper lollipops. The game continues until many children have lollipops. Pupils then say each word or write the word that is found on the lollipop. *Adaptations:* Use with phrases or sentences.

Use objects in keeping with various seasons instead of lollipops. *Example:* Halloween—jack-o'-lanterns; Thanksgiving—pumpkins; Christmas—Santa or toys.

f. *Learning Names of Colors.* Make tops from sucker sticks stuck through the center of milk bottle. Paint them different colors. One child spins his top and calls the name of another child. The child called must name the color of the top before it stops spinning. Later the second child runs to the chalk tray where word cards are and takes up the correct color card.

g. *Wheel of Chance.* Obtain a spinner device (like a clock face) numbered from one to fifteen or beyond. On chalkboard or oak tag print the same number of phrases or words. A child is called on; he flicks the hand on the spinner device, sees the number at which it stops, then reads the corresponding printed phrase or word from the chalkboard or oak tag. *Adaptations:* Sentences may be used as well as words.

h. *Dominoes.* Play with word cards. Matching is done according to words, word endings, word beginnings, or rhyming words. You play this game exactly as you do the game of dominoes.

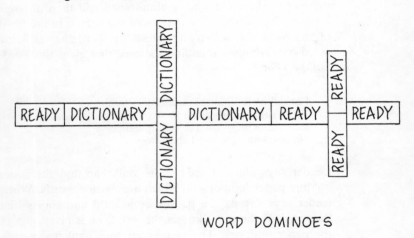

WORD DOMINOES

4. Special emphasis must often be placed on special words that are difficult for children to remember at the beginning stages of reading. Sometimes games help children to recognize the form of these special words.

a. *Special Words.* For teaching the word "it" have a large cardboard with that word printed on the front. Punch hole in top. Put a string in so it will go around a child's neck. Choose someone to be "it" and have someone chase him around the room.

b. *Hard Words.* To aid children to distinguish "was" from "saw," make folders of sentences in which either word has been omitted. Make small cards with the word "was" or "saw" printed on each. The child is to place correct word in blank.

Phonetic Analysis

Phonetic attack on words begins with the program for developing audio and visual discrimination, and the suggestions on pages 115–126 are appropriate in developing phonetic analysis skills. Many of them may be extended to a more direct approach of phonetic attack. The ideas suggested in Chapter II are worth reviewing as creative ways to lead children into a phonetic consciousness.

Because the creative personality enjoys seeing the order and logic behind life, an understanding of the structure of words can contribute to this aspect of the child's creative development.

Some general suggestions for teaching phonetic analysis skills follow:

Initial consonant sounds and rhyming endings. Children can imitate sounds they hear (trains, bells, and so on) and the sounds (choo-choo, ding-dong) can be placed on a chart to show the importance of sounds as a mode of communication even when these sounds are not really words. Known words can be constructed from these sounds by substituting initial consonant sounds (ding: sing, ring, king, wing).

1. Initial consonant sounds can be developed in several ways:
    a. Hearing beginning sounds that are alike (*d*og, *d*oor, *d*ump).
    b. Finding word in a group that starts with different sound (jump, jar, *cat*).
    c. Having children discover what is alike about all words in a series (oral or written)—*r*ug, *r*ake, *r*ing.
    d. Matching beginning sounds, both words and pictures.
    e. Calling attention to the fact that a new word begins the same as a familiar word.
    f. Completing a sentence with a word that begins with same sound as first word in the sentence:

    Dick has a _____. (dog)
                                    (doll)

    g. Changing the first consonant to make new words (ball, tall, call).
    h. Comparing words with names. "I am thinking of two

children whose names begin alike" or "I am thinking of a child whose name begins like Paul's."

   i. Listing words with similar beginnings.

   j. Identifying words, objects, and pictures with same beginning sound.

  k. Construct charts by placing an initial consonant sound at the top of a sheet of poster paper and have the children collect pictures of all the objects they can find which begin with this particular sound. This may be extended to speech consonants and consonant blends.

   l. Miss Jarmon had her children collect tongue-ticklers to help get across the initial consonant sound. The children enjoyed chanting "Peter Piper picked a peck of pickled peppers." After a while they made up their own tongue-tickling rhymes. Sally wrote, "Mamma makes much music"; Billy wrote, "Corky the clown can carry a cart," and Jimmy, who could not write many words, dictated, "Gary got a gallon of gas."

  m. *Which one is different?* All of these words begin with the same sound except one. Listen carefully. Tell me which word does not begin like the others.

     Example: sun, soup, ball, six (for initial consonants)

       1. girl ball bed book
       2. deer duck dinner bell
       3. red rose ring broom
       4. fire apron fish frog
       5. church chair child goat

   n. *Riddles.*

     "I am thinking of a word that begins the same as the words 'sun,' 'see,' 'sew.' It is the name of a number [six, seven]."

     "I am thinking of a word that begins like the words 'cook,' 'cut,' 'camp.' It hangs at the window [curtain]."

2. *Rhyming words* may be introduced by:

   a. Hearing and recognizing rhyming words (jump, bump, thump).

   b. Using nursery rhymes and poems to aid in discovery of rhyming words.

c. Saying words in series and discovering the one which sounds different because it doesn't rhyme (sun, *cat,* run).

d. Memorizing and repeating jingles.

e. Having children give a rhyming word for one the teacher gives (joy, toy, —).

f. Making a scrapbook of rhyming words (pictures and/or words).

g. Making up short rhymes. (Jack and Jill went up the _____.)

h. Using the children's creative writing for a study of rhyming words.

i. Some games provide a creative attack on the teaching of rhyming words and initial consonant sounds.

(1) *Verbal Tennis.* The children face each other across the room in two teams. One child gives a word such as "red." The child across from him must give a word that rhymes with it, such as "head." This goes on until no more rhyming words can be given. The team that cannot supply any words gets a point and begins another word. The team with the lowest score wins. The teacher may print the words on the board as they are given and then use time at the end of the game to teach some phonetic generalizations with their exceptions. Beginning consonant sounds can also be accented and the consistency of the beginning consonant emphasized. Miss Eggers began a chart from this experience on which children collected words which sounded alike at the ending but did not look alike (seed, bead; led, dead; rail, pale).

(2) Collect several sets of large pictures of objects (about three to a set) whose names rhyme. The teacher places two or three sets on the chalk ledge or on a flannel board and says, "Some of these things have names that rhyme." She may ask other questions: "Who can find pictures of two things that rhyme?" "Are there any others that rhyme too?" "Can you think of any other things that you know that would also rhyme?"

(3) Collect a set of small pictures of words that rhyme (man, fan, can; cat, hat, bat). Paint an egg carton an attractive color. A child can then sort the pictures and put the rhyming cards into the separate sections. (This exercise may be adapted for beginning and ending sounds.)

(4) The teacher opens the game with this riddle: "I rhyme with sled, you sleep in me. What am I?" The child who answers correctly may make up the next riddle.

(5) *Shopping at the Supermarket.* An adaptation (see page 118). Prepare word cards using the names of items that may be obtained at a supermarket (bag, book, bottle, cake, can, corn). (Duplicates are all right.) Choose a leader who can then distribute several cards to each player. The leader may say, "Who has bought something that rhymes with the word "bees?" The players whose cards answer the question will read them aloud and then give their cards to the leader. For more fun the leader may hold a grocery bag into which the children can deposit their "purchases."

(6) *Bingo* and *Lotto.* Make pictures or letters with same ending sounds.

(7) *Rhyming Endings.* The leader says, "I end with 'ook.' Can you guess who I am?" The player may take one guess in turn and say, "Are you look?" "No, I am not look," answers the leader if his word is, say, "book." The player who guesses correctly becomes next leader.

(8) *Rhyming Words.* Tell the two words that rhyme. Allow children to make up their rhymes or dictate one already known.

> Little Jack Horner
> Sat in a corner.
>
> Out in the snow
> Sat a black crow.
>
> One day when it was sunny
> I met a little bunny.
>
> I've looked high, I've looked low
> But I can't find my red bow.
>
> Fish, fish in the brook,
> I will catch you with my hook.
>
> Giraffes are tall
> But ants are small.
>
> Little boat, little boat
> All around I see you float.

(9) *Name a word that rhymes with:*

coat	(boat)	tree	(bee)
car	(star)	eye	(pie)
house	(mouse)		

(10) *Tell the word that rhymes with the first word.*

> *Ted,* ball, bed, train
> *play,* say, dead, palace
> *red,* balloon, head, candy

(11) *Riddles that rhyme*

> Something you eat
> (It rhymes with dandy) (candy)
> Something you wear
> (It rhymes with boat) (coat)

(12) *Tell the missing word and you will make a rhyme*

> We went so far
> In Daddy's new _____ (car)
> The snow is falling all around
> Floating and sailing to the _____ (ground)
> Bobby fishing in a brook,
> Caught a fish on his _____ (hook)

(13) *Bounce-a-Rhyme Game.* Let children try bouncing a ball to a chant consisting of rhyming words. Give a child a one-syllable "starter" word like "will" which rhymes with many others: bill, hill, sill, till, spill, fill, Jill. The youngster continues to bounce the ball as long as he can say a rhyming word each time he bounces it. Other good starters are "can," "and," "old," "it," "day," "red."

(14) *Lost Children.* The teacher appoints one of the children to act as "police captain." The other children are "policemen." The teacher announces to the police captain that she is "Mrs. Ill" and has lost her children while shopping. The police captain then tells the policemen to hunt for them. Some of the policemen might look through the "Bureau of Missing Persons" (a box containing a number of words, some of which belong to the "Ill" family). Others might look in the parks (along the window ledges

there are more word cards face down), or in the streets (on the desks or along the blackboard ledge, where there are more cards). The policeman who finds the most children may be rewarded by a "medal" or a "promotion."

j. Choral speaking provides an excellent opportunity for developing a consciousness to rhyming words (see Book II of this series, *Creative Teaching of the Language Arts in the Elementary School*, Chapter V).

3. Emphasis from rhyming endings and beginning consonant sounds can be extended by:

a. Finding the same sounds in consonants at the end of a word which were noted at the beginning of a word (*d*ark, pai*d*).

b. Noting likenesses and differences in beginnings (*c*an, *r*an) and endings of words (ma*n*, ma*t*).

c. Finding known word in a longer word (*some*thing).

d. Recognizing the same word beginning with capital and lower case letter (Jump, jump).

e. Framing words to show length and form

Sally   Something

f. Recognizing plural and possessive forms made by adding *s* or *'s*.

g. Finding similarities and differences in words such as "stop," "spot"; "Dick," "duck."

h. Noting configuration of words.

i. Noting word endings (car, cars [s]; box, boxes [es]; small, smallest [est]; like, liked [d]; call, called [ed]; sweet, sweetly [ly]; sing, singing [ing]).

j. Noting the same sound regardless of placement in words (*g*et, be*g*in, pi*g*),

4. Study letters having more than one sound by:

a. Recognizing that *x* and *k-s* sound alike. *Example:* boo*ks*, fo*x*.

b. Listing words that show how the same letter sometimes has a different sound. *Example:* Sally, busy.

c. Learning the hard and soft sounds of "c" and "g." *Example:* country, city; grass, ginger.

    d. Recognizing the vowel sounds with "r," such as "or," "ir," "er," "ur."

5. Mr. Markin used the book *Ounce, Dice, Trice* to help him develop a consciousness to sounds in his room. As a result of their experience with this book, children made charts for various purposes: "Words That Are the Same Coming or Going" (noon, Dad, gag, Nan, pop, pep, sees, toot); "Words That Are Quiet in Spots" (knife, beat angle, wren); "Words That Grow from One Word" (all, ball, tall, fall); "Words That Mean the Same Thing" (stand, rise; push, shove; box, carton); "Words That Go Together" (kiss, love, hug, dear, warm); "Words That Sound Alike But Aren't" (hair, hare; see, sea; hear, here; buy, by).

6. Children can be made aware of the many times they use the vowel and consonant sounds they are learning by:

    a. Noting the many times total words or similar uses of sounds are used by underlining them in the daily plans they write together on the chalkboard, in experience charts, or news bulletins.

    b. Underlining words that are alike from several sentences on the chalkboard, using the same color of chalk.

    c. Matching word cards with chart.

    d. Matching word card with manuscript (board).

    e. Finding and underlining words that are like the beginning word in a row of words.

    f. Playing recognition game—put word on board or show word card and then ask, "Where can you see this word somewhere else in the room?" (Word such as "one" may be in word chart, on the bulletin board, in the number center, in the daily news, and so on.)

7. Literature and the development of phonics may be blended when books such as *I Met a Man* and *The Reason for a Pelican,* by John Ciardi, are used by the teacher as springboards for fun with sounds.

8. Motivation for practice in sounds may be developed with a few interesting games:

    a. *Clapping Game.* Children clap when they hear a certain blend or letter sound at the beginning of a word; when they hear a certain variant ending; when they hear a long or short vowel.

    b. *Picture book of sounds.* Children find pictures of words beginning with various sounds, blends, and such, and paste them in appropriate page of book or on a chart.

    c. Teacher dictates a word such as "parrot," and children circle word in a list that begins with same consonant (doctor, fireman, policeman). Or dictate a word and have children circle word that has the same ending consonant. Again, dictate a word and have children circle word that has same beginning and ending consonants. *Example:* "foot": people,   forget,   lawn.

Speech consonants and consonant blends. After children have mastered many consonant sounds they can be led to discover that in combination consonants such as "ch," "sh," "th," "wh," "ck," "gh," "ph," "qu" and "ng" lose their identity and produce a different single speech sound. These are the speech consonants. They will also be aware that some letter combinations consist of two or more letters, each of which has its own distinct sound ("bl," "br," "cl," "cr," "dr," "dw," "fl," "fr," "gl," "gr," "pl," "pr," "sci," "scr," "shr," "sk," "sl," "sm," "sn," "sp," "spl," "spr," "st," "str," "thr," "tr" and "tw") and these are the consonant blends.

Like beginning consonants and initial vowel sounds, speech consonants and consonant blends are best understood when they develop from the oral vocabulary of the child. His spoken language, and the symbol language he already can read, should be the foundation for an understanding of the use of speech consonants and consonant blends as an attack on new words.

Once again, putting his "sounds" into printed form can be a good beginning for recognizing blends and speech consonants. The dog says "grr" (a blend). The train goes "chug-chug" (a speech consonant). Transferral of these discoveries to other words is a simple matter.

1. Many of the techniques used to introduce consonant sounds can be applied to the teaching of blends and speech consonants.

    a. Changing beginnings and endings of words to make new words. *Example:* eat, meat; meal, squeal.

    b. Making a list of new words with a part of a familiar word. Children say words. *Example:* rain, train, brain, chain, and so on.

    c. Having children underline beginning blends in a group of words. *Example: cl:* clouds, clams, climb.

    d. Making large charts of pictures illustrating words that begin with consonant blends (train, truck).

    e. Listening for and listing words that begin with the same consonant blends.

    f. Using riddles ("I am thinking of a word that begins with the same sound as *ch*air. It is where people pray on Sunday. What is it?" [church]).

    g. Collecting words that begin and end with the same speech consonant or consonant blends: *ch*ur*ch, sh*u*sh*.

2. Motivation for individual practice with speech consonants and consonant blends may be provided with some simple games:

    a. *Circle wheels.* One big wheel with a smaller one attached to it with a paper fastener. On the smaller wheel may be the blends of "ch," "wh," "st," and others. On the larger wheel the word endings may be placed ("op," "ip," "ick," and so forth). Children can make these from oak tag.

3. Increase skill in blending initial consonant with familiar part of word (rain, train) by:

    a. Applying results of word-building activities in attaching new words in context (cat, catch).

    b. Listing words with initial consonants and blends.

    c. Writing "br," "tr," "dr," "fr," and so forth on board and having children point to and name the sound they hear at the beginning of such words as "drink," "trip," "cream," "frog."

    d. Having children name words that begin or end with certain blends ("cl," "bl").

4. Increase skill in identifying hard and soft sounds by:

    a. Recognizing hard and soft "c" and "g": (*Example:* car, cent; girl, large.) Make chart collections of these contrasts.

    b. Ask the children to listen to first sounds in words pronounced. In a natural tone of voice pronounce words like "chilly," "cheese," "chicken," and so on. Elicit from the children the sound "ch." The children give other words with the same sound. As the list of blends increases, children may draw from a box cards on which are printed words beginning with blends they know. The child who draws a card gives another word beginning with the same blend as the word he draws.

        Use a shoe bag and staple a consonant blend or

speech consonant to each pocket and pass out word cards. Children say their word cards and place them in correct pocket.

On a large piece of paper or in a booklet put a different consonant blend ("br," "cr," "st," and so on) on each page. Cut out and paste pictures whose names begin with the blend.

c. *Finding endings.* A child is given an envelope containing sentences such as: Sally is play____ with her doll. Dick ride____ the horse. This tree is big____ than the house. An envelope containing endings accompanies the card. The child is to select the proper endings for the unfinished words.

Vowel sounds. While most consonant sounds are stable, the vowels can have many sounds. It is the vowels that give language the greater part of its tonal quality. This can be demonstrated by having children sing *America* by singing only the vowel sounds. The tune is unimpaired but it is not possible to sing the consonants and maintain the tune.

Discovery of the many differences in vowel sounds may be promoted by using the children's names. Jane and James have similar vowel sounds in their names, but Jack and Mary have different sounds. If the teacher has the children write their names on the chalkboard and pronounce them, the children can be led to see the differences in vowel sounds. The teacher may use this opportunity to help them establish some of the generalizations of phonetic attack.

1. While Clymer's study shows that only nine of the forty-five phonic generalizations are applicable 100 percent of the time and that seventeen of these generalizations are not applicable even 50 percent of the time, this does not mean that they should not be used to help children. It does mean that they should be carefully reviewed and *some* should not be used—especially the seventeen that do not work 50 percent of the time. To be a generalization, a "rule" should work most of the time. All generalizations should be taught as clues to unlocking the pronunciations of words—not as rules. Children may become even more sensitive to these generalizations if they are challenged to hunt for the exceptions. In Mr. Parker's second grade this chart indicated how he was using the generalizations in phonetic attack:

Clue: WHEN TWO VOWELS APPEAR IN
A WORD, THE FIRST ONE SAYS ITS OWN
NAME AND THE SECOND ONE IS SILENT.

Places where it works:

beat	lean
meat	bead
hear	tear
fair	road

Places where it doesn't work:

chief	tough
veil	sweat
soup	loin
cough	

Mr. Parker often used the chart to introduce a new generalization, as in the words "loin," "cough," "bough," each of which introduces a new phonetic sound. Children started another chart on which they placed all the double vowels that made new sounds. These charts created an exciting word hunt for the children, and any child could add a word to the chart when he found one that rightfully belonged there.

As soon as children are aware of differences in vowel sounds and have had many experiences with the different sounds, the teacher can concentrate on the different sounds for each specific vowel, provided, of course, she does so in a meaningful context rising out of the children's needs. Children can hunt for vowels in their words and sentences and learn to mark them. Words from their sight vocabulary should be heavily used during this discovery stage because the children already know the sounds of the vowels in their sight vocabulary and will see how generalizations fit or do not fit these known words.

2. Miss Horton used the color concept mentioned in Chapter III to help children understand the difference in vowel sounds. Long vowels were printed on her charts in red, short vowels in blue, and so on. Children quickly figured out strange words under this system, and then Miss Horton had them tell her what generalization had dictated the color she would use. This "color" reading was used to establish the generalizations, after which the children were exposed to new words in sentences without the color but with the commonly accepted vowel markings. This provided for a smooth transition into regular reading material.

3. Common ways of teaching vowel sounds are:
   a. Substituting medial vowels to stress sound changes (bad, bed, and so on).
   b. Having children tell the vowel sound they hear in a word that the teacher pronounces. *Example:* bit, bite.
   c. Detecting silent letters in words. *Example:* cream.
   d. Perceiving how final "e" changes the sound and meaning of such words as "cap" and "cape."
   e. Listing words under vowel headings (long or short sound of same vowel).
   f. Having children mark the long and short vowel sounds in their spelling words.
   g. Showing the difference in meaning and sound of words when a double vowel is substituted for a single vowel. *Example:* met, meet; bet, beet.
   h. Having each child try to find the most words with either long or short vowels in a given length of time in one verse of a poem by writing the complete word and marking its vowels in the proper way on paper. When the time is completed, check and verify the vowels marked.

4. Increase skill in hearing beginning and medial vowels, with recognition of both short and long vowels, by:
   a. Making separate charts for each vowel sound and finding pictures to illustrate each.
   b. Listening to two words and designating which has the short "i" (hit, hat); the long "a" (hide, hate), and so on.
   c. Listing words on the board to illustrate the effect of changing the vowel, or inserting an additional vowel in certain short words such as "rug, rag," "bat, bit," "met, meat."
   d. Showing the child how a final "e" changes the vowel sound and thus the meaning of words: "cap, cape," "can, cane," "hop, hope." Collect such words on charts.
   e. Showing the child the difference in the meaning and sound of words when a double vowel is substituted for a single vowel: "bet, beet"; "met, meet."
   f. Showing the effect of "r" on the vowels "a" (cart), "e" (sister), "i" (bird), "o" (color), "u" (hurt).
   g. Showing the differences in diphthongs represented by two letters: "ou" (ground), "ow" (cow), "oi" (noise), "oy" (boy).
   h. Comparing sounds of homonyms (sow, sew; road, rode).

5. Well-chosen games provide interesting practice for phonetic development.

    a. *Finding medial vowels.* On 3 x 5 cards print words with different vowel sounds, such as "pig," "hat," "wig," "can," "ran," "sat," "big." Shuffle the cards and give four to each child. A small pack should be left face down on the table. The first player reads a word from any of his four cards. If another player holds a card that contains a rhyming word, he must give the card to the player calling for it. The next player receives a chance to call any of his words. When a player fails to get a card from any of the others, he may draw from the pack on the table. If he still fails to get a rhyming word, or if he cannot read the card he has chosen, he must discard the card he called. The player with the most cards at the end is the winner.

Structural Analysis

The teaching of structural analysis begins in the development of visual discrimination. Many of the suggestions on the preceding pages help to develop structural analysis skills such as:

1. Listing words beginning with the same sounds.
2. Making word wheels.
3. Changing beginning consonants of root words.
4. Choosing from letters on the board those which indicate the beginning letter in a word pronounced by teacher.
5. Matching beginning and ending sounds.
6. Substituting beginning and ending sounds.
7. Naming root words.
8. Observing word endings.
9. Making new words from root words.
10. Substituting medial vowels to stress sound changes.
11. Detecting silent letters in words.
12. Learning basic rules about vowel sounds (double vowels and such).
13. Learning consonant blends.
14. Knowing and using basic rules about consonants.
15. Making larger words out of smaller words (and, stand).
16. Seeing little words in a larger word (*yester*day).
17. Recognizing compound words such as football.
18. Recognizing contractions.
19. Knowing and using the main rules for syllables.

a. If double consonants come together divide the consonants ("sum-mer," "lit-tle").

b. If the first vowel is followed by one consonant divide the word after the vowel. *Example:* li-lac, lo-cate.

c. If the ending syllable is "le," the first syllable ends after the vowel (ta-ble).

d. When two consonants come between two vowels, we usually divide the word between the two consonants. *Example:* fif-ty.

20. Using the dictionary as a helping device.

1. The activities suggested on pages 146–150 are appropriate for the introduction of word structure. Other ways children can be made sensitive to the structure of words are:

a. Mastery of *sight* vocabulary words to the point where they can be spotted in varying content by:

(1) Finding little words in larger words. *Example:* afternoon.

(2) Taking off beginning and ending prefixes and suffixes to locate root word.

(3) Finding words in a group which are exactly alike.

(4) Determining parts of words that are alike and parts that are different.

(5) Recognizing familiar words in compound or hyphenated words.

(6) Distinguishing between common prefixes and suffixes from root words.

(7) Having children scan to find answers to questions, descriptive terms, names, and so forth.

(8) Dividing words into syllables and marking the accent.

(9) Presenting new words in written sentences and discussing meanings.

(10) Recognizing compound words.

(11) Listing words that are alike except at the beginning (bell, fell, tell).

(12) Making a dictionary of words to use when writing stories or poems.

(13) Developing ability to recognize derivations formed by adding suffix "y" to a known root word (sleep, sleepy).

(14) Developing ability to attack words when final consonant is doubled before the ending (sit, sitting).

(15) Recognizing and understanding the final "e" being dropped before an ending and the changing of "y" to "i."

b. See how many words can be built from *one* root word and notice how the new words are all related to the root word in meaning. *Examples:* Root word "law." Words built by adding suffixes, prefixes, and compounds: "lawyer," "lawless," "lawsuit," "lawful," "unlawful." Root word "rain." Built words: "raincoat," "rainy," "raindrop," "raincheck," "raining," "rains."

c. Make collections of compound words whose meanings are obvious and some that are not. Mrs. Marr's third grade produced the following two contrasting charts:

Words That Tell Us Their Own Meanings	*Words That Do Not Tell Us Their Meanings*
evergreen	tidbit
shoelace	shamrock
scarecrow	shipshod
teabag	sandwich
boxcar	fanfare
sidewalk	ketchup
tiptoe	horse-radish
sandman	iceberg
airplane	handsome
seashore	nightmare
tattletale	

d. Make collections of words that go together but are not compounded. Mrs. Farr's list looked like this:

Words We Say Together But Do Not Put Together

tie tack
mince pie
eye ball
candy cane
window sill
window pane
lake shore
state fair
hope chest
ice cream
ferris wheel
fish pole
golf ball

2. Increase skill in identifying endings on nouns without change in base forms.

    a. Endings "s," " 's" and "s' " without adding an extra syllable (boats, uncle's, girls').

    b. Endings "s" and "es" adding an extra syllable (pieces, watches).

3. Increase skill in forming compound words.

    a. Making "solid" compounds (today, another).

    b. Building hyphenated compounds (make-believe, far-off).

4. Increased skill in forming contractions by substituting an apostrophe for one or more letters (I'm, can't).

5. Increase skill in identifying "s," "es," "est," "ed," "er," "ly," as forms of familiar words by:

    a. Naming the root word.

    b. Using the root word to make new words.

    c. Looking through a story or book to find words that were made by adding an ending to a known word.

6. Study word endings by:

    a. Observing word endings "s," "es," "est," "er," "d," "ed," "ly," "ing."

    b. Identifying root word in attacking new words (open, opening).

    c. Making new words from a root word. *Example:* want, wants, wanted, wanting.

    d. Choosing correct word ending to complete sentences. *Example:* Jane (play, plays) with her doll.

7. Some games and gimmicks are suitable in developing structure awareness in children:

    a. *Word pyramid.* Start at the top of the pyramid with the word *A*. The players take turns adding another letter to form a new and longer word and to build the pyramid. If the first player adds "t," the pyramid may develop as follows: a, at, eat, meat, steam, steamer, teamster. The pyramid may be built on the chalkboard.

    b. *Finding families.* The children are divided into four or five teams. The captain of each team holds a large card with a family name printed on it. Each team has a different family. Along the chalkboard ledge there are word cards facing the board. There are as many word cards for each family as there are children in each team. At a given signal the children hunt through the word cards to find one that belongs to their family, the name of the family being held in full view by the captain. The team that wins is the first to have each member show a card with the name of the family indicated by his captain.

   c. *Keeping prefixes in a box.* Drawing out a prefix and making a new word by adding the prefix. *Example:* using "like," take "dis" out of box and make "dislike."

Summary

Every day of a child's life he uses hundreds of words in multiple situations. Creative children have the particular characteristics of wanting to create order out of chaos, of wanting to be independent and able to initiate their own learning. Creative children are flexible, unique, have original ideas, are sensitive to problems, are individualists, have a fluency of ideas, like to redefine and rearrange, like to produce, have keen visual discrimination, keen intuition, and strong identification ability. These are actually the natural, healthy ways by which all children learn, if freed to do so—or if conditions have been properly set. In this chapter and the next are many suggestions for teaching reading through the development of each of these skills. If the teacher herself can be flexible enough, observant enough, and creative enough, she can use the hundreds of words she hears the children use to develop the above traits, all of which are necessary to the development of reading and creative skills.

TO THE COLLEGE STUDENT

   1. In the lesson described at the beginning of this chapter, Mr. Cline appealed to the sense of taste, smell, touch, sight, and sound. Little children learn best when what they are learning appeals to all their senses. Compare Mr. Cline's lesson with the one described at the beginning of the next chapter (VI). Did Mr. Banks also follow this principle in the intermediate grade lesson? How?

   2. Reread Mr. Cline's lesson and tell how you would develop some creative experiences in phonics development for the children involved.

3. Why did the author feel that the quote from Rumer Godden's book, *An Episode of Sparrows,* was particularly appropriate for this chapter?

4. How keen is your visual perception? Do you really notice things—*see* things? Check by trying some of the games suggested on pages 120–121. Also, try these exercises below:

    a. Turn to face the rear of the room and then write the answers to these questions:

        (1) What is hanging on the wall in the front of your classroom?

        (2) How many panels are there in the chalkboard?

        (3) Does the doorway to your classroom have a glass panel?

        (4) What picture is hanging before the room?

        (5) What is currently written on the chalkboard?

        (6) Is there a movie screen or a map in the room?

        (7) Is there an electric outlet in the front of the room?

        (8) What is currently on the teacher's desk?

        (9) Who is absent from your class today?

TO THE CLASSROOM TEACHER

1. Look at the next lesson you plan to teach in developing reading skills and see if you can do it with more creative, stronger motivational power by applying some of the ideas in this chapter.

2. Think of as many ideas as you can to check the comprehension ability of your children without using the workbook exercises.

3. Look at the words below and sound them out. Check your pronunciation with the dictionary. Often when children sound out words they encounter the same problem you just did. Knowing this, can you be more patient with children's experimentation with words? Of what value is phonetic analysis in this instance—might not it be as practical to drill on the memorization of the word?

tapetum, iatrophysical, erythrocyte

4. Check the reading materials you are using in your classroom. Which of them violates the basic principles of creativity by tracing,

unimaginative direction-giving, nontension-producing motivation, and so on? How many ideas can you substitute for some of these uncreative ones?

TO THE COLLEGE STUDENT AND
THE CLASSROOM TEACHER

1. Search through children's literature books and make lists of all those which might serve as a springboard for teaching phonetic analysis or structural analysis.

2. Make lists of all the children's *picture* books you can find that might serve to meet one of the objectives of the reading readiness program described in this chapter.

3. The specific qualities possessed by creative children which may be logically developed in the reading program were listed on page 58. Check the list against Mr. Cline's lesson and determine which of the creative components of divergent thinking processes Mr. Cline was developing.

4. Parties are a natural part of a child's heritage. Yet in some schools parties have been deleted from the curriculum because they are fun and not educational. Challenge this idea by planning a party where you would develop the following reading skills: the ability to follow directions, audience-type reading situations, the ability to develop audio and visual acuity, comprehension abilities, organizational skills, the ability to understand ideas in sequence, the ability to dramatize, and the ability to summarize and evaluate.

5. Patty came home crying from first grade about a week after the opening of school. She was clutching a paper on which was printed an apple, a small "a" and a large "A." When her mother asked Patty why she was crying, Patty pointed to a red check mark on the paper and said, "I did this wrong—the teacher said it was wrong." "What were you supposed to do?" asked her mother. "I had to tell her that "A" is for apple—that this is a big "A" and this was a small "a" and that "a" says 'm-m-m.' " "But, darling," her mother said, " 'A' doesn't say 'm-m-m.' " "Oh, yes it does," said Patty.

"Apples are good—'m-m-m,' " and she patted her tummy with her hand.

What was Patty trying to do? Was the teacher helping her conceptualize? Of what value was the lesson? Of what value are "marks" on papers at this stage of a child's development? Would you say Patty's teacher was creative? How would you introduce vowel sounds?

SELECTED BIBLIOGRAPHY

BROGAN, PEGGY and LORENE FOX. *Helping Children Read.* New York: Holt, Rinehart and Winston, Inc., 1961.

CARILLO, LAWRENCE W. *Informal Reading-Readiness Experiences.* San Francisco: Chandler Publishing Company, 1964.

CIARDI, JOHN. *I Met a Man.* Cambridge: Houghton Mifflin Company, 1961.

———. *The Reason for a Pelican.* New York: J. B. Lippincott Co., 1959.

———. *You Read to Me, I'll Read to You.* New York: J. B. Lippincott Co., 1962.

DECHANT, EMERALD V. *Improving the Teaching of Reading.* Englewood Cliffs, N.J.: Prentice-Hall, Inc., 1964.

FRANK, JOSETTE. *Your Child's Reading Today.* Garden City: Doubleday & Company, Inc., 1960.

GANS, ROMA. *Common Sense in Teaching Reading.* New York: The Bobbs-Merrill Company, Inc., 1963.

HEFFERNAN, HELEN and VIVIAN EDMISTON TODD, *The Kindergarten Teacher.* Boston: D. C. Heath and Company, 1960.

HEILMAN, ARTHUR. *Teaching Reading.* Columbus: Charles E. Merrill Books, Inc., 1961.

LANGDON, GRACE and IRVING W. STOUT. *Teaching in Primary Grades.* New York: Macmillan Co., 1964.

LARRICK, NANCY. *A Teacher's Guide to Children's Books.* Columbus, Ohio: Charles E. Merrill Books, Inc., 1960.

LEE, DORIS M. and R. V. ALLEN. *Learning to Read Through Experience.* New York: Appleton-Century-Crofts, Inc., 1963.

LeFEVRE, CARL A. *Linguistics and the Teaching of Reading.* New York: McGraw-Hill Book Co., 1964.

McKIM, MARGARET and HELEN CASKEY. *Guiding Growth in Reading in the Modern Elementary School.* New York: Macmillan Company, 1963.

MORRISON, IDA E. *Kindergarten Primary Education.* New York: The Ronald Press Company, 1961.

REID, ALASTAIR. *Ounce, Dice, Trice.* Canada: Little, Brown and Company, 1958.

RUDOLPH, MARGUERITA and DOROTHY H. COHEN. *Kindergarten: A Year of Learning.* New York: Appleton-Century-Crofts, Inc., 1964.

RUSSELL, DAVID and ETTA E. KARP. *Reading Aids through the Grades.* Columbia University: Bureau of Publications, 1951.

SMITH, NILA BANTON. *Reading Instruction for Today's Children.* Englewood Cliffs, N.J.: Prentice-Hall, Inc., 1963.

UNIVERSITY OF THE STATE OF NEW YORK, BUREAU OF ELEMENTARY CURRICULUM DEVELOPMENT. *The Teaching of Reading.* Albany: State Education Dept., 1963.

VEATCH, JEANNETTE. *Individualizing Your Reading Program.* New York: G. P. Putnam's Sons, 1959.

The Creative Teaching of Reading in the Intermediate Grades

I have learned . . . that the head does not hear anything until the heart has listened, and what the heart knows today the head will understand tomorrow.[1]

JAMES STEPHENS

TO THE READER

This chapter is a continuation of Chapter V. The student will need to skim it to get a total picture of the reading program. It will be of most value to him when he is in his student-teaching situation. The primary teacher will benefit from this chapter in many ways: (1) there are many ideas here that may be adapted to her reading program; (2) she will understand how the work she accomplishes becomes the foundation for the development of reading skills in the intermediate grade; (3) by knowing this, teachers may give greater continuity to the reading program between grade levels; and (4) the preparation she gives her children may become more meaningful when she understands the skills required for a good intermediate reading program.

The intermediate-grade teacher will find in this chapter many ideas which, I hope, will spark her own imagination for designing a creative intermediate reading program.

Introduction

The following account is a combination of a lesson plan prepared by Mr. Banks, a fourth-grade teacher, and the notes taken by an observer during the lesson.

[1] James Stephens, *The Crock of Gold: Irish Fairy Tales* (New York: The Macmillan Co.).

A Lesson Plan

1. To build a reading vocabulary through the creative approach to teaching.
2. To foster creativity in the children in terms of creative thinking and creative writing.
3. To develop the following reading skills:
    a. Selecting the main idea of a communication medium.
    b. Extending reading vocabulary through the oral vocabulary.
    c. Audience-type reading.
    d. Word study—the importance of using the most effective word in a special place.
    e. Good oral reading expression.
    f. Sequence of ideas.
    g. Sight reading.
    h. Structural analysis.
    i. Phonetic analysis.
    j. Ability to classify.
    k. Choral speaking ability.
4. To diagnose some reading problems.
5. To apply reading skills as a tool and integrate them with art, language arts, and social studies material.

Motivation

Discussion of purposes of lesson.

Procedure

1. *Discussion: the importance of words.* Mr. Banks placed a series of cards on the chalkboard which said:

> 1. Words Are Important
> 2. Words Take Us Far Away
> 3. Words Work For Us
> 4. Words Make Us Feel
> 5. Words Help Us
> 6. The *Right* Word Is Important in the *Right* Place

The children discussed the cards and explained what each meant to them. Then they played the "Adjective Game" (Book II of this series)[2] to show how important it was to get the right word in the right place.

[2] James A. Smith, *Creative Teaching of the Language Arts in the Elementary School* (Boston: Allyn and Bacon, Inc., 1967), Chapter V.

2. *A survey of children's oral vocabulary and a check on the children's ability to classify words.* Mr. Banks held up some 9 x 12 pieces of construction paper. On the top of each sheet he had printed a topic. Among the topics were: World's Fair, Space Age, summer, spring, baseball, beautiful, old-fashioned, a scare, sports, school, home, airplane, travel, hobbies, pets, farm, city. He asked each child to choose a topic in which he was interested and, with a flo-pen, list on cards all the words he knew that were appropriate to this topic. These could be descriptive words, related words, or action words. The children worked on the cards for five minutes. Then Mr. Banks asked them to exchange cards and make the lists longer by adding to each other's cards. A second exchange was encouraged. The children then stood by rows and read their word lists, which were then placed on the chalkboard ledge. Mr. Banks suggested some new words for each chart. Soon twenty-two charts of classified words appeared before the class.

3. *Some creative writing.* The children were then encouraged to select one topic on which to work together, and they chose Space Age. Mr. Banks had them work with him and write a poem, using the words on the card and any others they could think of. Soon the poem was composed and the children put it on the tape recorder as a choral poem. They listened to the tape, evaluated it, made some changes, and recorded it again.

4. *Preparing individual reading materials.* Mr. Banks then encouraged the children to get their own charts from the chalkboard and to write a poem, a story, a description, or a joke, using all the words they could from the list on the chart. Those who finished first could either take another card or illustrate their own writing. As soon as each child finished, he was given a large sheet of chart paper, and he printed his story on the paper with a flo-pen so that all the children could see it. They were encouraged to give their writing titles.

When they were done, the children brought their writings to the front of the room and put them between two large colored cardboards which served for the covers of a "Big Book" of twenty-two original stories. One child decorated the cover while waiting for the others to finish and gave it a name: "The Big Little Book of Big Ideas."

5. *Audience-type situation.* While two children held the book open to the proper page, the author of each creative bit of writing shared his work with the class by reading it. In some instances the

children read each other's work. Each story or poem was evaluated.

6. *Sight-reading: new material.* Mr. Banks had dittoed a choral play called *America Today.* In it he had anticipated the many words that might arise. The play was about America in the Space Age—and was to be read by both groups and solos. Mr. Banks assigned readings; the children were allowed to read the material through once to learn any words which they did not know. At this point Mr. Banks kept a record of the words that gave group members trouble and made entries in his notebook. After the dry run, Mr. Banks introduced a recording of "The Battle Hymn of the Republic" and played it as musical background while the children read the choral play once more. This time it was recorded. After the playback, the children evaluated their work.

7. *Building reading skills.* Mr. Banks then told the children he had some notes he had taken which he felt would help them. He spent time reviewing some vowel generalizations which they had trouble reading aloud, and he introduced some work in structural analysis, using words from the children's charts to show how suffixes and prefixes changed meanings. He introduced the prefixes "un," "re," and "dis." Children applied them to words from their charts and changed meanings as follows:

"un" (*to make opposite*)		*from chart on:*
happy	unhappy	(spring)
exciting	unexciting	(World's Fair)
comfortable	uncomfortable	(summer)
afraid	unafraid	(airplanes)
related	unrelated	(home)
necessary	unnecessary	(school)

"re" (*to do again*)		
visit	revisit	(World's Fair)
make	remake	(World's Fair)
shape	reshape	(World's Fair)
strict	restrict	(old-fashioned)
pay	repay	(World's Fair)
call	recall	(home)

"dis" (*to make opposite*)		*from chart on*
enchanted	disenchanted	(World's Fair)
engage	disengage	(travel)
order	disorder	(school)
interested	disinterested	(baseball)
organize	disorganize	(school)

The children also made lists of words which had opposite meanings to the ones on their charts but the opposites of which were *not* obtained by adding the prefix "un" or "dis." Their list included some of the following:

fragile	strong
beautiful	ugly
colorful	drab
pretty	homely
rural	urban
love	hate

8. *Evaluation.* Mr. Banks asked the children to review what they had learned about words, about the prefixes studied, and what they had learned about oral reading. He asked them, too, if they had enjoyed the afternoon. He told them the "Big Little Book of Big Ideas" would be left in the reading center and he expected them to read each other's stories some time during the week and to ask each other for help with troublesome words. He also put three pieces of chart paper on the chalkboard with the prefixes "un," "re," and "dis" printed at the top and asked that each child add a word to these charts any time they found one in their reading.

*   *   *

Mr. Banks met his objectives well. He also is a creative teacher. Almost all of the principles set up in Chapter I of this book were utilized in his plan.

In developing reading skills Mr. Banks was also developing creative skills—flexibility of thinking, ability to generalize, ability to abstract and conceptualize, fluency of ideas, originality and individualism, visual and audio discrimination, the ability to discern differences and likenesses, ability to rearrange, ability to produce reactions, retention ability, and the ability to adapt and elaborate. A reference to Book I of this series,[3] Chapter V, will show that research in the social-emotional structure of creative people indicates that each of these qualities and abilities is found in creative people more than in average or noncreative people. And training children in these skills is fostering creative development as well as reading efficiency.

The creative teaching of reading is enhanced as children learn

---

[3] James A. Smith, *Setting Conditions for Creative Teaching in the Elementary School* (Boston: Allyn and Bacon, Inc., 1966), Chapter V.

more and more words and more reading skills, for they are better equipped to put their reading abilities to new uses and new experiences and to create new products. Reading in the intermediate grades should be a powerful tool in the development of creativity.

The instructional jobs of the intermediate-grade teacher, as listed on page 50, will be reviewed below with frequent illustrations of creative teaching. In the lesson above Mr. Banks taught many of these skills in a meaningful and creative way.

Continued Development and Expansion of Primary Reading Skills

Most of the skills to be discussed in this chapter have been introduced in the primary grades. Continued work in developing visual perception, oral vocabulary, sight vocabulary, phonetic and word analysis, word-attack skills, and the use of various context clues continue throughout the child's reading instruction program.

Continued Independent Reading

Power in reading at the intermediate grade level comes from many experiences including:

1. The *mastery of word attack skills* described in Chapter V.
2. The *careful building of a meaningful vocabulary* as each child is exposed to many topics in his science, social studies, arithmetic, and other studies.

It must be remembered that word-attack skills only aid a child in pronouncing a word; they give no clue to its meaning. Consequently, new words should be introduced for the first time at the meaningful experience level, which can be either a direct or a vicarious experience.

The continued development of a sight vocabulary. Many words can be learned all through life simply by remembering the shape of the word. The continuous building of a sight vocabulary provides the teacher with a backlog of known words on which she can build phonic generalizations and exceptions, and on which she can develop reading skills such as those demonstrated by Mr. Banks in the reading lesson above.

Mrs. Ames used a homemade tachistoscope for quick recognition of many words. She cut a piece of oak tag about 5″ x 8″ and

Children need broadening association with many topics for creative reading experiences.

A strong program in children's literature is a part of the creative reading program.

folded it back one-half inch along each of the long sides. This served as a tray to hold her printed materials. She cut an opening in the center of the oak tag strip wide enough to allow for the usual size printed material and fastened another piece of oak tag over this opening with a piece of masking tape to make a hinged shutter. Printed words on slips of paper cards were slipped into the folds on the back of the oak tag and the shutter was flipped for a second to see if the children could recognize new words at a glance. Children used this device in drilling each other.

A workable group plan. Various plans for grouping have been outlined in Chapter III and the merits of each discussed. Rigid ability grouping at the upper elementary grade level is hardly justified (see page 51). At this age children have a variety of reading problems, and the grouping should be centered around their *problems* rather than their *ability*. Very slow children will need to be handled separately much of the time, but those within the average range (and this will constitute 84 percent of the class) can be grouped in a variety of ways to work on a variety of problems. Children should have many opportunities to read together as a total class in lessons similar to the ones described on pages 3 and 105 and at the beginning of this chapter. An independent reading program that is highly individualized is the most logical grouping plan for children of this age and can best foster creative teaching and learning.

Many books and materials on all levels of reading and about many topics. This is an essential requisite if all reading abilities and problems are to be met. The materials for the upper elementary reading program should include copies of many text books, many commercial trade books, SRA materials, reading machines, some workbooks for individual practice, and programmed reading materials for some children. A school library is a *must* for a good intermediate-grade reading program. Three or four sample books from many sets of social studies, science, and arithmetic books are a wiser choice in stocking room libraries than are twenty-five books from one series which are all alike. At least one newspaper and several magazines should be available to children.

A strong program in children's literature. The skill of writing and the joy of reading should be shared daily as a motivation for reading and as a practical way to help boys and girls apply their reading skills. Chapter VII deals with this subject in detail.

Individual records of reading growth and power. Careful records must be kept of each child's reading power. At this age this is possible because children can keep their own records. The SRA materials offer help in this direction. Teachers and children can devise check sheets and record sheets which keep a record of each child's problems, the books he has read, his reading power and the areas where he needs help.

Strong incentives for reading are necessary in order to help each child read independently. Some creative teachers have used the following gimmicks with success in motivating children for independent reading.

1. Keep records of books read on cards or book-jackets. Use the card file to which each child contributes as a master file for the class. In selecting books, children read the file cards to guide them in choosing books classmates have enjoyed.

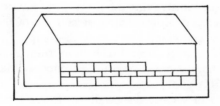

2. Build a reading house of bricks. Each brick represents a book read by a student. A large cardboard contains an outline of a house. Each student, when he finishes a book, writes its name on a brick with his name at the bottom. They start building the house from the bottom and can see it grow as their reading progresses.

3. Build a resource file to help children select books for independent reading.

   a. At the first part of the school year, as the students read books from the room library they write the name of the books, the authors, and one or two sentences about the books on 6 x 9 cards, which are placed in a box in front of the library books. The cards are in constant use—the students seem to select books after reading the cards.

4. Children can make a "bookworm" bulletin board. Cut circles from colored construction paper. Each child makes one to resemble a worm's head, then on assorted colored circles they write the name and

author of each book they read. The circles are pinned overlapping slightly on the bulletin board to make the "bookworm."

5. Many other suggestions are presented in Chapter VII of this book, "The Creative Teaching of Literature and Poetry."

Expanding the Vocabulary and Range of Materials

In the intermediate grades, the child is often introduced to a world of new words through the social studies program of the school and through the expanding, varied number of activities in which he finds himself. Up to this time, most children have been reading material in their social studies books which is familiar to them. They have studied their own community, contrasting communities, and then the history of communities. In each instance, the children have added unique words to their base oral and reading vocabularies, but the bulk of the words were learned in studying their own communities. These vocabularies were developed with meaning, since most of them were derived from the child's common, local, everyday experiences. These base vocabularies made it possible for him to transfer meanings into a study of other communities because all communities are alike to a degree.

In the area of science, especially in topics related to the Space Age, children have acquired a unique vocabulary by the time they reach the fourth grade. Through television, newspapers, movies, and other forms of mass media, children at this age have often integrated a larger vocabulary in some of these areas than their teachers. In selecting and constructing reading and instructional materials, teachers need to recognize this fact, threatening though it may be to some of them.

Also, by the time the child reaches the fourth grade he has learned many things from reading. He is now capable of living many experiences in his mind; that is, word symbols suggest experiences about other people which he can visualize and which he no longer has to experience directly or vicariously in order to understand. His own vast background has given meaning to word symbols to the degree that he can now use them in new thought patterns and imagine the experience being described on the printed page. This ability makes it possible for children of this age to learn a great deal more from books than the early primary child who can only read with understanding about those experiences which are much like his own.

One precaution should be taken in order to avoid reading disability at this time, however; *new* words should still be introduced at the experience level. Social studies books, at best, are a collection of important concepts, and any one page may contain several concepts outside the realm of the child's comprehension. One of the first jobs of the teacher is to be sure that the vocabulary of new words to be introduced for any social studies unit is done at the experience level. For instance, a group of children who are going to study Mexico will need to develop a vocabulary unique to that country in order to be able to use these words with meaning as the unit develops. Such a list might contain such words as "adobe," "sombrero," "serape," "fiesta," "siesta," "tortilla," "frijole," "burro." All of these words can be meaningfully introduced through a good film that shows each and where the teacher stops the film to discuss with the children those parts which give meaning to the words. A word is assigned to an object or an experience in meaning and context so that it has equal meaning when read later in the context of the social studies book.

In addition to the ever-expanding social studies vocabulary of the middle grades, there are several other experiences for which the children need to build new vocabulary—current events, regional experiences, introduction to new heroes, sports and political events, and the ever-widening world of the child as he travels with his family. Reading power can be developed most logically if the child is helped to develop the meaningful oral vocabulary first, then see the words he is speaking put into print as suggested by the language sequence chart in Book II of this series.[4]

A creative teacher will recognize that learning words is a social and academic skill which children of this age must develop and will find many ways to continue to develop the oral and reading vocabulary of every child.

Ideas for building vocabulary in the intermediate grade child:

1. Reread the section on vocabulary development in the chapter on oral vocabulary (see Book II of this series, Chapter V).[5]

2. Keep a vocabulary chart at the front of the room to which all new words discovered or experienced by the class or by individuals are added. Remember that the *sight* of the word will help the child to read it and that children still learn words this way most quickly,

[4] James A. Smith, *Creative Teaching of the Language Arts in the Elementary School* (Boston: Allyn and Bacon, Inc., 1967).

[5] *Ibid.*

even though they now possess many phonetic and word analysis skills.

3. Introduce units by films, film strips, trips, and so forth, so that the oral vocabulary of the material to be developed in the unit is acquired in a meaningful way at the *beginning* of the unit.

4. Refer to Chapter VII (page 208) for ways of using bulletin boards, puppet shows, and such, to develop reading vocabulary.

5. Have children make individual card files of the new words they find. Each child can make a box for his own words and keep them filed alphabetically in his desk.

6. Make individual scrapbooks of words.

7. Play "descriptive" games. Take a word such as "tree." List all the words that could be used to describe a tree—green, tall, stately, rough, smooth, leafy, majestic, twisted.

8. Print sentences or phrases on strips of paper; leave out descriptive words and then print on the chalkboard all the words that would fill the space. Some examples are:

> The _____ house stood in the woods.
> I like to see the _____ light in children's eyes at Christmas.
> The _____ smell of the pine trees.
> The _____ odor of smoke.

9. Make a matching game with new words in one column and meanings in the other.

10. Have each child make his own dictionary of new words. Illustrate dictionaries with verbal descriptions or pictures.

11. Have children make up descriptive riddles.

12. Play guessing games, such as: I am thinking of a word that means a large tank or well in which water is kept. It begins with a "c" and ends with a "d." (Be sure the word is printed on the chalkboard after it is guessed.)

13. Use picture cards with word cards to match. A child who has a picture must find the child with the matching word. Then they sit together to study spelling words or for some other paired activity.

14. The feltboard and stickboard can help to develop new words and new word skills.

15. Flash cards can be used effectively to check reading vocabulary—especially with difficult words.

16. Make word trees. Bring in a branch and set it in a container. Print a key word on a piece of brightly colored construction

paper. Children tie on related words as they discover them. One tree may contain words unique to Alaska, one may contain words describing Canada, one may be built around a new science unit.

17. Print individual stories of each child on shelf paper. Have the child draw an illustration for his story. Make a roll movie of it, and each child can read his story to the class as it comes into view.

18. Use games to develop vocabulary, such as:

    a. *Word Lightning.* The object is to name in one minute as many English words beginning with the letter being worked on as you can. The one who can think of the most will be the score-keeper next round. This would be very helpful in stimulating reading and vocabulary study.

    b. *Word Parchesi.* A parchesi board may be made or drawn on the chalkboard. The spaces will contain words from the vocabulary of the class. The child must give the word definition before he goes on. This can be worked in teams also.

19. *Vocabulary using.* Put several or all of the vocabulary words on slips of paper and/or on the board. Divide the class in groups and have them create original stories around these words. Read the stories to the class or have them exchange stories and read them in groups. This can aid to stimulate the imagination, reinforce the vocabulary, and give practice in oral expression.

Developing More Refined Techniques of Effective Comprehension

Reading without comprehension is not reading. Throughout the primary grades reading comprehension is checked with each day's reading lesson in a variety of ways. Comprehension will be no problem if the child's reading is based on material within his own experience. When he begins to read widely and independently, however, he meets many words he has not experienced, or his experience is limited, and the word does not make sense as applied in a new situation, so comprehension often breaks down. More frequent checks on comprehension are needed, and skills in helping children obtain the meaning of new words and old words used in new situations need to be taught.

Comprehension may be checked in many interesting ways in these grades, as in the following:

1. Listen to children tell stories they have read.
2. Give interesting and unusual book reports (see page 222).

3. Refer to the many good exercises listed in the teacher's manual accompanying basic readers.

4. Show children how to select the most helpful facts to answer a specific question.

5. Prepare exercises with children where they are asked to reorganize a series of closely related thoughts.

    a. Make up and solve cross-word puzzles in subject areas.

    b. Follow directions for making a diorama, slides, roll movies, and so forth.

    c. Read dramatizations and write plays of favorite stories.

6. Prepare cards of more difficult directions for children to follow.

    a. During a class party have a treasure hunt, with clues planted at various places for children to find.

7. Keep a file of individual cards for independent activities with directions for children to follow in preparing materials for the room.

8. *Activity Game.* Teacher can distribute slips of paper with some secret activity to all the children. For example, one might read, "Get out the new book from the top of teacher's closet. Look it over and see what it is about." This will give children an opportunity to talk about something new and of interest to the class at the end of the activity period.

9. Use many methods of studying to develop study techniques. (See Book V of this series[6] for detailed discussion on study techniques for social studies.)

    a. Using guide words to study.

    b. Using outlines to study.

    c. Using dramatization as a study skill.

    d. Setting up questions for study.

    e. Studying by committees.

10. Use outlining as a means of developing comprehension (see Book II of this series[7] for ideas for teaching outlining). Outlining is especially useful in helping children to select minor items that are related to a central thought.

11. *Selecting main ideas.* Use techniques to help children select the central thought in short and long selections.

---

[6] James A. Smith, *Creative Teaching of the Social Studies in the Elementary School* (Boston: Allyn and Bacon, Inc., 1967), Chapter X.

[7] James A. Smith, *Creative Teaching of the Language Arts in the Elementary School* (Boston: Allyn and Bacon, Inc., 1967), Chapter VIII.

a. Collect baby pictures and have children write clever captions for them.

b. Pictures of animals in various poses may be used the same way.

c. Read paragraphs or stories together and then make up titles for them.

12. Read a paragraph and draw a picture showing the main idea *or* read a story and draw many pictures showing a succession of main points. These pictures can be used in a roll movie or a classroom mural.

13. Make a bulletin-board display showing the central idea of a story.

14. Run off a series of paragraphs on a ditto sheet, and at the bottom of the sheet ask a series of questions that point out the main idea of each paragraph. Children match paragraphs and questions.

15. Have the children write paragraphs with the main idea (or sentence) missing. Have each child type or print his paragraph on a 5 x 8 card. On another card print the missing sentence that expresses the main idea. Children will have fun reading each other's paragraphs and matching them to the main ideas.

16. Show children that riddles are often paragraphs without a main idea. Have them write riddles and allow the rest of the class to guess the answers. Then rewrite the riddles as a paragraph with a main idea and use these paragraphs to show that clear, uncluttered writing gives the main idea immediately.

17. Give the children paragraphs to read from which the main idea has been omitted so that they will see how the lack of one sentence in a paragraph can render it meaningless. One such example follows:

It was a lovely place, full of fun and laughter. We saw all the characters from the famous moving pictures made by the inventor. We rode on every sort of ride; for a moment we were Alice in Wonderland and then Peter Pan flying to Never-Never Land. We went from the underwater world of Atlantis to the depths of the African jungle. It was an experience we shall never forget.

This paragraph leaves the reader with an odd, unsatisfied feeling. The sentences are complete, but the explanatory sentence is missing. Read it again but this time add this sentence at the beginning.

Last summer we visited Disneyland.

Now the paragraph takes on a complete meaning. Point out to the children that each paragraph and each article they read will have a main idea. Collect newspaper and magazine articles and underline the main idea in each paragraph.

18. Ask pupils to bring to class colored pictures from calendars, magazines, or advertisements. Mount and number all pictures. On worksheets made of sheets of paper numbered to correspond with the pictures, have each child write a caption appropriate to each picture as it is passed along. Later, when the pictures are placed on the bulletin board, the captions are read and the one that best shows the main idea of the picture is printed below it.

19. *Writing headlines*. By writing headlines children have the experience of writing a complete but brief summary of the BIG idea of the story or article. Collect some short newspaper articles. Paste them on white paper for convenience in handling. Number each article for identification and discussion.

Have each child read an article with the purpose of finding the BIG idea. On a worksheet numbered the same as the articles, write a brief headline telling what the article is about. After all the children have had the opportunity to read and brief the articles, the headlines each wrote may be shared. Who was able to write the most appropriate headline?

20. Help children to select and judge relevant materials. (See Book V of this series,[8] for aids in using research materials.)

    a. Send for material from various resources by writing letters and then judge the material received.

    b. Learn how to use a film catalogue to select classroom films.

    c. Learn how to select, order, and use filmstrips.

21. *Stage-Coach Game*. Equipment: A list of parts of a stage-coach, equipment, and passengers, such as wheel, bridle, harness, springs, cushion, cranky old gentleman, young college girl, maiden lady, young farmer, sacks of apples, newspaper. Also brake, seat, window, laprobe, white-and-black horse, dashboard, foot warmer, suitcase, cane, parasol, canary bird, hat box.

Formation: Players are seated in a circle. One extra player is chosen as Story Teller and gives each player in the circle a name from a list such as the above. The same name may be given to more than one player if the circle is very large.

[8] James A. Smith, *Creative Teaching of the Social Studies in the Elementary School* (Boston: Allyn and Bacon, Inc., 1967), Chapter X.

A story is made up by the Story Teller in which he brings in as many references as possible to the passengers, parts, and equipment. As each name is mentioned, the player who represents that part must stand quickly, whirl around once, and sit down. If the Story Teller should bring in the words "and the stage coach upset" all the players change seats, and the Story Teller tries to get one of the seats. The player who is left without a seat takes up the story and the game continues.

22. Study pictures and paintings to find specific items, such as: Did the artist use any other color besides white to show snow?

23. Develop skills in reading graphs, charts, and maps. (See Chapter X, Book V of this series,[9] for detailed discussion of skill building in this area.)

24. Develop a vocabulary for each unit to be taught in science, social studies, literature, and so forth. (See Book V of this series,[10] for help in developing these skills.)

25. Keep an individual vocabulary notebook in which many word-comprehension skills are recorded: varied meanings, homonyms, synonyms, antonyms, definitions, pronunciations.

26. Help children to adjust speed to purpose; that is, help them to realize that some assignments require skimming, some, careful reading for details.

    a. Teach children to skim by using supplementary reading material printed in columns rather than across pages. Children are told to run their eyes down, selecting key words in each line of print, and to try to reconstruct the story through use of these key words.

    b. Collect headlines and guidelines from newspapers and use them to anticipate story. Check to see how this helps speed comprehension.

    c. Scan sports pages to find batting average, etc.

27. Help children develop skills in rereading for such specific purposes as finding specific facts, slecting general ideas, drawing conclusions.

    a. Have children reread to find clues as to what should be included in a mural or in scenery.

[9] *Ibid.*
[10] *Ibid.,* Chapter VI.

28. Use materials to help children think critically (see Book V of this series[11] for teaching suggestions in this area).

29. Use note-taking to write reports, prepare dramatizations, and so on. (See Book II of this series,[12] for suggestions for the development of this skill.)

30. Provide many books (on all reading levels and on a variety of topics) in the reading center to broaden the scope of the child's leisure reading.

31. Use the teacher's manual of a basic series for ideas for developing comprehension with specific textbook stories.

Developing the Skill of Critical Thinking

A discussion of critical thinking with suggestions for teaching it will be found in Book V of this series.[13]

Developing Techniques for Effective Reading Rate

In a culture where much reading material is available and where the average citizen must read a great deal to remain literate in national and world affairs, speed in reading becomes an essential skill. But speed in reading is a skill only if the reader comprehends what he reads. Part of the problem in developing speed in reading is helping the child *think* about what he reads. The *type of thinking* must help determine the speed. Is he, for instance, reading to think *critically, evaluatively, imaginatively, appreciatively, analytically?* The purpose of reading determines the proper speed for reading. Part of the problem in developing speed for reading, then, is to help the reader recognize material which should be read with speed and that which must be read slowly. Parts of the daily newspaper may be skimmed without losing the essential point of the article, while other parts must be read with great care in order not to confuse essential points of any given issue. Much of the work of the teacher in developing reading rate is to help children determine the intensity of speed to be used with any given article. Children may make lists of material

[11] *Ibid.,* Chapter VIII.

[12] James A. Smith, *Creative Teaching of the Language Arts in the Elementary School* (Boston: Allyn and Bacon, Inc., 1967), Chapter VIII.

[13] James A. Smith, *Creative Teaching of the Social Studies in the Elementary School* (Boston: Allyn and Bacon, Inc., 1967), Chapter VIII.

which should be read carefully and that which should be skimmed. One such list in a fifth-grade classroom looked like this:

Things We Read Carefully

1. Arithmetic problems.
2. Directions.
3. Science experiments.
4. Research material to get facts.
5. Things we read for details.
6. Charts, graphs, maps, globes.

Things We Read Quickly

1. Newspaper articles.
2. Stories.
3. Articles, when we want the main idea.
4. Material in which we are trying to locate something.
5. Cartoons.
6. Comic papers.

Some suggestions for helping children develop speed in reading follow:

1. Examine each article or story the children plan to read together, determine the purpose for reading it, and decide whether it can be skimmed or should be read carefully.

2. To help children develop a skimming skill, have them use their supplementary school reading materials, such as the *Weekly Reader,* or any other paper arranged in columns. Throw one sample on a screen with the opaque projector. After one child has read the column aloud, work with the class in reading each line separately and have them then select and underline the main *word* in each line. Then read the column by reading the key words *down* the page. After awhile try this with other news items without reading the whole item first. After reading down the page, discuss the article, glean its meaning, then check by reading it carefully. Before long, comprehension may be checked by having children read articles in their school papers, textbooks, or supplementary reading materials in this way, and then giving a comprehension test on it. If children can read this way with 70 percent comprehension or more, they are doing well.

3. Poor reading rate generally means a child has a short eye span. He sees only a few words with each eye fixation as his eyes cross a page. Lengthening the eye span helps his reading rate. This can be done by various drills that train the child's eye to recognize a wider span of material.

Put numbers on cards and flash them before the children or on a screen. Have the children tell you the numbers on the card (for example, 3628). As soon as they can do this easily, add numbers to each end of the series (such as 236289). Work a while with these numbers and then add more. Finally, change all the numbers.

Pictures placed on strips of cardboard will also help the children notice more things in one sweep of the eye. Make the strips longer as the children gain proficiency in recognizing and remembering the number of objects and their names.

4. Miss Hartness, a fourth-grade teacher, made a simple television screen from an old mattress box and left a slit in the middle of the screen where she could flash a series of objects or numbers. She had put her series of objects and numbers on shelf paper with a flopen; then she simply rolled each series into view by attaching the roll of paper to long dowels which protruded from the sides of her "TV set," like a large roll movie. The children read these each day as part of a television quiz program.

Later Miss Hartness substituted phrases, such as "in the afternoon," and "around the corner." Then she flashed whole sentences, such as, "John went to the party in the afternoon," and "The party was at Betsy's house, which was just around the corner."

5. Use easy material to improve the children's speed. Familiar material (that which has been read before) may also be used if children are remotivated to reading it. Tell them that you are going to try to develop their speed, so you will use something they know. Then check their comprehension by asking general questions—but not the usual ones.

Easy books with good stories which are new to the children provide good material for reading quickly. Mrs. Frank set aside one period each week in her sixth grade for easy books she brought into the classroom from the town library. Each child was to see how many of these books he could read in one half hour. Comprehension was checked by the discussion that followed.

6. Teacher's manuals accompanying the basic series used in the classroom offer excellent suggestions for increasing speed in reading.

7. Anticipation of material helps children read with speed. Use clues (guide lines, headlines, pictures, charts, graphs, or cartoons) to help children get the gist of the article quickly before they begin to read it. The nature of the material helps children anticipate the vocabulary necessary to read it.

Developing the Skill of Reading Carefully for Directions and Details

Some reading must be slow to the point of being laborious in order to be effective. Reading for directions and for details may fall into this category. In teaching children to read carefully without destroying the speed essential to other kinds of reading, probably the first step again is to help them recognize material that will require slow reading.

In Mrs. Mead's fourth grade, the children made an analysis of their reading over a period of two weeks and listed all the material they had read slowly and carefully. Their list looked like this:

Things We Read Slowly

1. Directions for our test.
2. Stage directions for our play.
3. John read slowly when he learned how to stock the terrarium.
4. Recipes for making candy for our bake sale.
5. Mary read the new fire drill directions to us slowly.
6. Our daily plans.
7. Mrs. Mead read the new playground rules to us slowly.
8. We read our workbook exercises slowly.
9. We read the directions in our girl scout and boy scout manuals slowly.
10. Mrs. Mead read "Uncle Remus" slowly to us.

Later these children made lists of times they had seen their parents read slowly at home.

Times Parents Read Slowly

1. Mother reads recipes slowly and carefully.
2. Father reads slowly when he assembles new furniture, the new lawn mower, or a new toy.
3. Mother reads slowly when she makes out the family schedule for the week.
4. Mother reads her grocery list slowly.
5. We read the bulletin board with rules for using the park slowly.
6. Dad reads the road map slowly.
7. We read directions in our erector sets and science sets slowly.
8. We read our school homework assignments slowly.
9. Mother reads the notices I bring home from school slowly.
10. Mother and Dad read the church bulletin slowly.

A summary of such experiences in Mrs. Mead's room resulted in a chart like this:

Materials We Read Carefully and Slowly

1. Directions.
2. Rules.
3. Recipes.
4. Schedules.
5. Maps.
6. Bulletins and programs.
7. New material.
8. Our daily plans.
9. Dialects.

Once a sensitivity has been built up to what should be read slowly, children will learn to identify this kind of material by glancing at it. A word from the teacher will often help act as a guide while children are learning about differences in material.

Many techniques and methods can be employed to help children read for detail.

1. Just as anticipation of the nature of the article helps build speed, it can help the student read for details. Use headlines, guide-lines, pictures, and maps to determine the nature of a story or article, then have the children list questions which, if answered, would fill in the unknown details of the article. Read to find these answers.

2. Unit teaching offers ample opportunity for helping children find material and read it for detail. In listing and classifying questions at the beginning of a unit, children are setting up realistic conditions for reading for details. (See Book V of this series.) [14]

3. Time tests can be effective in developing speed when used in situations that are fun. Children are given a selection to read in a book related to their independent reading level. The teacher starts them reading and stops them at the end of three minutes. Children estimate the number of words they have read and find the number they are reading per minute. Then they read the same material again to see how much faster familiar material can be read. The results can be graphed so that each child can see his progress over a period of time. Frequent comprehension tests should be given along with the reading to be sure the child is getting meaning from his reading.

Developing Skill in Oral or Audience Type Situations

Oral reading is used much less than silent reading in actual life ex-periences. Consequently, it is not emphasized as heavily in the reading

[14] *Ibid.,* Chapter VI.

program as it once was. Excessive oral reading reduces rate in speed and comprehension. The use of oral reading in the classroom should be restricted to those purposes for which children use oral reading in life. Intermediates use oral reading:

1. To impart and provide information or background material, such as reading to a class about a famous scientist.

2. To prove a point or verify information.
   a. Have children look up populations of countries in several books. Note differences and determine which source is most reliable.
   b. Check with original sources when a debatable or incorrect piece of information is given by a child during a report.
   c. Use newspapers to check batting averages, store prices, etc.

3. To answer questions in a check on content.
   a. See section on social studies in Book V of this series[15] for ideas for teaching this skill. Also see Chapter VIII, Book V, on reading maps and charts.

4. To read written reports (social studies, book reports, reports from interviews).

5. To an audience:
   a. Miss Holmes set up a Story Telling Bureau at a table in the rear of her room. Whenever a child finished a story or a book that he liked well enough to tell to the rest of the class, he put an ad in the bureau offering the name of his story and his services in telling it. Time was provided in the daily program for one such story each day.

6. In giving directions (one child reads directions for making cake or candy for a party while others follow them). Also when one child reads directions from the principal's office for fire drill, air raid drill procedures, or other civil defense drills, and other children listen.

7. For "walking out" a dramatization which children are reading.
   a. See section on sociodramas, Book V of this series.[16]
   b. See section on literature, p. 208, Chapter VII.

8. For reading plans from charts or dittoed sheets which were originally made by the children, such as plans for studying, plans for a play, a field trip or an exhibit, or questions or other material that needs frequent reviewing.
   a. See teaching suggestions, Book V of this series.[17]

[15] *Ibid.,* Chapters VIII and X.
[16] *Ibid.,* Chapter IX.
[17] *Ibid.,* Chapter V.

9. For reading from minutes or notes for class meetings, meetings of book clubs, and so on.

10. For appreciation and fun, such as:

    a. Listening to stories.

    b. Watching filmstrips while a child reads a story (Weston Woods Filmstrips are especially suited to this).

    c. Reading captions on filmstrips.

    d. Reading for dramatization.

    e. Choral reading from books or chalkboard.

    f. Reading reports of favorite books to each other.

    g. Reading poems aloud.

    h. Reading for sociodramas (see Book V of this series).[18]

    i. Reading in role-playing or problem stories.

    j. Reading to accompany flannel-board stories or panto-mimes.

    k. Reading certain verbal games.

11. Have children read stories to each other, or take turns reading parts of the story aloud. Tape the readings and play them back so they may hear themselves. This is an excellent way to improve expression and correct gross mistakes.

Developing More Skilled Approaches to Word Study

Among the word-attack skills developed in most intermediate grades (if they have not already been developed in the primary grades) are the following. Each child:

1. Gains auditory perception of diagraphs and diphthongs, as "oa," "ea," "oo," "ow," "ou," "oi," "oy."

    a. Make a list of words containing the above letters.

    b. Play flashcard game using above letters in words.

    c. Use telephone books to find words having above letters.

    d. Use magazines, *Weekly Reader,* to find words containing such letters.

2. Recognizes phonograms useful in attacking new words ("aw," "ou," "ight," "ick," "ack," "ock," "ing," "old," "ill," "all," "est," "ake," "orn," "ong."

    a. Make a list of words containing letters above.

[18] *Ibid.,* Chapter IX.

3. Recognizes "x," "k," and "s" sound alike (boo*k*s, fo*x*).
    a. Pronounce rhyming words (box, fox).
    b. Give lists of words and have child strike out word that doesn't fit (box, chair, books).
4. Recognizes "s" sometimes has sound of "z" (vi*s*it, bu*s*y).
    a. Use flashcards where necessary.
    b. Use lists of such words for pronunciation.
5. Recognizes words with both voiced and unvoiced "th" (they, their, thin, thought, through).
    a. List words to pronounce orally.
    b. Make up sentences and underline words having voiced or unvoiced "th."
6. Knows that "wh" has sound of "w" in *wh*en, *wh*ere.
7. Knows "wh" has sound of "h" in *wh*o, *wh*ole.
8. Learns the principle of contractions (apostrophe used in place of one or more letters) (see Book II of this series).[19]
9. Learns meaning and uses of common suffixes and prefixes, as "ful," "less," "re," "un."
    a. A wheel with word roots and prefixes and suffixes can be designed to turn so that the words change when new prefixes and suffixes are added to the root words.
10. Receives continued instruction in using the context to develop meaning in passages read.
    a. See teaching suggestions, Book V of this series.[20]
11. Learns that words can have more than one meaning, as "run *fast*," or a "*fast* color."
12. Learns that meanings of words may shift from line to line or page to page.
    a. Make cards showing this:

It was a *fair* day. The Joneses were going to the *fair*.

13. Learns that some words have no meaning until seen in context, such as the word "cleave."

Example: The butcher will *cleave* the beef into several parts. The barnacles will *cleave* to the side of the ship.

[19] James A. Smith, *Creative Teaching of the Language Arts in the Elementary School* (Boston: Allyn and Bacon, Inc., 1967), Chapter VIII.

[20] James A. Smith, *Creative Teaching of the Social Studies in the Elementary School* (Boston: Allyn and Bacon, Inc., 1967), Chapter VIII.

14. Learns that there are exceptions to all rules.

Example: The prefix "in" often negates a word, as in "destructible" and "indestructible"; "valid" and "invalid."

Exception: "valuable" and "invaluable." Meaning not negated—both mean "valuable."

15. Be sure to read Book II of this series,[21] Chapters V, VI and VII, for ideas for expanding the vocabulary of children.

Teaching the Efficient Use of Reference Techniques

To become independently adequate in applying reading skills to the subject-matter areas, the intermediate-grade child will need to master many reference techniques. Specific skills he will need are:

1. The ability to locate information easily (see Book V).[22]
2. The ability to take notes (see Book II).[23]
3. The ability to outline (see Book V).[24]
4. The ability to summarize (see Book V).[25]

Suggestions for teaching these skills are discussed on the pages under each chapter indicated above.

Teaching the Application of Reading Skills

No reading skills should be taught without direct application of the skill to the particular child's reading program. For a highly developed teaching program, a few skills must be extracted, taught and then the learned skill should be applied through continual usage to reading material. Skills are often taught as another part of the language arts program and then applied to reading.

A list of skills needed in the intermediate grades (if not developed

---

[21] James A. Smith, *Creative Teaching of the Language Arts in the Elementary School* (Boston: Allyn and Bacon, Inc., 1967).

[22] James A. Smith, *Creative Teaching of the Social Studies in the Elementary School* (Boston: Allyn and Bacon, Inc., 1967), Chapter VIII.

[23] James A. Smith, *Creative Teaching of the Language Arts in the Elementary School* (Boston: Allyn and Bacon, Inc., 1967), Chapter VIII.

[24] James A. Smith, *Creative Teaching of the Social Studies in the Elementary School* (Boston: Allyn and Bacon, Inc., 1967), Chapter VIII.

[25] *Ibid.,* Chapter XII.

before) in order to promote independent reading and reading power would include:

Dictionary skills: Use the dictionary to—
1. Recognize alphabetical arrangements.
2. Train in the use of guide words.
3. Learn divisions and parts of dictionaries.
4. Learn pronunciations and how to use pronunciation keys.
5. Select suitable meanings for words used in varied context.
6. Understand phonetic spelling and syllabication (using syllables as an aid to spelling and pronunciation).
7. Find single and blended sounds of letters.
8. Interpret diacritical marks.
9. Find and use homonyms, synonyms and antonyms.
10. Recognize simple parts of speech.
11. Recognize symbols for nouns, verbs, and adjectives. (See Book II of this series.)[26]

Book skills: Use various books to learn how to—
1. Use exact title of book in making references.
2. Use author's name in making references to book.
3. Use index and table of contents.
4. Use glossary.
5. Use paragraph headings.
6. Use cross-references.
7. Use preface.
8. Be aware of copyright date.
9. Introduce classification of books and library procedures.
10. Use letter keys of encyclopedia or reference book.
11. Use simple footnotes.

Skills of locating information: This involves the development of—
1. Use of dictionary.
2. Use of encyclopedias (see Book II).[27]
3. Use of almanacs and similar reference materials.
4. Use of film and filmstrip catalogues.
5. Use of television guides.
6. Use of newspapers.
7. Using magazines and periodicals.
8. Using the telephone book with particular emphasis on the yellow pages section.
9. Use of cross-references.
10. Use of free materials indexes for sending for materials.

[26] James A. Smith, *Creative Teaching of the Language Arts in the Elementary School* (Boston: Allyn and Bacon, Inc., 1967), Chapter VIII.

[27] *Ibid,* Chapter VIII.

11. Use of book skills.
12. Use of the school library (call cards, picture files, materials files, and the Dewey Decimal System).
13. Use of periodicals.
14. Use of children's guides to locate materials.
15. Use of room files.
16. Reading maps and charts.

Applying Skills in Selecting Main Ideas

1. See suggestions pages 186–190.
2. Refer to teacher's manual of basic reading series for suggestions and ideas.

Applying Skills in Reading for Beauty and Appreciation

1. See Chapter VII, on children's literature.

Applying Skills in Reading Dialects and Other Levels of Vocabulary

1. In Book II[28] an example was given of the levels of vocabulary to which children are constantly exposed. One such level, often called the "homely" level, includes dialect. For many years textbooks failed to print stories containing dialect because dialect was considered too difficult for children to master. Many children were deprived of the joy of reading such stories as "Uncle Remus" because of the inability to use this skill.

Yet children *do* learn to read dialect. Some of the current comics (such as "Snuffy Smith") are written in dialect. As dialect becomes more and more a part of our printed literature, children are exposed to it more frequently and should be taught to read it.

Dialect is a phonetic reading. Familiar words become unfamiliar because they now appear in different shapes. Teaching dialect reading cannot precede basic training in phonics. As with all reading, children must have oral experiences with dialect before they can hope to pronounce it with phonetic skills. The teacher can read dialect and explain it to children. Most children are exposed to many forms of dialect on television shows (southern dialect, cowboy, Irish). They are as eager to read it as to hear it, for dialect gives the language its contrasting rhythms and patterns.

[28] *Ibid.,* Chapter III.

Other levels of vocabulary should also be taught in the intermediate grades. Classical literature can be introduced as part of a program in literature and creative writing, and at that time children can be taught how to read this level of writing.

One fifth grade was studying the New England States. Kenny brought "The Courtship of Miles Standish" to school because it was about the people they were studying. The teacher realized the reading was above the children's vocabulary level, so she told them the story. She then explained the style in which it was written. She typed and dittoed those parts which she felt the children could read, and they read them first silently, then in an oral audience-type situation. They discussed the beauty of the writing. Many children volunteered to read parts to the class. The entire class enjoyed it so much they decided to dramatize it. Later they included it in a moving-picture film which they made.

At no time during this experience was the beauty of the writing lost to the group. The original was not rewritten or "watered down." To do this is to destroy the literary quality of the writing. Instead, the teacher helped the children bridge the gap between their own inadequacies and the skills required to read the poem. If children are unable to read certain pieces of literature they should not do so without some teaching that gives them the new skills required to enjoy it.

Part of the joy of learning reading skills comes from applying these skills to unexplored areas and making them work. Application of word analysis skills to dialect and classical literature can be a challenging and satisfying experience for intermediate-grade boys and girls.

Reading Levels

Throughout the reading program the teacher must realize that all children operate on three basic reading levels: the independent, the instructional, and the frustration reading level.

At the independent reading level, the child can read with enjoyment and without help from his classmates and teacher. It will generally be below the level of instruction. At this level many easy books are read, and most children enjoy rereading stories they have previously enjoyed. The independent reading level is recognized by the fact that the child can read almost 100 percent of the material selected.

The instructional reading level is that level of reading where the child reads fairly well but needs help in certain reading skills or in the mastery of new vocabulary. It is at this level that actual teaching occurs. The criterion for the instructional level is that the child is reading 80 percent of the selected material independently.

The frustration reading level is that at which the child cannot read well enough to receive enjoyment or understanding from his reading. The criterion is that he reads little of the selected material with comprehension.

Evaluating the Reading Program

A teacher can best evaluate her reading program by noting how the children read, their attitudes toward reading, and their selection of reading materials. Many good reading tests are available, although their frequent misuse has spoiled their effectiveness. Standardized tests help teachers find the ability levels of their students and, in many cases, will help the teacher identify the specific problems of each child. When utilized in this manner the tests can be of extreme value, but when teachers spend their time trying to get children up to "grade level" they are defeating the purpose of such tests. They must remember that the tests are based on norms and norms are averages and, by that very token, half the class must fall above the midpoint and half below. If this is not true, the chances are that the teacher has either a brilliant or a retarded group.

The best readers are those who have a wide background of experience and basic reading skills from which to draw, and who enjoy reading immensely. The most effective way of evaluating a reading program is through the use of individual check sheets that show each child's abilities and needs in reading and indicate clearly his frustration level, his independent level, and his instructional level. Such charts used over a period of time will clearly show the child's progress and will remove threatening grade-level classifications and useless grade indicators. Children can help teachers keep these charts in diagnosing their own difficulties, in planning their own instruction, and in evaluating their own growth. Many excellent charts and scales[29] are available

---

[29] Emmett A. Betts, *Foundation of Reading Instruction* (New York: American Book Co., 1957); and Reading Clinic, Syracuse University, *The Informal Reading Inventory* (Syracuse, N.Y.: Syracuse University Reading Clinic, 1964), mimeographed.

commercially, but children and teachers can do some creative thinking in making their own. The activity of constructing such a chart helps the children understand the teacher's objectives for the entire reading program and creates a high motivational interest in their own reading progress—the first step in the creative process.

Summary

Reading is a skill that develops as a result of a mixture of instruction and the many components making up the personality of the child. Basic to all reading instruction is the awareness on the part of the child that, through reading, he may find the answers to many of his problems and curiosities and experience adventures far removed from his own life. To each child, reading is a personal thing—it serves to round out the knowledge, experience, and concepts his own living cannot afford him. It is a skill he must acquire in order to live effectively in his society.

The teaching of reading must, above all, be exciting, practical, and individual. No child should be hindered in his reading by being forced to wait for a poorer reader. Nor should any child be pushed into material that does not communicate to him. No child should waste time learning skills he already knows. Nor should he be handicapped in his reading ability through lack of adequate materials that are on his level and interesting to him.

The basic purpose of teaching reading is to refine the skills to communicate. The development of these skills gives the child the ability to do new things with his life. Reading, for many children, can unlock the doors to creativity. Most of the skills needed for the good reader are the skills necessary to develop creative people. Teaching reading can contribute substantially to creative development.

TO THE COLLEGE STUDENT

1. Have one class member make a report on "The Individualized Reading Program" from the following viewpoint: The Individualized Reading Program is the most creative approach to the teaching of reading.

2. Work out a series of grouping plans for a reading period of

one hour in any intermediate grade of thirty-two students when the following conditions are present:

1. There are five different ability levels, and on this particular day the teacher is grouping by ability. She has two readers who are two years above grade level, four who are a year above grade level, eight who are reading at the top of the grade, ten who are average, six who are a year or more below grade level, and two who are reading almost nothing.
2. A particular teacher has discovered through the use of a diagnostic reading test that half of her class of thirty children does not comprehend at the 60 percent level, six others are very slow readers, and the remaining nine all have difficulty making generalizations.

In planning this one-hour period, be sure to plan work for all groups so that they may work independently when you are not working with them directly, and *be sure each group is creatively occupied, not just engaged in busy work.*

3. Divide your class into groups and assign each group the job of demonstrating the development of one of the skills listed in this chapter. Try to create an idea of your own, but, if you have difficulty, demonstrate one of the techniques suggested in this chapter.

4. In a fifth-grade classroom a teacher recently said, "I follow the reading manual religiously. After all, the men who write it are experts in their field and know a lot more about reading than I do." What is the fallacy in this teacher's reasoning?

5. Discuss this statement: Reading can be taught creatively without knowing all the things about reading presented in this chapter. What part does knowledge play in creative teaching?

6. Check Mr. Banks' lesson against the objectives listed at the beginning of the chapter. Did he accomplish each? If so, how?

TO THE CLASSROOM TEACHER

1. Make a chart of the skills listed in this chapter so that you can check each pupil's name against it. Then ask yourself what you are doing to develop these skills in each child. If you are not doing much, plan a program that will start you working in the skills-building direction.

2. Do your children know *why* they are reading *every* time you have a reading lesson? Try informing them and see if it makes any difference in their attitude. Reading is a tool and is put to use for a reason. Let the children in on the reason.

3. What program do you have for your slowest and poorest readers? Try meeting with them once a day and printing individual stories, which they dictate, for them to read. Perhaps a good reader who also prints well may do this for you. Allow the slow reader to make as many stories as possible just as fast as he can read them. Spring a surprise story on him once in a while using the same words he is using. Encourage him to bind his stories in book form. Check his speed, comprehension, and vocabulary development over a period of weeks. Is this creative, open-ended learning and teaching?

4. Most reading manuals give lists of questions that can be answered by the children after they have read a specific selection in a reader. This is closed, uncreative learning, for it does not put knowledge to new use. Look over some of the lessons you plan to teach within the next few days and decide on ways you can change them to open-ended lessons where the new knowledge acquired is put to use. For example: The children may be reading about a great invention, such as the telephone. Instead of asking many uninteresting questions, why not start your lesson with this approach: "Today we are going to read about an invention which did a great deal for the world but also created many problems. Let's read to see how that invention came to be and what good it did. You will have to then think about the problems it could and did create."

TO THE COLLEGE STUDENT AND
THE CLASSROOM TEACHER

1. Look at the list of instructional tasks of the intermediate teacher on page 50. Plan a lesson for developing each task which will be creative in that it places children in a situation where they use old skills to develop some new ones.

2. Here are two questions taken from two different sixth-grade reading books:

1. Why was the Battle of New Orleans fought after the War of 1812?
2. Why did Vermont lose population in 1961 while a desert state, Nevada,

and a swamp state, Florida, became the two fastest growing states in the United States?

Which of these two questions is more likely to result in a lesson of critical thinking? Why?

3. Think of five ways you might increase your own reading rate and reading comprehension. If your college has a reading clinic, check to see what methods are used to increase reading speed and comprehension in adults. Are any of these methods applicable to children?

4. Analyze your own study habits. In what ways are you weak? In taking notes, outlining, selecting main ideas from a lecture, taking exams? Try to remember whether you were ever *taught* these skills or whether you just picked them up as you went along through school. How many of these deficiencies are due to improper reading habits? Do you see the value of teaching these skills in the elementary school? Try to work out a plan to help you remove your deficiencies. One resource that will help is *Effective Study,* by Francis P. Robinson (New York: Harper and Brothers, 1948).

5. Review the lesson Mr. Banks taught, which is presented at the beginning of this chapter. Check the skills described in this chapter against his lesson. Note how subtly he taught the skills in his presentation. Discuss these statements:

   a. An integrated language arts program is more meaningful than isolated periods of reading, spelling, and so on.
   b. Mr. Banks spent too much time (a whole afternoon) on teaching reading.
   c. Mr. Banks' lesson was a good example of the language method approach as described in Chapter III.
   d. Mr. Banks met individual needs well without stratifying the children.

6. Review the lesson described at the beginning of this chapter and notice how many objectives Mr. Banks attempted to accomplish in his work. It is more customary for small reading groups to meet and work at one or two objectives. In terms of the philosophy of creative teaching summarized in Chapter I, which of the two approaches sets conditions more conducive for teaching creative reading and developing creative potential?

SELECTED BIBLIOGRAPHY

BOND, GUY and EVA BOND WAGNER. *Teaching the Child to Read* (3rd ed.). New York: The Macmillan Co., 1960.

CUTTS, WARREN G. *Modern Reading Instruction.* Washington, D.C.: Center for Applied Research in Education, Inc., 1964.

DARROW, HELEN FISHER and VIRGIL M. HOWES. *Approaches to Individualized Reading.* New York: Appleton-Century-Crofts, Inc., 1960.

DEBOER, JOHN J. and MARTHA DALLMANN. *The Teaching of Reading.* New York: Holt, Rinehart and Winston, Inc., 1960.

DECHANT, EMERALD. *Improving the Teaching of Reading.* Englewood Cliffs, N.J.: Prentice-Hall, Inc., 1964.

GRAY, LILLIAN and DORA REESE. *Teaching Children to Read.* New York: The Ronald Press Company, 1957.

HARRIS, ALBERT J. *Effective Teaching of Reading.* New York: David McKay Company, Inc., 1962.

HEILMAN, ARTHUR W. *Teaching Reading.* Columbus: Charles E. Merrill Books, Inc., 1961.

KRESS, ROY (ed.). *That All May Learn to Read.* Papers presented at Syracuse University Reading Conference, 1959. Syracuse: Syracuse University Press, 1960.

MCKIM, MARGARET. *Guiding Growth in Reading in the Modern Elementary School.* New York: The Macmillan Company, 1955.

LEFEVRE, CARL A. *Linguistics and the Teaching of Reading.* New York: McGraw-Hill Book Company, Inc., 1964.

RUSSELL, DAVID H. *Children Learn to Read.* New York: Ginn and Co., 1949.

RUSSELL, DAVID and ETTA E. KARP. *Reading Aids Through the Grades.* Columbia University: Bureau of Publications, 1951.

SCHONELL, FRED J. *The Psychology and Teaching of Reading.* New York: Philosophical Library, Inc., 1962.

SMITH, NILA BANTON. *Reading Instruction for Today's Children.* Englewood Cliffs, N.J.: Prentice-Hall, Inc., 1963.

SPACHE, GEORGE and PAUL BERG. *The Art of Efficient Reading.* New York: The Macmillan Company, 1955.

STRANG, RUTH and DONALD LINDQUIST. *The Administrator and the Improvement of Reading.* New York: Appleton-Century-Crofts, Inc., 1960.

TOOZE, RUTH. *Your Children Want to Read.* Englewood Cliffs, N.J.: Prentice-Hall, Inc., 1957.

WOOLF, MAURICE and JEANNE WOOLF. *Remedial Reading.* New York: McGraw-Hill Book Company, Inc., 1957.

# The Creative Teaching of Literature and Poetry

Books are no substitute for living, but they can add immeasurably to its richness. While life is absorbing, books can enhance our sense of significance. When life is difficult, they can give us momentary release from trouble or a new insight into our problems, or provide the rest and refreshment we need. Books have always been a source of information, comfort, and pleasure for people who know how to use them. This is as true for children as for adults. Indeed, it is particularly true for children.[1]

MAY HILL ARBUTHNOT

TO THE READER

The above quotation bears special significance for teachers, for they may enter the world of children through reading children's books. Last year in this country there were as many children's as adult books published. If you have not read any children's books lately, read several before you read this chapter. It will take on more meaning for you if you do.

Introduction

Miss Wilson typed the story of "The Elephant's Child" on ditto paper for her fourth grade and numbered each paragraph. Today's reading lesson was to be a combination of teaching new words in meaningful context and enjoying a good piece of literature. And it was to be a period when *all* children might enjoy reading together for a change rather than in small reading groups. Miss Wilson planned one such period each week, and the children always looked forward to it.

Miss Wilson knew her children well. She was well aware of their reading skills and abilities. She knew which of those numbered paragraphs Sammy and Julia could read and which they could not. She knew which words would be new to the entire group and which would be new to certain children.

[1] May Hill Arbuthnot, *Children and Books* (Chicago: Scott, Foresman and Co., 1957), p. 2.

She had many objectives in mind in planning her lesson. For one, she intended to use it as an audience-type situation in order to check the children's oral expression in reading. For another thing, she planned to use the lesson as a means of developing certain word analysis and phonetic skills. She also intended to build a picturesque vocabulary among all the children while realizing that some children would learn more words than others. She planned to use the whole of Friday afternoon to integrate literature, oral expression, reading, music, and art.

The children had been studying jungle life and jungle animals. This accounted for Miss Wilson's choice of "The Elephant's Child." Miss Wilson planned to do a great deal with Kipling's work and this was to be the children's introduction to him.

At school time she asked all the children to take their seats. She told them she had a story about some animals who lived in the jungle and she wanted to read it to them. The children were ready at once, and Miss Wilson read the story with all the expression and drama she could muster. A discussion followed—and then a hunt for new words, which were placed on the board.

"I knew you would enjoy this story," said Miss Wilson, "and I ran off some copies for you so that we might read it together. While I am passing out these copies, will you think of someone to choose in this room who can make a voice like a baby elephant—like the elephant's child?"

Soon five names were suggested, and each of the five children was asked to read a selection from the dittoed papers, speaking like the elephant's child. After each had tried out for the part, they were asked to leave the room, and the children voted for the one they thought was best. Mark was chosen, and the children returned to the classroom.

Miss Wilson asked the children to take the dittoed sheets and find a paragraph which they could read well. While they were scanning the sheets, she walked around the room and assigned certain paragraphs to her slower or poorer readers.

When all the numbered paragraphs had been assigned, Miss Wilson suggested that the children read the story through once so she could help in the pronunciation of new words and they could all "feel" their voices. Mark, of course, read each time the elephant's child spoke.

"Now," said Miss Wilson, "I have here several records and I am going to play a small part of each one. While I'm playing them, will each of you think of the one you feel goes best with this story because it has the same rhythm, the feeling of the jungle, and seems to make a good background—just like they have a musical background in the movies."

She played excerpts from five different records. The children chose *The Theme from the Sundowners* as the one they felt to be most appropriate.

Miss Wilson then suggested that the children think of a way they might announce the story if they were to read it and put it on tape while the music played in the background. The ideas were written on the chalkboard; the class finally agreed on this one:

Miss Wilson's Fourth Grade Class
Presents
THE ELEPHANT'S CHILD
by
Rudyard Kipling

Mark was asked to read it. The children then read the story into the tape recorder (while the music played in the background) passing the "mike" from one child to another.

"Before we hear how the story sounds on tape," said Miss Wilson, "I have something else here that I know you will enjoy doing. Here are some frosted and plain pieces of glass, which will fit into our lantern slide. Now, I want you to think about what will happen if we draw pictures on these slides and put them in the projector. Remember our science unit on light? How might we make colored pictures on these glass slides which will show up as colored on the screen in the front of the room?"

The children discussed this problem. Many new words were introduced and placed on the vocabulary chart at the front of the room—words like transparent, translucent, projection. Some experimentation took place; they tried different media on the slides and tested to see whether the color would project onto the screen. The children found out that ordinary wax crayon cast only a shadow on the screen and that the color was lost. At this point, Miss Wilson introduced transparent Eastman crayons, which do project color. Soon a list of media that project color appeared at the front of the room, including the following: flo-pen ink, water colors, colored cellophane, Eastman crayons, colored ball-point pens, tissue paper, regular ink.

The children also discovered that some media could be applied directly to the frosted glass while others, such as the cellophane and tissue paper, had to be arranged and held in place with two pieces of clear glass, taped together with masking tape.

Each child then decided how he would make a slide to go with the paragraph he read—he could use any medium from the box of materials that Miss Wilson had placed in the front of the room. After each child had selected his materials and was working at his desk, Miss Wilson again played the music from *The Sundowners* to help the children keep the mood of the story. Each child was instructed to number his picture in the left-hand corner to correspond with the number on his paragraph. Children who finished early were set to work making and decorating title slides and one that said "The End." As each drawing was completed the children brought it to the front of the room and put it in a box in the proper order.

Soon the production was ready. Miss Wilson chose two capable children to run the slides with the tape, and the children saw their own interpretation of "The Elephant's Child" in a combination of music, picture, color, and voice. They were so delighted with the project that they burst into applause at the end. Immediately they proposed showing it to other children in the school. So a list of the classes that might enjoy it was made on the chalkboard. A date was set to show it and a committee dispatched to the principal's office to sign up for the auditorium on the chosen date. Invitations were written and delivered, and, before the children went home, they had to see the story once more.

*   *   *

In the above account we have an excellent example of the creative teaching of literature and reading. In her lesson, Miss Wilson employed all the basic principles of creative teaching discussed in Chapter I. On subsequent days the children used their vocabulary chart to discuss word structure and phonetic structure. They were asked to show their project at a PTA meeting, and this resulted in poster-making and the study of the writing of announcements and letters of thanks. The basic "conforming" skills were learned by every child while all kinds of creative, individual products were being produced. Creative teaching accomplishes so much more than traditional teaching in the same length of time.

The following suggestions and illustrations are ideas that creative teachers have used to develop an enthusiasm and love for reading, literature, and poetry among children while at the same time developing their own creative powers.

General Conditions That Build Appreciations and Standards in Literature

1. Have a library corner with good books easily available.

2. Keep a bulletin board of good books before the class. Discarded book jackets, posters, and pictures of favorite authors will help make these bulletin boards attractive.

3. Read a poem or story to the class at least once a day.

4. Encourage children to share the good books they have read by providing time during "sharing" periods.

5. Provide time every day for children to choose favorite books and to read silently.

6. Encourage the children to tell and write stories, poems, and books.

7. Take the class to good motion pictures of great pieces of literature or show these films in the classroom.

8. Use film strips, such as those of the Weston Woods, to create an interest in new books.

9. Use creative book reports for children to share each other's literature experiences (see page 222).

10. Draw or paint pictures of favorite poems, books, or characters.

11. Encourage children to share their home libraries with the class. Ask them to bring three or four books from home and tell the others about them while they show the pictures.

12. Encourage frequent trips to the town library or the school library.

13. Reserve time occasionally for the school librarian to come into the room and show new books from the library or tell a story.

14. Encourage children to take advantage of local children's theater groups or traveling companies who do a notable adaptation of some piece of children's literature.

15. Watch the paper for good commercial television shows that portray some great children's literature.

16. Play some of the better commercial recordings of dramatiza-

tions of children's stories, such as *Hansel and Gretel, The Littlest Angel, The Christmas Carol, Peter and the Wolf.*

17. Organize a Book Club that meets once a week in your class-room.

18. Children can make their own book jackets for their favorite books.

19. Make up good book lists for parents and have them dittoed to be sent home. This may be done around Thanksgiving time as a guide for parents in purchasing children's books for Christmas gifts.

20. Watch for radio programs that dramatize children's literature.

21. In art class, have the children make posters of books they like. When made in three dimensions these posters add interest to book exhibits, library displays, and bulletin board exhibits.

22. Devote a few assemblies each year to programs about books. If each grade would take responsibility for putting on one assembly program during the year to which other classes were invited, the children would be constantly exposed to books on all reading levels and all topics.

23. Celebrate Book Week with assemblies, exhibits, visits from authors, library trips, story hours, displays, and special programs. Be sure all children have a part in preparing for Book Week. (Many ideas for Book Week programs may be found on the following pages.)

24. Hold at least one or two Book Fairs a year where the materials made by the children may be exhibited. However, a fair should expose children to hundreds of new and exciting books. It will be necessary to arrange for traveling commercial exhibits and book companies to exhibit. The books should be covered with strong plastic covers so that they may be handled and skimmed by children.

25. Correlate literature with all your classroom work. In social studies, read great books to help children understand the life of any given country. *Heidi* correlates well with a study of Switzerland, *The Secret Garden* with England. Kipling's stories relate well to India, and *The White Stag* is perfect reading when studying the countries of central Europe (see Book V of this series[2]). Many books provide excellent material for dealing with social problems and may be used in bibliotherapy (see Book V).

26. In grammar classes, styles of writing may be studied by reading from various authors. Much literature has been set to music, such

[2] James A. Smith, *Creative Teaching of the Social Studies in the Elementary School* (Boston: Allyn and Bacon, Inc., 1967), Chapter VIII.

as "The Lord's Prayer," "The Owl and the Pussycat," "Little Boy Blue," "A Nautical Ballad," "Cradle Hymn," "The Nutcracker." Less notable ones that are, nonetheless, part of the children's rightful heritage, are "The Night Before Christmas," nursery rhymes, and folk ballads of the west, the mountains, and the plains. Music and literature can be closely correlated by singing some of the great poems set to music or by hearing them sung by great artists on high fidelity recordings. Every aspect of the school curriculum may be correlated with some great children's story or poem.

27. Art work is a close companion to literature. Correlations in art have already been suggested in bulletin-board displays; creative book reports; drawing and painting pictures of stories, books and poems; making posters, and book week exhibits and displays. Other ways art may be correlated are:

1. Use cut-out illustrations for children's favorite selections.
2. Use crayon sketches.
3. Use block print designs for posters and for covers for Book Week Programs.
4. Have the children fingerpaint pictures of the literature they read.
5. Spatter-paint designs can be used as variety in illustration.
6. Make silhouette designs of favorite scenes from their readings.
7. Colored chalk lends variety to illustrations, especially in covering large surfaces such as murals or backdrops for dramatizations.
8. Favorite characters can be depicted with soap carvings.
9. Sand-table scenes of favorite stories may be constructed.
10. Wood models may also be constructed.
11. Dolls may be dressed to represent story-book characters (real and paper dolls).
12. Prints (potato prints, cork prints, and linoleum prints) may be used to make book covers, program covers, and invitations to Book Week programs.

On the following pages, other art activities are suggested through clay modeling, mural painting, puppet shows, shadow plays, map-making, costume-making, and flannelgraph presentations.

28. Development of good oral expression can be closely allied with the development of an appreciation of good literature (see Book II of this series).[3] In reading stories to the class the goals of good oral presentation—poise before the group, clear enunciation, correct pronunciation of words, correct phrasing, the use of a pleasant and in-

---

[3] James A. Smith, *Creative Teaching of the Language Arts in the Elementary School* (Boston: Allyn and Bacon, Inc., 1967), Chapter V.

teresting speaking voice, and the ability to read with expression—can be developed.

29. In addition to the many activities suggested in Book II of this series[4] which may be correlated with literature, children will enjoy many described on the following pages. Other possibilities include making tape recordings of their favorite selections or stories; story-book quizzes made up by the children; the reading of favorite selections to each other; telling the saddest part or the most humorous part of the story; holding a tall tale contest; reading or quoting favorite poems; showing and telling about the illustrations; and holding round-table discussions of favorite books, stories, characters, incidents and authors.

30. We have already seen how written expression can be correlated with literature in many ways in Book II of this series.[5] When the children create their own literature they will appreciate that of the writers. Some activities to develop written expression are: writing plays and radio or TV scripts, writing character sketches, making dictionaries or reference books containing new or strange terms, collecting sayings, making riddles, keeping individual records of books read, writing short reviews for a local or school newspaper, making and working crossword puzzles, writing letters to friends about books, making animated book lists for children in another grade or of another age, and writing biographies of authors.

31. Keep a good, up-to-date anthology of children's literature on your desk so that, at your fingertips, you have a story or poem to use on any occasion.

Contrived Conditions That Build Appreciations and Standards in Literature

Dramatization. Most obvious of all the ways to live literature is through dramatization, which helps the children get the feel of the characters and sense the mood of the story. Many stories and poems lend themselves well to dramatization. The dramatizing of a poem or story can be creative in itself if children are encouraged to interpret characters, improvise props, and develop moods.

If we apply the principles of the creative situation to dramatization, however, we must go beyond a simple dramatization of a story in

[4] *Ibid.,* Chapter V.
[5] *Ibid.,* Chapter VI.

Creative dramatization builds a "feel" for literature

order to build up those qualities which make for creative and critical thinking. Mr. Brooks, a sixth-grade teacher, read *The Adventures of Tom Sawyer* to his children. They then chose to dramatize the fence-painting scene. Many children volunteered to play the parts. Mr. Brooks chose a cast and gave them a few minutes to get simple props and to establish a crude setting. Then the group dramatized the scene. When they had finished, Mr. Brooks and the rest of the sixth grade told what they had liked about the scene and also made suggestions as to how it could be improved.

Then another cast depicted the scene. In the discussion that followed, Mr. Brooks pointed out that the differences in the interpretation were good, since different characters could be portrayed different ways without spoiling the plot of the story. The children also noted that the character of Aunt Polly lent itself least to a varied interpretation.

Through evaluation of this sort, children come to understand characterization very well. They also use words that describe the characters they are portraying, thus developing a good oral vocabulary for later use in their own writing.

Dramatization does not always have to be a story. Little children dramatize freely—they will mimic ducks, chickens, and pigs as easily as they mimic people. Intermediate-grade teachers might well make use of this technique to build up the idea of character. Here are some kinds of dramatizations other than stories teachers may use.

1. Pretend you are an animal. Act like the animal you choose and let the class guess what you are.
2. The next time you go to a shopping center watch one person closely. Then dramatize this person for us and we will see if we can tell what he was doing.
3. Show anger, pain, hunger, fear, joy.
4. Working in groups, dramatize a scene you saw during the past week at home or in school. Use no voice, just pantomime.
5. Dramatize a holiday using no sound, only action.
6. Dramatize a day and have the class guess what the weather is like on that particular day.
7. Dramatize such words as "airy," "beauty," "hopeful," "tremble," "painful," "exciting."
8. Dramatize your spelling words.
9. Dramatize one line of poetry.
10. Pretend you are in a circus. Show us what you do.

Poetry also lends itself well to dramatization. Mr. Palmer's sixth grade dramatized "Casey at the Bat"; Miss Hobart's third grade did

Kindergarten children build "Little Toot" during their free play period.

"The Elf and the Dormouse." In both instances the children came to understand the drama and humor in the poems.

Some books lend themselves to other kinds of dramatizations such as pageants, shadow plays, or puppet plays. A discussion of some of these forms of dramatizations appear in Book V of this series, *Creative Teaching of the Social Studies in the Elementary School,* Chapter IX.

Telling and reading stories. Both telling and reading stories have a place in presenting good literature to children. Some stories, poems, and plays are written in such a way that to tell them would be to spoil them. This is especially true of books where the script rhymes or where especially beautiful words are used to set a specific tone for the story. Dr. Suess's rhyming books need to be read (unless the teacher can memorize the script). Robert McCluskey's *Time of Wonder* is a book that needs to be read because of the way this particular author uses the soft sounds of "s" and "c" to give the impression of the softness of fog and rain, and the way he uses other sounds to develop an audio atmosphere for his story.

Literature comes alive in a creative dramatization of
Robin Hood.

Other books should be read because of the close relationship between the story and the pictures. Many primary books are written in such a way that the pictures help tell the story. McCluskey's *Blueberries for Sal* and *Make Way for Ducklings* are good examples of such books. When books of this nature are read, it is essential that the teacher set proper physical conditions so that all children can easily see the pictures.

When the teacher *tells* a story, something different happens. When read the book is the focus of attention for both teacher and children; but when a story is told the focus of attention is the teacher's face. Her voice inflections, her expression, her degree of animation, and her own enthusiasm play the major part in putting the story across. The art of storytelling has almost become a lost one. It is due for a revival. Children gain something unique and special from this kind of experience with literature.

In telling stories the teacher need not memorize them; this often makes for a stilted and wooden performance. She needs to know the story well, with the logical sequence of events carefully organized in her mind. Even more important than this, she must memorize the words, lines, or phrases that give the story its personality and charm—and repeat them in exactly the right places.

Because folk tales have always been passed along from mouth to mouth, they lend themselves especially well to telling. Such stories as "The King of the Golden River," "The Man Who Kept House," "The Gingerbread Boy," "East of the Sun and West of the Moon," and "The Princess of the Glass Hill" are especially suitable for telling. Legends and fairy tales fall into the same category.

Proper physical conditions are essential in storytelling. All distractions should be removed. Children should probably sit facing the quietest wall in the classroom. The teacher should stand if children are seated—at any rate she must be easily seen. Her own voice must be sure and clear. Her face must show the animation and expression necessary to project the story as well as the mode or feeling of the words. She must see herself as the author, telling the story directly to the audience for which it was written.

Storytelling becomes highly personal in that it is person-to-person, with no barriers or distractions. It is communication in its most elementary and most beautiful form. The great literature of the past was all passed along this way before man could read and write. All children should experience the joy of hearing their teachers tell stories, since this is the way young children will communicate at home before *they* can read and write. Storytelling is an art children should be encouraged to keep through their lives, and teachers can set conditions for this art to develop in their classrooms.

Making films. Film-making is less expensive today than it was, and children can have many worthwhile experiences making a real movie and showing it to other children. Actually, making a moving picture is not much different from making a play—only much more permanent! An 8mm camera can be used with black and white or colored film. Taking movies is so simple with modern built-in viewfinders that children can be taught quickly how to do it.

Mrs. Briggs's fourth grade enjoyed reading "Hansel and Gretel" so much that they decided they would make a moving-picture film of it. Mrs. Briggs borrowed a camera for the shooting of the film. The children had raised some money for classroom activities and they used it to purchase the film.

First they adapted the story to a movie version. Then, as they had no indoor lighting equipment, they obtained some large sheets of cardboard from a box manufacturer, and on this they painted a cottage scene to set up outdoors. For the woods scene, they used the woods behind the school. They also painted, on heavy cardboard, a gingerbread house to set up in the woods.

Costumes were simple and were made for the most part from crepe paper. Props were gathered from around the school or brought from home.

A book on moving-picture making was obtained from the library. The children learned a movie-making vocabulary and talked in terms of "going out on location" or "building the set."

The cast of main characters was chosen through a discussion where criteria were established for each part; then children tried out for the parts. Voting was done in terms of the established criteria and performance.

While only a few children were chosen for the main parts, all of them took part some way. Some made titles, some painted scenes, some cared for costumes. There were scene designers, directors, camera men, editors and a make-up crew. All the children took part in one dance, "Brother Come and Dance with Me," which they called their "production number."

The scenes were shot in true Hollywood style, not in sequence but whenever they were ready, providing, of course, that the weather was suitable.

After the film was developed, returned, edited, and shown, the children decided to put the songs, music, and script on a tape to go with the moving picture.

The entire project cost $12.00 and keeping track of the expenses provided some excellent arithmetic experiences.

The children showed the film at a P.T.A. meeting, where Mrs. Briggs explained the learning values that came from the work. They called this showing their "World Premiere" and advertised it as such.

These children lived this story with every fiber of their beings. Such an experience made them appreciate good stories and gave them the opportunity for many social and academic experiences.

Book reports. There are many ways of giving book reports so that they are creative and challenging to children. Too often, books are read for the primary purpose of making a report on Book Report Day,

A dramatization of "Hansel and Gretel."

which makes the literature secondary. Book reports assigned in this manner often make a child hate a book. If he has liked the book he will *want* to tell others about it! The inventive teacher will find many ways to encourage the child to *tell* about his book.

*   *   *

Miss Wagner organized her class into a Book Club that met from one to two o'clock every Friday. Each Friday morning the members of the class were divided into five groups. Then the children took their weekly trip to the library, where, in addition to other books, each child chose one book he wanted to read for fun and brought it back to the classroom.

During Book Club time the groups met around five tables, and for the first five minutes everyone looked at the books each child chose for fun reading. Then each group selected one book and a child to read it to them. The five groups sat at different places in the room where a story was read to them. After half an hour they discussed whether they wanted to report on their book to the rest of the class. If they did, they decided on interesting ways in which they might present the book and selected one. During the following week they had time to prepare their report.

The last fifteen minutes of each Book Club meeting was spent in the presentation of one group's report. Thelma's group read "The Five Chinese Brothers," and with Miss Wagner's help they gave the following presentation:

The six girls on the committee made flowers for their hair from colored facial tissues. They made their eyes look oriental with an eyebrow pencil. Then each made a picture of one of the Chinese brothers, accenting his unique feature—such as the legs that stretched or the neck that could not be cut off. These pictures were made on wrapping paper so they rolled up easily. Each girl brought an oriental Hallowe'en costume from home, or a kimono or house coat.

At the beginning of the presentation, the children played the record, "The March of the Siamese Children." Then Thelma tiptoed into the room and stood before the group. The five other girls minced in behind her, holding their rolled-up pictures, and stood in a row behind Thelma. Thelma bowed deeply to Miss Wagner. "Honorable Teacher," she said. Then she bowed to the class, "And Honorable Classmates," she added, "I would tell you a story about five

Chinese brothers. Now each brother had something very strange about him. One had a neck that could not be cut off." At this line, Becky tip-toed to the front of the improvised stage and let her picture unroll. Each character was introduced in this way.

After this, Thelma invited the class to read the book to find out what happened to them, and the six Chinese sisters minced out of the room while Miss Wagner turned off the record player.

Bill and Sid gave their book report by using a flannel board. It worked out very well for *Robinson Crusoe,* because new characters and objects could be added to develop the scene as they went along.

A group of five boys gave scenes from *Treasure Island* by using a sheet with a light behind it to make a shadow graph. Scenery was made by simply tearing or cutting shapes from wrapping paper and pinning them to the sheet so that the shadow made a setting. Another group chose different scenes from their story and pasted them in sequence on shelf paper from which they made a roll movie.

Projects such as these not only arouse children's creative thinking, they serve the additional objective of making literature live.

Bulletin boards. Bulletin boards can be exciting condition-setters for experiences with good literature. Throughout this book frequent mention has been made of the bulletin board as an instructional device.

A "Book Report" Fair using dioramas.

Bulletin boards may be arranged for a variety of objectives; in the realm of children's literature some of them are:

1. Motivation to interest children in new books or poems.
2. To have the children share their writing and reading with their classmates.
3. To summarize an experience in literature.
4. To impart information.
5. To provide individual instruction or individual work for the children.
6. To share beautiful passages, phrases, or words.
7. To encourage creative writing on the part of the children.
8. To advertise or announce new books and events about books.
9. To display first editions, unusual books, or illustrations in books.

Let us see how some teachers used the bulletin board to fulfill each of these objectives.

*   *   *

Miss Lowe used book jackets to motivate the children to read new books in the room. She put a sign above the colorful jackets which read, "Have You Read These New Books?"

On another occasion she used riddles. She pasted on cards pictures from the book jackets and then beside them printed "Who was it that became lost in the haunted house?" or "What book in this room tells about a family that lived through a terrible hurricane?"

Miss Lowe also kept a record of the children's favorite authors. When one of these authors published a new book, she put a picture of him on the bulletin board and surrounded it with titles of his works or a book jacket, captioning the bulletin board with "A new book by Dr. Suess!"

Book catalogues were also clipped apart and used to make summary cards of books. Miss Lowe used these first of all on a bulletin board, and then in a file to guide children in selecting books that were of interest to them.

*   *   *

Miss Gilbert used her bulletin board to post the children's own writings. She often built the bulletin board around a theme such as, "It is snowing, and our authors have written about the snow," or "Poems for Children *by* Children."

Often she asked the children to choose lines of poetry or selections of prose and print them on a 5 x 8 card. Each child then painted or drew a picture to go with his selection. This material provided a great deal of interest over a long period of time.

Miss Gilbert also used some of her own favorite selections illustrated by a picture or a painting. Once she had the children finger-paint for her, with the purpose of selecting a line of poetry to go with each painting. The next day the children found poetry of their own to match the paintings.

Bulletin boards provide motivation for editing any sort of personal writing or printing so that it will be in proper form to share with other people.

*   *   *

Miss Nelson used her bulletin board a great deal as a summary of experiences with literature. After her fourth grade had read Kipling's "How the Camel Got His Hump," the children built a scene of the story from cut construction paper.

On another occasion Miss Nelson used Carl Sandburg's "Fog" as motivation for some creative writing on a foggy day. She printed the poem on a cardboard and centered it on a bulletin board. After the children had discussed it, and then discussed the fog, they made up phrases and poems describing the fog, which were posted around the poem. One child suggested the title "Foggy Ideas," which was printed and placed over the bulletin board.

Miss Nelson brought in an armful of old magazines one day. After she read them the poem, "America the Beautiful," the children went through the magazines and found pictures to illustrate the poem. These were then mounted on the bulletin board around a printed copy of the poem. On another occasion, the children drew their own pictures.

Miss Nelson used the bulletin board a great deal to integrate social studies with literature. Bulletin boards built around such topics as "Stories about Mexico," "Children in Other Lands," "Children in Trouble," "Books About Living Together" helped Miss Nelson direct the children's attention to the literature dealing with the topic being studied.

When the fourth grade was studying Indians, Miss Nelson introduced the unit by reading "The Song of Hiawatha" while she played soft drum music on the record player. From this reading came a dramatization followed by questions about Indian life. This led to a

bulletin board built around the questions and pictures of Indians depicting the answers.

A bulletin board can be invaluable in summarizing experiences
in literature.

*   *   *

Mr. Lowery used bulletin boards a great deal to impart information. Beside the more common uses of the bulletin board (such as
posting announcements of school functions, radio and television programs worth seeing, and the like), he used it for current events,
community activities and problems, and outstanding current world
problems.

Often Mr. Lowery used his bulletin board to impart news about
a certain author in whom the children were interested. Generally he
found a picture of the author and selected interesting facts about his
life to dramatize by printing and illustrating them on cards. He always
made a bulletin board on the Newberry and Caldecott award-winning
books.

Mr. Lowery found the bulletin board was of great value in summarizing stories. Often he wrote a summary of a book and encouraged
the children to fill out the bulletin board by providing space for their
book summaries on it.

When Mr. Lowery was teaching a unit, he often used the bulletin
board as a reference center. Under the title "Resources for Our Unit,"
he would pin envelopes to the bulletin board with titles such as these
printed on them: "Legends of Mexico," "Stories Written in Mexico,"
"Mexican Authors," "Picture Books of Mexico," "Books for Research
on Mexico." Inside the envelopes were cards on which were printed
the author, title, publishing company, and publishing date of many
books under each category. A sign at the bottom of the bulletin
board ("Can You Add to These Packets?") encouraged the children
to make a record of the books they found.

*   *   *

Mrs. Gaines used a bulletin board in her room to meet individual differences and as a means of providing individual instruction.

One day the children decided to make a marionette show of
Alice in Wonderland. The day after the show was planned, a simple
set of directions for stringing a marionette appeared on the bulletin
board and below this the necessary materials for doing so. This gave
the children a worthwhile independent activity to pursue when their

other work was finished and freed Mrs. Gaines to work with those children who needed her most.

On another occasion, Mrs. Gaines placed step-by-step directions for binding a book on the bulletin board; she also used the board to instruct the children in the basic process of cutting a block print; and at one time she showed them how to take a book out of the library by use of the call numbers.

Mrs. Gaines used one bulletin board next to the chalk board to meet individual differences in children's reading ability and interests. Each child was given an envelope on which to print his name. Each envelope was pinned on this bulletin board under the sign, "Here Are Some Special Books You Will Enjoy." Mrs. Gaines then made simple cards of books best suited to each child's ability and interest and dropped them into the child's envelope. All the children were encouraged to go to these envelopes when they had any free time during the day. The envelopes were also explored previous to each trip to the school library so that the children could look for definite books while they were there.

Sometimes Mrs. Gaines suggested special activities in the children's envelopes. Billy, who was a slow reader, was not only directed to read a certain book whose vocabulary was compatible with his reading level; he was also encouraged to make a picture of it for the bulletin board. And Maxine, who was reading on a grade level three years in advance of her own grade, was encouraged to read a more adult book and to write an illustrated summary of it for the bulletin board.

*   *   *

Many suggestions have already been given as to how to use bulletin boards to share beautiful passages, phrases, or words (see pages 97, 183, 225) and as a motivation for encouraging creative writing (see Book II of this series). The teacher can readily see that bulletin boards can be made exciting by displaying original illustrations borrowed from publishing houses or by displaying first editions of great children's classics.

Mrs. Eggert selected some great paintings and tied art and literature together in various ways. One day she mounted a lovely reproduction of Winslow's "Blue Boy" on the bulletin board. Below the bulletin board she opened a book to Eugene Field's "Little Boy Blue." Then she printed beneath the picture, "An artist expressed his idea of a blue boy this way. A poet expressed his idea about Little Boy Blue this way. How would you do it?"

One day she displayed a picture from a magazine showing an icy abstraction done in shades of blue. Above it she lettered, "This picture made me think of these poems. What does it make you think of?" Around the picture she mounted such poems as Robert Frost's "Stopping by Woods on a Snowy Evening," excerpts from Lowell's "The First Snowfall," Shakespeare's "When Icicles Hang by the Wall," James Stephens' "White Fields," and Sara Teasdale's "February Twilight." Books of poems below the bulletin board on a table encouraged the children to look for other poems.

Often Mrs. Eggert found a beautiful picture from a magazine or a calendar which she saved for the bulletin board, using this caption, "List the poem this reminds you of." A cardboard of empty lines with a flo-pen attached encouraged the children to write titles under the picture.

*   *   *

Bulletin boards can be very creative and helpful in setting conditions for the enjoyment of literature. To be creative they must be ingenious, fresh, and interesting so as to provide an outlet for creative expression much as a painting or a clay modeling will. Here are a few suggestions that should be considered in making bulletin boards that place no restrictions on the creator.

1. The overall effect of the completed bulletin board should be as good in design and as pleasing to the eye as a painting. Too much material can make bulletin boards confusing and cluttered.
2. Any lettering should be as much a part of the total design as the other material on the bulletin board. It should not be tacked on as an afterthought.
3. Bulletin boards are more attractive if material is grouped according to related ideas rather than simply spread out in any manner. Rest spaces for the eye help the purpose of the bulletin board to become more apparent.
4. Every bulletin board should be centered around an idea or purpose and that idea or purpose should be outstanding enough both to be immediately recognizable and to be conveyed across the room. The main idea should attract the children so that they are drawn to the bulletin board to read or see the subtopics. Importance can be obtained for the outstanding idea by having it larger in size, brighter in color, or more prominently placed than any other idea on the bulletin board.

Displays and exhibits. Displays and exhibits can help children develop a love of books. Many schools have Book Fairs during Book Week when all the grades display the creations they have made which relate to good children's books. Often, assembly programs are given to stimulate an interest in stories and poems. Exhibits of commercial books, original sketches for various books, and bulletin boards of the authors and their lives can add a great deal of interest to such an exhibit. To make the exhibit even more meaningful and "live," films may be scheduled at various times. Many schools invite an author to be present to tell stories or to sketch for the children.

Commercial publishing houses will supply catalogues for such exhibits. Children should have the opportunity to handle books and help select those which are to be purchased for the school library. Good children's magazines and periodicals should constitute a portion of book exhibits.

Often the neighborhood library advertises a children's book exhibit. School personnel should take advantage of these exhibits by taking children on excursions to see them.

The value of displays and exhibits is enhanced when children have a part in setting them up. This involves careful planning, however. Haphazard exhibits are often so confusing that they become ineffective. Material should be grouped topically, by authors or by reading level. When tables are used, they should be elevated at the back in some way so that all books are readily exposed to view and some are not hidden behind others. Books that are to be handled should be on tables low enough for the children to see them easily. Often a theme for the exhibit (such as "A Book Is Like a Ship" or "Adventures Through Books") makes it possible to organize the exhibit more logically and interestingly.

Although a large exhibit once a year is a worthy activity for any school, smaller exhibits and displays should be used constantly. The school library should always have displays of new books and bulletin boards which excite an interest in reading. A showcase near the main entrance of the school building can provide notice of the new books in the library as well as develop an interest in a special gem recently acquired. Such a showcase or bulletin board can also keep children informed of the worthwhile television shows built around children's literature. It can draw attention to fine films in town based on great writing. The showcase can be used to announce unusual events, such as the Book Fair, special noon-hour film showings, and current neighborhood library displays. Such announcements and displays create even more interest among children when they have had a part in creating them.

Peg-board displays. Peg board is invaluable in the modern classroom. With the variety of hooks, metal pockets, and bars manufactured for the peg board, the teacher is able to display three-dimensional objects very effectively as part of her bulletin-board display. The books themselves can be placed in the pockets; through the use of the adjustable wires, they can be displayed open to selected passages. Pegs help to hold pictures in place. Bars make it possible to construct simple shelves where clay modeling or other three-dimensional objects may be displayed. Peg board is very adaptable to many uses and purposes, especially in the promotion of children's literature.

Contacts with authors. Nothing is more thrilling for a child than to become acquainted with an author through his writings and then to correspond with that author, or, what is even more exciting, to see him. Teachers can develop a great love for literature, and for reading, by writing to live poets and authors, or by influencing a local organization to bring one to visit the children during Book Week or any appropriate time. Writers of children's books love children—and are most gracious with them. Acquaintance with these fine people is a constructive and inspiring experience for children.

Dioramas. Dioramas serve the purpose of providing children with a three-dimensional picture of the images created in their minds by the stories and poems they read. Similar to a shadow box in construction, the diorama provides an opportunity for the creative use of materials in group or individual projects. They can be made from cardboard cartons or can be constructed as a real art form with heavy cardboard and wood.

Dioramas are especially effective at book fairs and exhibits. A series of them can show scenes from several stories or poems, or can show several scenes from the same story. Sometimes dioramas can be made in various forms to add uniqueness to an exhibit.

*   *   *

Each child in Mr. Rogers' sixth grade made a small diorama. The children worked in groups and built three or four scenes for each of several stories. They then framed their dioramas by cutting poster board in the shape of an open book. A hole the same size as the diorama was cut in the open book so that the resulting effect was a three-dimensional picture on one page of the open book. On the page facing the diorama was the name of the book, the author, and the passage that best described the diorama.

Later in the year, Mr. Rogers' group tried to depict various moods with the creative use of materials in dioramas. One group of children made the locked-up room in *Great Expectations*. They created the illusion of the old, dusty wedding table by spraying a table set with miniature dishes with Christmas snow. Across the front of the box they used string to suggest cobwebs. Old strips from plastic bags cut with ragged edges hung from the ceiling like cobwebs and dust.

Another group depicted *McGillicutty's Pool* by painting the inside of their box to resemble water and suspending the fish and undersea animals on strings from the top of the diorama to give the illusion of swimming. Across the front they pasted pale blue cellophane to complete the impression of an underwater scene.

*   *   *

Teachers can set conditions for the creative interpretation of children's literature through dioramas by discussing the stories and poems that the children read and by emphasizing the mood or feeling of the poem as much as the story. The teacher can help children see the relationships between available materials and the mood or scene they are trying to depict. Patty's teacher suggested clothespins for bedsteads in the scene from *Peter Pan*. Patty's teacher also suggested that facial tissues be used to make miniature pillows. Once Patty caught on to this type of thinking, she suggested making a three-dimensional fireplace with crumpled cellophane behind it. Patty then cut a hole in the box so light came through the cellophane, giving the appearance of a lighted fireplace. It was also Patty's idea to poke holes in the box outside the window so that the light would represent stars. After Patty added Tinkerbell on a string before the fireplace, she hung a real little bell behind the fireplace which could be tinkled by pulling on a string. Thus Patty added color and sound to her diorama. From discussions of the use of materials, teachers can help children find creative ways of making dioramas both realistic and attractive.

Puppet shows. Puppet shows sustain the quality of make-believe that permeates much of children's literature and are, therefore, very well suited to dramatizing children's stories and poems. The use of various kinds of puppets has been developed in Book II of this series.[6]

[6] *Ibid.,* Chapter V.

A creative use of materials: Patty's diorama of Sir James M. Barrie's Peter Pan.

Children who use puppets a great deal to interpret literature soon become skilled in using them creatively.

*   *   *

Mr. Hunter's fifth grade decided to dramatize Robert Browning's "The Pied Piper of Hamelin" with marionettes. Certain production problems were discussed, and many unique ideas were offered to solve them. One problem was how to give the illusion of the Pied Piper walking down a long street with the rats following him and then, later, the same street with children following him. One child suggested that the Pied Piper go through the motions of walking while the scenery went by. The children put a sheet of shelf paper on the floor and painted houses, lamp-posts, fences, trees, bushes, and shops on it. Then, using the roll-movie technique, they rolled the scene up on two dowels which they inserted through holes in the back of the puppet stage. Two boys rolled the street scene from one dowel to another while the Pied Piper walked in place. The effect delighted the children.

The same technique was later used to dramatize *The Little Engine That Could* for a second grade. The engine stayed in one place on the stage while the scenery went by. In this way the engine was able to go up one side of the mountain and down the other.

*   *   *

Marionette shows and puppet shows of various kinds delight children of all ages and provide an excellent opportunity to play out beloved stories and to acquire the language of the authors.

Box theaters. Box theaters provide another form of dramatization which can be adapted to many different uses in presenting children's literature. Some suggestions for using boxes creatively were made in Book II of this series.[7] Box theaters are actually dioramas with some sort of movement added. Sometimes the movement comes simply from slits in the bottom of the box through which stick figures make their appearance on the stage. Larger box theaters can be used with hand puppets.

One group of children who were studying magnets used a box with a thin cardboard bottom and made their characters move about the stage through the use of magnets. This was done by making cardboard figures and inserting a paper clip in the base that held each figure upright. The powerful magnet, when touched to the cardboard

[7] *Ibid.,* Chapter V.

floor, attracted the paper clip. By moving the magnet about on the underside of the floor, the figures in the box theater moved about also. To stop them in a particular place, the magnet was simply pulled away from the cardboard floor. One group of children used this technique very effectively in dramatizing *Hans Brinker and the Silver Skates,* where the magnet was especially effective in making the skaters glide.

Box theaters can be adapted to finger puppets or simple marionettes, or to using commercial figures effectively. They are especially effective if the teacher wants to depict a scene or a story without too much preparation. In presenting the poem "Wynken, Blynken and Nod," Miss Carey used a box theater and made the wooden shoe sail about the sky simply by making a cardboard shoe and fastening it on a thin dowel with a tack. The dowel was left protruding from the back of the box; a slit was cut there so that Miss Carey could grasp the dowel, and, by moving it in the slit, could give the illusion of a wooden shoe sailing the skies. She also used this simple idea to present "The Duel." The gingham dog and the calico cat could really fight when she moved the dowels protruding from the back of the box theater. With this simple device, trains and cars can move, ships can rock, Jack can climb the beanstalk, and Humpty Dumpty can fall.

Box theaters are effective for giving book reports, for use at school exhibits, and for sharing books read at home.

Shadow pictures. Shadow dramatizations are excellent for depicting favorite stories when the scenes are complicated or foreign to the natural environment of the children. A realistic dramatization of a story can be obtained by fastening cardboard figures on wire coat hangers (which have been straightened) with masking tape and then moving the figures about on a screen of unbleached muslin pasted over an opening cut in a large box. (See Book II of this series.)[8] A light between the child and the figure being manipulated casts a clear-cut shadow on the screen. Scenery of detailed design can be made on heavy plastic wrap with a black flo-pen and then simply pushed against the unbleached muslin. To change scenes, the children turn out the light, pull off one piece of plastic wrap, apply another, turn on the light, and continue with the story. Shadow dramatizations are especially effective when one child reads the words from the story and others shadow-play it. Stopping at intervals to allow the players to speak parts adds interesting variety to the scenes.

Shadow boxes. A large shallow box can be made into a shadow

[8] *Ibid.,* Chapter V.

box that will serve as a focal point for arousing interest in good literature in the classroom. The front of the box can be cut out, leaving a frame. It is then painted and hung on the wall. Because of its depth, three-dimensional objects may be displayed in a variety of ways to obtain many interesting effects. A feeling of greater depth may be obtained by painting heavy cardboards to represent various aspects of a scene and placing them one behind the other. Sometimes lights (the Christmas tree variety) can be added to gain more realistic effects.

*   *   *

Miss Arnold's fourth grade made an interesting shadow box of "The Night Before Christmas." They poked holes in the back of the shadow box to allow light to come through to represent stars. The back of the box was then painted a deep blue. Near the bottom, about one-half inch from the back of the box, they set cardboard mountains covered with snow. In front of this they set a cardboard row of fir trees covered with snow. Along the very front of the box they made flat cardboard houses, with windows cut out and covered with tissue paper. Using a string of Christmas tree lights, they set some blue lights before the trees and mountains, and some colored lights behind the windows of the cardboard houses. To top off their scene, they cut out a cardboard Santa and reindeer and suspended them on threads between the top of the box and the houses, giving the illusion of a Santa flying before a star-studded sky.

Shadow boxes can provoke a great deal of interest in poems and stories, and they can provide rich creative activity when the children themselves make them. Often they can serve as a place to put an exciting or colorful object—a lovely arrangement of driftwood and flowers, a place to suspend two or three lighted Japanese lanterns, a coveted shrine to exhibit an artistic madonna, or a center where objects to be seen and not touched are displayed.

Shadow plays. Shadow plays are the same as shadow pictures except that the children themselves act out the parts, casting their shadows on a sheet behind which there is a bright light. Scenes for shadow plays can be made by cutting simple shapes from wrapping paper or newspaper and pinning them to the sheet. Almost any story or poem lends itself to shadow play. Shadow plays may be done in pantomime or with voices and movement.

The lap story. Lap stories are very effective in helping children become involved in a piece of literature, and many variations are possible. Lap stories serve as another way to make interesting book reports. They may be planned by individuals or by groups of children.

*   *   *

Commercial materials are often well adapted to the lap-story technique. Miss Ames found the characters of Red Riding Hood printed on a Post Toasties box. She punched them out and used them for a lap story. The paper dolls were designed in such a way that Miss Ames could insert two fingers in the holes near the base of the figures and thus, by moving her fingers, make them walk. "Dr. Suess" figures, purchased at the department store, also served as the core for a good lap story. Paper dolls can well be used for this purpose.

Sometimes children's toys lend themselves to use in a lap story. Michael received a miniature steam shovel for Christmas; he and Miss Ames used it to tell the story of "Mike Mulligan and His Steam Shovel." Building blocks often provide good props for lap stories. Arthur brought a cardboard castle to school, and it was used to tell several lap and "table top" stories of "King Arthur and His Knights." Edith made puppets that fit over her hand so that they walked when she moved her fingers, and her puppets danced, talked, and walked when she told "Hansel and Gretel" as a lap story.

Often little objects cannot be used for audience-type situations because they are not visible in an auditorium or classroom seating arrangement. Some of these objects (delightful dolls, intricate carvings, and clever gimmicks) can be easily and advantageously put to use in the informal closeness of a lap or table-top story.

Felt-o-grams and flannel boards. Felt-o-grams and flannel boards are especially effective for stories that are developed by adding a character or two as the story progresses (such as "The Gingerbread Boy") or for those stories where there are not many scene changes but there is a building up of one or two scenes (such as "The Duchess Bakes a Cake").

Stories with several scenes can be effectively depicted by tacking several layers of flannel along the top of a board and drawing a simple scene on the flannel with crayon. The pieces of flannel can then be flipped as the scenes unfold and the characters and scenes added in their logical sequence.

Many creative effects can be developed with the flannel board if children are cautioned to keep alert to find all materials that might adhere to the flannel. Colored pipe cleaners can be bent quickly into many shapes and they will stick readily to felt or flannel. Blotters will also stick to felt and flannel, and many figures and objects can easily be cut from them. Decorative materials, such as glitter or Christmas snow, also adhere to flannel and can create interesting illusions.

In telling the story of "The Night Before Christmas," Mr. Torsey sprinkled Christmas snow over the last scene as he said, "Happy Christmas to all and to all a good night!" Mrs. Cohen used silver glitter on her flannel board to create the illusion "Sailed on a river of crystal light, into a sea of dew," from "Wynken, Blynken and Nod."

Light-weight tiny objects can be backed by flannel and are effective in telling stories. (Other ways for using a flannel board were described in Book II of this series.[9])

Pictorial maps. Picture maps serve many purposes in helping to develop a love for literature.

Mr. Jones's sixth grade made a large outline map of the United States. In each state they located the authors about whom they studied as a class during the year.

Miss Young's fifth grade made individual maps of each state and of other countries and drew in the appropriate places pictures that best symbolized the stories they read as a class.

The children in Mr. Barrett's third grade made a small book of every book they read by folding a piece of construction paper and printing the title and author on the front page and their own names on the inside page. These were then pasted on a large outline map over the state about which the story was written.

Mrs. Martin's fourth grade made a large map of the United States and pasted around it pictures of stories and poems written by their favorite authors. A ribbon from the picture to the correct place on the map showed where that author lived.

More elaborate maps made by some children had flaps that opened. On each flap was a clue about a great piece of literature, such as, "A story was written here about a famous rabbit." On lifting the flap one read, "The Tar Baby," by Joel Chandler Harris. Another clue read, "Spare your country's flag!" and under the flap was printed "Barbara Fritchie," by John Greenleaf Whittier.

Pictorial maps tend to help develop concepts of time and place with children as they relate to authors and their creations.

[9] *Ibid.,* Chapter V.

Peep boxes. Peep boxes are constructed much like shadow boxes. They allow the children to put into visual form the images that words from their favorite stories create in their minds. They are especially useful for individual projects. The element of mystery added by "peeking" at the scenes is high motivation for children. Peep boxes can be used effectively in school book exhibits, at book fairs, and for book reports.

Clay modeling. Children enjoy using plasticine or clay to model their favorite characters or scenes. Clay modeling helps the child capture the feeling of the character he is depicting. Sometimes this can be done by a facial expression, a stance, a posture, or a gesture.

*   *   *

In Miss Arnold's third grade, the children modeled the characters from *Treasure Island*. Long John Silver was especially well-portrayed with his peg leg. Each pirate had a personality of his own. The modeled figures were used to make a series of box scenes of the story. Over each box the children placed the words chosen from the text which best described the scene. One scene depicted Jim clinging to the deck of the Hispaniola with the pirates, gazing at Treasure Island. On a placard over the box scene the children had printed the following passage:

The Hispaniola was rolling scuppers under in the ocean swell. The booms were tearing at the blocks, the rudder was banging to and fro, and the whole ship creaking, groaning and jumping like a manufactory. I had to cling tight to the backstay, and the world turned giddily before my eyes; for though I was a good enough sailor when there was way on, this standing still and being rolled about like a bottle was a thing I never learned to stand without a qualm or so, above all in the morning, on an empty stomach.

Perhaps it was this—perhaps it was the look of the island, with its gray, melancholy woods, and wild stone spires, and the surf that we could both see and hear foaming and thundering on the steep beach—at least, although the sun shone bright and hot, and the shore birds were fishing and crying all around us, and you would have thought anyone would have been glad to get to land after being so long at sea, my heart sank, as the saying is, into my boots; and from that first look onward, I hated the very thought of Treasure Island.[10]

On another occasion, the children in Miss Arnold's class modeled their favorite characters chosen from all the literature they had

[10] Robert Louis Stevenson, *Treasure Island.*

read. The models were displayed before a backing made of a folded piece of cardboard on which the children had printed the words best describing their character. Sometimes these words were written in phrases taken directly from the original text; others were made up by the children.

Rosanne made a model of Pinocchio with a long, long nose. Behind it, in her own words, she printed:

> He was naughty
> He was bad,
> Always in trouble
> It really was sad.
>
> Sassy and insolent
> Always on the go
> Silly and sweet:
> Adorable Pinocchio.

Bill modeled Homer Price and made a cardboard counter to go before him. On the counter he had piles of Cheerio cereal to represent miniature doughnuts. On the cardboard behind his model, Bill printed:

> Homer Price was a real boy. He was full of fun. He was always in trouble. The biggest trouble he ever had was the day he could not stop the doughnut machine. This is my favorite story about Homer Price.

Kenny, who read every Paul Bunyan story ever printed, modeled a huge lumberyard, and on the card behind him printed directly from the text his favorite description of Paul.

> Paul Bunyan was of tremendous size and strength, the strongest man that ever swung an ax. Now a lumberjack always measures things by ax handles instead of by feet or yards—a thing will be so many ax handles long or so many ax handles high—and the various estimates as to Paul's size are given in this way. Accordingly, the estimate which seems most nearly correct is that Paul was so big that ninety-seven ax handles would just barely measure him from hip to hip. This estimate is a little misleading, however, as no one is sure whether the ordinary ax handle is meant, or one of Paul's, which was seven—or perhaps it was seventy—times as long as the ordinary one. At any rate, it can easily be seen that he was no little fellow.
> He had curly black hair which his loving wife used to comb for him every morning with a great crosscut saw, after first parting it nicely with a broadax, and a big black beard that was as long as it was wide and as

wide as it was long. He was rather proud of this beard, and took great care of it. Several times every day he would pull up a young pine tree by the roots and use its stiff branches in combing and brushing it smooth.[11]

Clay models can be used for making table-top or sand-table scenes of favorite stories. Children become more aware of qualities of their favorite characters in literature when they try to translate them into visible forms.

Mobiles. Mobiles are especially fascinating when units on literature are being taught. Miss French's second grade was reading Dr. Suess. The children and the teacher read all the Dr. Suess books they could find. They also read and collected material about Dr. Suess as an author.

Their five favorite Dr. Suess stories were listed on charts. Each child signed his name under the story he liked best of the five. Then the children met by groups and planned what they would like to put on a Dr. Suess-mobile. Each group worked out its mobile, which was suspended from the ceiling, in its own way. One group used a tree branch, which they painted white. From it, suspended by threads, were Horton, Maizie, the two hunters, an egg, a circus tent, and a ship. Another group crossed sticks and balanced many grotesque and unique animals to represent *If I Ran the Zoo*.

In the center of the room hung a mobile with a picture of Dr. Suess surrounded by tiny books on which was printed the name of every book he had written.

Mobiles lend themselves to an excellent representation of poetry and well-written prose. The movement of the floating mobile symbolizes the flow of characters and words through the child's mind. An imaginative teacher can find many ways to match the free, fluent action of a mobile with the free-flowing words of a good poem or story.

Fingerplays. Many works of literature lend themselves to adaptation to finger plays. This is especially true of nursery rhymes and counting poems. Children can make up rhymes for finger plays or they can use their fingers to create table puppets to act out stories or selections. (See Book II of this series.)[12]

Games. Certain games, such as charades, lend themselves to de-

[11] From *Paul Bunyan and His Great Blue Ox*, by Wallace Wadsworth. Copyright 1926 by George H. Doran Company. Reprinted by permission of Doubleday & Company, Inc.

[12] James A. Smith, *Creative Teaching of the Language Arts in the Elementary School* (Boston: Allyn and Bacon, Inc., 1967), Chapter V.

veloping an interest in literature. Children can act out the titles of books while the rest of the class tries to guess what it is. Games such as "Who Am I" or "What Am I" also lend themselves to descriptive word usage.

Often the games that children play regularly in gym periods can be adapted to a game dramatization. Bombardment is an excellent game to play along with the reading of *The Adventures of Robin Hood* or "The Charge of the Light Brigade."

One game many children like is "telephone conversation" where they tell about a book over a toy telephone and the class must guess the book. (See Book II of this series.) [13]

Of course, in the primary grades imitative rhythms can be readily applied to the stories the children read. They hop like Peter Rabbit, strut like Paul Bunyan, chug like the Little Engine, and generally pantomime the characters they love.

A physical education teacher will have many suggestions as to how games may be adapted to literature in such a way that children "live" it.

Creating ballads. Another way that music and literature can be correlated is to help the children put their favorite stories into ballads. They can pretend they are singing the story just as the old minstrels did long ago. In free or rhyming verse, the story can be retold. Atmosphere can often be added if someone in the room strums a guitar or the teacher plays a recording of guitar or string music. Often one child begins the story and points to another to continue. Children who cannot make rhymes are not pressured to do so; they just tell their portions of the story in their own ways. The musical background will help to determine the tempo and rhythm with which they tell it.

Impersonations. One very effective way of creating interest in an author's ability to describe characters is to encourage the children to impersonate characters from the books they have read together while the rest of the class guesses who the character is. These impersonations can be done in many ways. Children can dress in costume and tell about themselves; they may act out a character silently; or they may use the "I Was There" technique, where they sit before the class and pretend they were eyewitnesses to a particular scene of the story in which the character they are depicting took an active part. Some primary teachers have encouraged this sort of activity by using a large

[13] *Ibid.,* Chapter V.

cardboard box as a television set on which children tell about themselves.

Impersonations help the children to focus attention on those bits of description in the author's writing which make his characters different and notorious.

Miss Empy used impersonations as the theme of a tea she gave for her fifth-grade mothers. She held a fashion show of children's famous story-book characters, using the boys and girls in her room as the models.

Dance interpretations. Many poems and stories lend themselves well to dance interpretation.

After the children in the second grade had read "The Elf and the Dormouse," Miss Bradford asked them if they would like to dance the story. A large umbrella was used as the toadstool; it was set in the middle of the room. Some of the children then made up "elf" steps. Others made up "mouse" steps. The children selected two interpretations they liked best, and then Miss Bradford composed music to go with their steps. After one group had danced the story, another group gave their interpretation.

In Miss Harmon's fourth grade the children made up a dance for "The Night Before Christmas." There were many step patterns to be planned—the prancing reindeer steps, the heavy, plodding "Ho-ho-ho" steps of Santa Claus, the airy steps of the sugar plums "dancing through their heads," the fast steps of the "wind and the leaves before the hurricane fly." Miss Harmon used a Fred Waring recording as a background for this dance. At another time her children dramatized "The Elves and the Shoemaker," and she composed music for the dance.

A group of fifth-grade girls and boys created a dance for their Book Week Assembly program from "Snow White and the Seven Dwarfs."

Whenever possible, children should have the opportunity to see literature translated into dance interpretations; for example, a corps de ballet dancing the *Nutcracker Suite, The Red Shoes, Peter and the Wolf, Hansel and Gretel, Cinderella, Robin Hood,* and other famous stories.

Types of reading with moods. Since literature often creates a mood, teachers should be conscious of the mood or "tone" of stories and should set conditions for the full enjoyment of these stories.

Some, such as ghost or mystery stories, are effectively told with the lights out in the classroom and the shades drawn. One candle burning on a table in the center or at the front of the room often lends additional mystery to the situation.

Some stories are told more effectively against a background of soft music. This is especially true of poetry, which lends itself to mood very well. Interesting combinations of voice and music can be developed, both when the teacher reads to the children and when they read to each other.

Sound effects sometimes enhance the feeling of a poem or story. A music box makes an excellent background for reading Dorothy Baruch's "The Merry-Go-Round." The teacher can work with a child who might add sound effects as she reads a mystery story—a creaking door, a loud bang, the sound of footsteps, a dripping faucet. Some commercial recordings are excellent for providing "sound" introductions to stories or sound effects during the story.

The children's positions also can be used to develop a mood for a story. Some stories are best felt when children put their heads down on their desks and close their eyes; others lend themselves to reading or telling while children are stretched out on the floor ready for a mid-morning nap. Some stories are best told when the children are grouped at the feet of the teachers, others when they are seated at their desks.

The weather may help decide the mood of a story. Foggy days help set the mood for certain poems, just as rainy days, snowy days, and sunny days do for others.

In all instances, the teacher should take advantage of every possible opportunity to set the appropriate physical conditions for presenting literature to children. Often the initial association a child has with a story or poem determines at once whether he enjoys it and whether it will bear repeating. Every attempt should be made to recreate the author's mood when he wrote the selection. If a similar mood is experienced by the child, the message is communicated. Children come to understand the importance of using the right word in the right place. They get to the heart of the selection so that it becomes an emotional, as well as an intellectual, experience for them.

Roll movies. Roll movies can be an excellent way to introduce stories and poems, to develop the sequence of a story, or to utilize the author's language to translate words into visual imagery.

Miss Fry's class made a roll movie of trees as a result of reading "A Tree Is Nice." Almost all stories lend themselves to roll movies, which provide a fine opportunity for children to express themselves creatively in a group project. (Ways of using roll movies were discussed on page 234.)

Radio and television shows. Almost all children these days have the opportunity of putting on a live television or radio performance. But too often the "showy" aspects of a school program are exploited in such presentations. Children's literature could be used much more than it is for these programs. This would not only help educate parent viewers as to good literature for children but would motivate child viewers to watch better television shows. Simple or elaborate props can be used for such programs. It is important for the teacher to remember that it is the beauty of the words that makes good literature, so the author's words should be used as much as possible. Many of the suggestions in this chapter are well-suited to television programming: choral speaking, puppet shows, shadow plays, dramatizations, reading with music, dance interpretations, pantomimes, book reports, displays and exhibits, dioramas, interviews with authors, flannel boards, pictorial maps, and impersonations.

It is well to remember that although most of this material should grow out of regular classroom work, the class is justified in striving for a polished performance when it is to be presented before the public.

Choral speaking. Both poems and many prose selections lend themselves well to choral reading or choral speaking exercises. In Book II of this series,[14] many illustrations of the effective use of choral speaking were given. Choral speaking can enrich the enjoyment of literature by giving the teacher a method of using the words of the author in beautiful and varied ways. It can often be used *with* many of the activities for promoting children's literature which have already been mentioned in this chapter. Choral speaking provides an excellent background for shadow plays, puppet shows, and pantomime. Probably no other device is as effective in enriching a child's oral vocabulary (see Chapter V, Book II).

Booklets. All kinds of booklets can be made as a result of experiences in children's literature. These range from simple booklets containing book reports and illustrations to very highly developed scrapbooks of collections of all kinds.

Book-binding can be taught to children so that they can make their own scrapbooks or booklets. Attractive covers dealing with

[14] *Ibid.,* Chapter V.

themes built around their favorite characters will enhance the value of these booklets. Booklets and scrapbooks can contain many interesting materials relating to children's literature:

1. Clippings about children's books.
2. Written book reports.
3. Children's illustrations of favorite books.
4. Autographs of authors.
5. Catalogues and brochures collected at exhibits and book fairs.
6. Children's original poems and stories.
7. Records of books children have read.
8. Book lists for children.
9. Book jacket collections.
10. Magazine or newspaper articles about children's authors or children's books.
11. Copies of programs from book fairs, assemblies, and exhibits.
12. Dittoed material given to children by the teacher, such as Caldecott and Newberry Award winners, books listed under certain topics, and reference materials.
13. Copies of favorite selections from literature.
14. Clippings of TV shows, moving pictures, and recordings made around children's literature.
15. Copies of letters written to various places for materials (catalogues, book lists, and such).

Often the "big book" idea can be used to dramatize favorite books. One class constructed a cardboard big book of *The Adventures of Robin Hood* which opened. One page of the opened book suggested print; the other was cut out so that each time the book opened the children pantomimed a new picture for each chapter. At intervals the pictures came alive and the children came out of the book and onto the stage to dramatize a scene.

Murals. Literature can be expressed in mural painting very well. Tempera paint, cut-out construction paper, and colored chalk lend themselves well to the creation of brightly colored murals for the classroom, the school corridors, or the school library.

Murals can grow out of the telling of one story or poem, or they may be a composite of many of the works of literature which the children have read.

*   *   *

Mural-making may be the motivation for art work also. Mr. Harrison taped a long piece of mural paper over the chalkboard along the side of his classroom one day. Then he said to the children, "In

Literature comes to life through a creative mural interpretation of My Friend Flicka.

the center of this paper I am going to draw a crossroads with this colored chalk. This is where four roads meet. It is Banberry Cross. Remember how all the people came to Banberry Cross to see the fine lady ride on the fine horse? Now each of you will take a section of the paper and we will chalk in all the people, the animals, the houses, the trees—everything, but with everyone running to Banberry Cross. Let's see how many different ideas we can get and how well you can connect your work with your neighbor's." The result was delightful.

Later Mr. Harrison had his children do a similar mural on "The Pied Piper of Hamelin" with all the children headed for one end of the mural where one student had drawn a river.

Another teacher in Mr. Harrison's school used his idea to make a Christmas mural with all the people and animals heading to the manger.

Murals may be developed like this to convey impressions, or they can be carefully planned in order to express more lasting ideas. Variations of mural-making may be obtained when children make them three-dimensional. Pieces of discarded cloth can be pasted on for clothing; green burlap can represent grass; yarn can be glued on for wires; corrugated cardboard, flannel, and novelty papers can represent house fronts; cereal can represent bricks or pavement blocks, and so on.

Murals can be used for scenery in puppet shows (see page 234). Large murals painted on big sheets of cardboard cut from mattress boxes or obtained from box companies make excellent backgrounds for the enactment of plays at assembly programs, especially when the cardboards are taped together with wide masking tape and can be folded accordion-wise as the play progresses.

Poetry Is Fun

A special word must be said about the teaching of poetry. So few children above the primary grades seem to love and know poetry that it seems essential to give poetry some extra attention and explore ways of reviving an interest in it.

Poetry is part of a child. It exists in the rhythm of his walking, his speech, his dancing, his movements, his singing. By setting the proper conditions for learning, teachers can bring out the poetry to be expressed in written form. Once a child writes his own poetry he needs little motivation for enjoying the poetry of others. However, teachers should constantly present poetry in new and exciting ways so that the children may gain deeper appreciations and skills in using it as a creative outlet. Much of the tension in children can be positively released if they can put their feelings down on paper in a creative form. A revival of interest in poetry is a must in a world full of the tensions of the Space Age.

All of the ideas suggested in the preceding pages are applicable to setting conditions for the creative teaching of poetry. Because poetry is a unique form of written expression, however, some additional suggestions are entered here.

1. Use choral speaking for the teaching of many poems.

2. Write a poem on the chalkboard and divide the class into groups. Encourage each group to think of a different way to present the poem through choral speaking.

3. Print a rhyming poem on a large sheet of paper. Cut the poem into rhyming strips and pass out the strips. Allow the children who have the strips to go to the front of the room and reassemble the poem by rhyming it. Then allow them to do the poem in choral speaking.

4. Create special moods by reading such poems as these to the children:

"The Song of Hiawatha" (with drum beats).
"The Bells" (Edgar Allan Poe) (with bells).
"Gerald McBoing-Boing" (with "boings" and other sounds suggested by the story).

5. Read action poems and then have the children create sounds or actions to go with them:

"Jack-Be-Nimble," while some children jump the candlestick.
"The Midnight Ride of Paul Revere," while children make the clip-clap noise of the horse in rhythm to the reading.
"The Highwayman" (Alfred Noyes) with accompanying hoof beats or music.

6. Look for "swinging poems." Do the action suggested by the poem as in:

"The Swing" (R. L. Stevenson)
"Polly Put the Kettle On"
"A Swing Song" (William Allingham)

7. Collect "noisy" poems and weave the noises into the poem. Some good ones are:

"Taxis" (Rachel Field)
"Chicago" (Carl Sandburg)
"The Duel" (Eugene Field)
"Frolic" (G. W. Russell)
"Motor Cars" (Rowena Bastin Bennett)

8. Collect "hopping" poems and hop to them:

"The Frog" (Hilaire Belloc)
"Ladybird, Ladybird" (Vachel Linsday)
"This Is the Way the Ladies Ride" (nursery rhyme)
"Grasshopper Green" (Walter de la Mare)

9. Collect "quiet" poems and read them to soft music:

"The Little House" (Christopher Morley)
"Hiding" (Dorothy Aldis)
"Hush-a-bye Baby"
"The Rock-a-bye Lady from Hush-a-bye Street" (Eugene Field)
"Antique Shop" (Carl Carmer)

10. Collect "swaying" poems and sway to their rhythm:

"Who Has Seen the Wind" (Christina Rossetti)
"Daffodils" (William Wordsworth)
"Wynken, Blynken and Nod" (Eugene Field)
"Sweet and Low" (Alfred Tennyson)
"Slumber Song" (Louis V. Ledoux)

11. Collect "walking" poems and walk to them:

"The Little Turtle" (Vachel Lindsay)
"Twinkle, Twinkle Little Star"
"The Rock-a-bye Lady" (Eugene Field)
"Goblin Feet" (J. R. R. Tolkien)
"Marching Song" (Robert Louis Stevenson)

12. Find a mood picture and place it on the bulletin board. Under it place a placard saying "What poems tell how these people feel?" or "What poems describe the feeling of this picture?" Help children find appropriate poems by providing books of collections of children's poems.

13. Some poems lend themselves especially well to dramatization, such as:

"The Pied Piper of Hamelin" (Robert Browning)
"A Tragic Story" (Albert Von Chamisso)
"Casey at the Bat" (Ernest Laurence Taylor)
"Concord Hymn" (Ralph Waldo Emerson)

14. There are poems especially suited to puppet shows, such as:

"The Pied Piper of Hamelin" (Robert Browning)
"The Duel" (Eugene Field)
"Robin Hood and Little John" (old ballad)
"The Leak in the Dike" (Phoebe Cary)

15. Some poems lend themselves especially well to pantomime:

"In School Days" (John Greenleaf Whittier)
"The Village Blacksmith" (H. W. Longfellow)
"The Blind Men and the Elephant" (John Godfrey Saxe)
"Abou Ben Adhem" (Leigh Hunt)
"Evening at the Farm" (John Townsend Trowbridge)

16. Poems especially suited for shadow plays are these:

"The Elf and the Dormouse" (Oliver Herford)
"The Night Before Christmas" (Clement Moore)
"The Courtship of Miles Standish" (H. W. Longfellow)
"The Owl and the Pussycat" (Edward Lear)

17. Some poems are especially suited to group action, such as:

"The Merry-go-Round" (Dorothy Baruch)
"Fog" (Carl Sandburg)
"Riding in an Airplane" (Dorothy Baruch)
"Tugs" (James S. Tippett)
"Riding in a Motor Boat" (Dorothy Baruch)
"The Little Jumping Girls" (Kate Greenaway)

18. Fingerplays provide a good way to introduce poems.

19. Collect unusual pictures and put them on the bulletin board. Encourage children to find poems that *describe* the pictures.

20. Find many pictures for one poem and make a bulletin board display of them. An example of a good poem to use for this activity is Joyce Kilmer's "Trees."

21. Collect poems "to make things to." If the children are making boats, such poems as these can be read:

"Sea Fever" (John Masefield)
"I Saw Three Ships" (folk song)
"A Good Play" (Robert Louis Stevenson)
"A Nautical Ballad" (Charles Edward Carryl)
"Old Ships" (David Norton)

22. Occasionally children can read a classic together and re-write the ending or imagine the story with a different ending, such as:

"A Visit From St. Nicholas"
"Little Boy Blue"
"Casey at the Bat"

23. Scrapbook collections of poetry can be encouraged. Collect poems under various headings and enter them in the class scrapbook. Examples:

HOLIDAY POEMS

"Birthdays" (Marchette Chute)
"At the Seaside" (Robert Louis Stevenson)
"Thanksgiving Day" (Lydia Maria Child)
"Christmas Bells" (Henry W. Longfellow)

FUN POEMS

"Mr. Nobody" (Robert Louis Stevenson)
"The Owl and the Pussycat" (Edward Lear)
"The Plaint of the Camel" (Charles Edward Carryl)
"A Nautical Ballad" (Charles Edward Carryl)
"Eletelephony" (Laura E. Richards)
"Father William" (Lewis Carroll)
"The Purple Cow" (Gelett Burgess)

TASTE POEMS

"Pop Corn Song" (Nancy Byrd Turner)
"The King of Hearts" (nursery rhyme)

"Animal Crackers" (Christopher Morley)
"The Ice Cream Man" (Rachel Field)
"The Sugar Plum Tree" (Eugene Field)

ANIMAL POEMS

"The Rabbit" (Edith King)
"Wooly Lambkins" (Rossetti)
"The Little Turtle" (Vachel Lindsay)
"Mouse" (Hilda Conkling)
"Choosing a Kitten" (author unknown)
"My Dog" (Marchette Chute)
"The Tiger" (William Blake)

POEMS OF ADVENTURE

"To China" (Leroy Jackson)
"A Boy's Song" (James Hogg)
"The Wonderful World" (William Brighty Rands)
"It Is Not Far" (Sara Teasdale)
"A Vagabond Song" (Bliss Carman)

24. Make collections of poetry for people. Examples:

POEMS FOR MOTHER

"Mother" (Theresa Helburn)
"Cradle Hymn" (Martin Luther)
"The Courtin' " (James Russell Lowell)
"The Vinegar Man" (author unknown)
"The Rock-a-Bye Lady" (Eugene Field)
"When Mother Reads Aloud" (Theresa Helburn)
"Her Words" (Anna Hempstead Branch)

POEMS FOR FATHER

"The Deacon's Masterpiece" (Oliver Wendell Holmes)
"Sea Fever" (John Masefield)
"In Flanders Fields" (John McCrae)
"I Hear America Singing" (Walt Whitman)
"Chicago" (Carl Sandburg)
"Father's Story" (Elizabeth Madox Roberts)
"The Thinker" (Berton Braley)
"Father" (Frances Frost)
"Automobile Mechanics" (Dorothy Baruch)
"Daddy Fell Into the Pond" (Alfred Noyes)

POEMS FOR BABY

"The Baby" (George MacDonald)
"Infant Song" (William Blake)
"A Baby's Feet" (Algernon Charles Swinburne)

"Little" (Dorothy Aldis)
"Slippery" (Carl Sandburg)
"Cradle Song" (Sarojini Naider)
"Slumber Song" (Louis V. Ledoux)
"Cradle Hymn" (Martin Luther)

POEMS FOR SISTER

"Skating" (H. Asquith)
"Sisters" (Eleanor Farjeon)
"Little Orphant Annie" (James Whitcomb Riley)
"In School Days" (James Whitcomb Riley)
"Our Silly Little Sister" (Dorothy Aldis)
"Marjorie's Almanac" (Thomas Bailey Aldrich)
"The Playhouse Key" (Rachel Field)
"The Lost Doll" (Charles Kingsley)

POEMS FOR BROTHER

"The Rum Tum Tugger" (T. S. Eliot)
"A Feller I Know" (Mary Austin)
"Big Brother" (Elizabeth Madox Roberts)
"The Quarrel" (Eleanor Farjeon)
"The Fishing Pole" (Carolyn Davies)
"A Good Play" (Robert Louis Stevenson)
"A Boy's Song" (James Hogg)
"My Dog" (Marchette Chute)
"Mr. Nobody" (Robert Louis Stevenson)
"Little Brother's Secret" (Katherine Mansfield)
"Hiding" (Dorothy Aldis)

25. Find interesting pictures and then find poems to go with them.

26. Combine the reading of poems with the humming or soft singing of music, such as:

"The Landing of the Pilgrims" with "The Doxology."
Excerpts from "Snowbound" with "Jingle Bells."
Reading of the Christmas story with "Silent Night."
"The 23rd Psalm" with "The Battle Hymn of the Republic."
"The Daffodils" with "April in Portugal."

27. Read poetry while children fingerpaint or paint pictures.

28. Have children show especially well-worded passages in paint or fingerpaint. *Example:* paint "The Humble Bee" by Ralph Waldo Emerson.

Poetry, like all literature, must be a source of enjoyment to children in order to be appreciated. The study of the structure of poetry has little place in the elementary school except as it relates to helping children structure their own poems.

In selecting poems for children, certain criteria can be kept in mind. A poem should do one or more of these things:

> . . . it should catch moments of beauty; it should penetrate the honest feelings of the author and the reader; it should picture interesting people; it should release hearty laughter or it should tell appealing stories.[15]

Teachers should be very skeptical of poems that attempt to teach lessons, contain remote adult ideas, or drip with sentimental doggerel.

Poetry can be *lived* by children and *loved* by children.

Summary

Literature is the record of man's living which contains his feelings as well as his way of life. Children can capture the spirit of literature because they have inherited the same feelings as other men even though they live in a different age. Literature is a common bond of communication of feelings across the continents, across the countries, and across the years. The beauty of living in all times is captured in it. It is the rightful heritage of all children everywhere. Teachers can help children relive and refeel the history of the world by helping them read and experience their great literary heritage.

> Books are not men, and yet they are alive.
> They are man's memory and his aspiration,
> The link between his present and his past,
> The tools he builds with, all the hoarded thoughts
> Winnowed and sifted from a million minds,
> Living and dead to guide him on his way.[16]

[15] Leland B. Jacobs, "Children's Experiences in Literature," *Children and the Language Arts,* ed. Virgil E. Herrick and Leland B. Jacobs (Englewood Cliffs: Prentice-Hall, Inc., 1955), p. 195.

[16] *They Burned the Books,* by Stephen Vincent Benet, Holt, Rinehart and Winston, Inc. Copyright, 1942, by Stephen Vincent Benet. Reprinted by permission of Brandt & Brandt. P. 12.

TO THE COLLEGE STUDENT

1. One of the most valuable references you can have in your teaching is a file of children's literature. Explore children's books by having each member of your class bring one to class each day to read. Have each member find out something about the author and the other books he has written. Each class member can take notes on these readings on 3 x 5 cards and can begin to build such a file.

2. Also start to collect magazine articles and pictures of children's books and build a file of these for use in your student teaching.

3. There is a great deal of trash sold as children's literature today. Have each member of the class bring a book of recent publication to class. Using the criteria for selecting children's literature as defined in this chapter, evaluate the books brought in by the class members.

4. There are many children's magazines on the market. Some are excellent, others are tawdry. Collect copies of various kinds of children's magazines and assess them for their literary value.

TO THE CLASSROOM TEACHER

1. The best way to use children's literature as a part of the reading program is through an individualized reading program. Note the books listed on individualized reading at the ends of Chapters VI and VII. If you have not tried such a program, read these books and try to individualize your top group as a starter, allowing the children to select their own materials and keep their own records. Later you can try it on your other reading groups.

2. One way to help children become interested in literature is to afford the opportunity for them to share books through creative book reports. Some ideas for such book reports were mentioned in this chapter. Take one reading period a week and devote it to this kind of activity rather than to skills reading. Watch to see if it pays dividends. Do children become more interested in books? Is the library frequented more often? Do the children carry books home more often?

3. In planning your next unit, use the *Periodical Guide to Children's Literature* to see how many ways literature can be used in correlation with social studies, science, arithmetic, and the creative arts.

TO THE COLLEGE STUDENT AND
THE CLASSROOM TEACHER

1. Make a list of all the current television shows that are based on children's literature. View some and discuss them in class with the following aspects in mind:
   a. Did the presentation catch the flavor of the story?
   b. What justifiable changes were made for television presentation?
   c. How creative was the producer in transferring the book to the television screen?
   d. Do you think television programs of this sort encourage or discourage the children from reading good literature?

2. Obtain a copy of the report of the National Library Association's Annual Conference and look for these facts:
   a. How many children's books were published in the past year?
   b. How many children's books were published in 1940?
   c. Note those books which were the most popular with children. How many of them do you remember as being translated into television shows?
   d. From these observations, can you tell whether children are reading more or less than they did twenty years ago and can you make some conclusions about the effect of television on children's reading?

3. Many children's stories have been made into motion pictures or cartoons. Among the many popular ones of the past years have been: *Snow White and the Seven Dwarfs, Bambi, Peter Pan, Treasure Island, Hansel and Gretel, Cinderella, Pinocchio, Lassie Come Home, Ivanhoe, Mary Poppins,* and a host of others. In translating these classics to the screen, is the producer justified in taking liberties with the original manuscript? Do you feel his interpretation for any particular one was creative or commercial? Do you think films of great

literature endear the writing to children or just make it easy for them to get the idea of the book? Discuss this.

4. The next time a children's classic is being shown at a local theater, call the manager and ask for an approximate attendance figure. Then call the local library and check on the circulation record of the particular book being shown in the film. Also check with your school library. Check other evidence to determine whether or not films encourage or discourage the reading of the book.

5. The *New York Times* publishes a Sunday supplement of children's books once a year. This is a very valuable resource. Watch for it and add it to your files.

6. Which are your favorite children's stories? Can you determine why they remain so dear to you after all these years? Think about the situation under which you were first introduced to these stories and of succeeding experiences with them. How much of the content of the story contributed to your liking it. The mood? The circumstances under which it was first read? Are conditions important in introducing literature to children?

7. A description of bibliotherapy is given in Book IV of this series, *Creative Teaching of the Creative Arts in the Elementary School*. Discuss this question: Is bibliotherapy a creative way of using children's literature?

8. List all the ways that Miss Wilson's lesson (see p. 208) developed creativity in the children and followed the principles of creative teaching.

9. Many creative thinking skills can be developed through the use of children's literature in the classroom. Select some well-known children's book and study it for answers to the following questions:

   a. What creative thinking skills does the author develop—challenge in arriving at a creative solution of the plot, appeal to imagination, clever use of words, challenge to the reader's ability to use empathy?

   b. What kind of personality characteristics are encouraged or discouraged by the story?

   c. Does the author tell a story, moralize, develop a "cautionary" tale or set a mood, or a combination of any of these? If so, does the work ring true?

SELECTED BIBLIOGRAPHY

ADAMS, BESS PORTER. *About Books and Children*. New York: Henry Holt and Company, 1953.

ALLEN, PATRICIA (compiler). *A Catalog of 3300 of the Best Books for Children*. New York: R. R. Bowker Co., 1963.

ARBUTHNOT, MAY HILL. *Children and Books*. Chicago: Scott, Foresman and Company, 1957.

ARNSTEIN, FLORA J. *Poetry in the Elementary Classroom*. New York: Appleton-Century-Crofts, Inc., 1962.

CASS, JAMES (ed.). *Books in the Schools*. New York: American Book Publishers Council, Inc., 1961.

DUFF, ANNIS. *Bequest of Wings*. New York: The Viking Press, 1963.

————. *Longer Flight*. New York: The Viking Press, 1956.

EATON, ANNE THAXTER. *Treasure for the Taking*. New York: The Viking Press, 1957.

EAKIN, MARY K. *Good Books for Children*. Chicago: University of Chicago Press, 1959.

EMRICH, MARION VALLAT and GEORGE KORSON. *The Child's Book of Folklore*. New York: The Dial Press, Inc., 1947.

FENNER, PHYLLIS. *The Proof of the Pudding*. New York: John Day Co., 1957.

FRYATT, NORMA R. (ed.). *A Horn Book Sampler*. Boston: The Horn Book, Inc., 1959.

HANNA, GENEVA R. and MARIANA K. MACALLISTER. *Books, Young People, and Reading Guidance*. New York: Harper & Row, Publishers, Inc., 1960.

LARRICK, NANCY. *A Teacher's Guide to Children's Books*. Columbus: Charles E. Merrill Books, Inc., 1960.

MARTIGNONI, MARGARET E. (ed.). *The Illustrated Treasury of Children's Literature*. New York: Grosset & Dunlap, Inc., 1955.

MEIGS, CORNELIA, ANNE THAXTER EATON, ELIZABETH NESBITT and RUTH HILL VIGUERS. *A Critical History of Children's Literature*. New York: The Macmillan Co., 1953.

SAWYER, RUTH. *The Way of the Storyteller* (rev. ed.). New York: The Viking Press, 1962.

SMITH, LILLIAN E. *The Unreluctant Years*. Chicago: American Library Association, 1953.

WALSH, FRANCES. *That Eager Zest*. New York: J. B. Lippincott Co., 1961.

Conclusion

My book and heart
Shall never part.

—THE NEW ENGLAND PRIMER

There is no one approach to reading that works with all children. Many teachers today use the best of each of many suggested methods, and this is as it should be. Research on which one of several systems of teaching reading at best is plentiful but not conclusive. Together, all the systems emerge as one of two basic approaches: the analytic-synthetic or the synthetic-analytic. Children actually need both analytic and synthetic skills in order to be effective readers. They need to observe both the whole word and the characteristics that individualize words. Consequently, there is little dispute over *what* a child must know in order to be able to read. This leads us to believe that many of our reading problems at present must result from the *way* the child is taught. Strict adherence to any preconceived plan can be deadly in the teaching of reading, just as the omission of the mastery of many basic skills can be deadly to the child's reading powers.

The imposition of pseudo-scientific methods of reading on children destroys creativity in teachers, which conversely cuts off the creative teaching of reading. Uncreative teachers become rigid conformists in their slavish addiction to manuals and textbooks, and somewhere in the shuffle *individual* children from whom we expect *differences* are lost. Such teachers quickly lose sight of the importance of individuality and the need for a variety of ways to teach reading.

Near Schenectady, New York, one group of teachers threw suggested systems to the winds and looked at reading from the standpoint that it is *perceptual* process and that all children *perceive* differently and *learn* differently, so consequently they must *learn to perceive* printed words differently. As a result of their reasoning they attempted, at the kindergarten level, to identify the mode of perception and learning of each child: (1) Did he approach learning analytically, that is, did the particular child see parts of things more readily than wholes? (2) Did he learn synthetically, that is, did the particular child approach learning by seeing wholes (as the kindergarten child mentioned on page 26)? or (3) Did he learn kinesthetically, that is, did the particular child learn best through touch, feeling, emotional reaction, and so forth?

A series of instruments were used to determine the child's approach to learning, and children were grouped according to their *approach to learning* when they entered the first grade. Although all the children were taught synthetic-analytical skills, the emphasis in the analytic group was on phonics, word analysis, and a study of word parts. The emphasis in the synthetic group was on sight vocabulary and learning by sentences or whole meanings. In the kinesthetic group, emphasis was placed on feeling words and letters with the use of water, sand, clay, cut-outs, and other methods suggested by Grace Fernald in her book, *Remedial Techniques in Basic School Subjects.*[1]

These teachers defined a reading problem as one where any child was not reading up to his ability level in all the various components of reading. Using mental ages as their measuring sticks, it was significant that, at the end of the three years of experimentation with the project, *not one single child* was identified as having a serious reading problem.[2]

This report is not presented here with the intent of influencing the reader to approach the teaching of reading as the Schenectady teachers did. It is presented as an example of how creative teachers work. These teachers place their children—not a system, a series, or a text—*first* in the teaching of reading. They identified the problems unique to their children. They are professional people who study and apply their studies to their work. Because they work with a creative principal who encourages their creative thinking, the above project was born and developed. This sort of creative thinking applied to a research design is another way creative teaching can be fostered.

When all is said and done, the one great variable in the teaching of reading, as in all teaching, is the teacher. No system will work if the teacher is not behind it, but the chances are strong that any system will work if the teacher considers the children first, and then is creative enough in her approach to make reading a stimulating, exciting experience and pastime for every child every day regardless of his ability level.

---

[1] Grace Fernald, *Remedial Techniques in Basic School Subjects* (New York: McGraw-Hill, 1943).

[2] Dr. Sanger Steele, dittoed report, Niskayuna Central School District, 1958.

Little has been said about remedial reading in this volume because the author believes that remedial reading implies what it says—a remedy—that something has gone wrong. He has seen too many limp, unhappy, meaningless remedial reading classes to have much faith in them. Some corrective reading may be necessary in any program. Children have illnesses, or defects, or need extra help, or misconceive, or misinterpret. A good reading program diagnoses children's ability *continually*—every day, in fact—and these flaws are *corrected* before whole blocks of remedial teaching are needed. In the creative teaching of reading, children at times read as an entire class (see page 173), at times in small groups (see page 223), at times individually to the teacher (see page 74), at times to each other (see page 107), at times to themselves (see page 209)—but rarely in a strange room to a strange person with strange material. Creative teaching should eliminate the need for remediation in reading because creative teaching does not see the deficiencies of a child as something for which he is to blame. Creative teachers accept what a child *has* and draw it out to help him to grow, and they do it in such a way that his own creative powers and his passion to learn lead him forward into new discoveries, into continuous growth, and toward self-realization.

Index